THE BLUE JEANS MILLIONAIRE!

By T.J. Rohleder
a.k.a. *America's Blue Jeans Millionaire*

The 26 SECRETS That Took Me from $300.00 to Over $10 Million Dollars in Less Than Five Years... And How You Can Do It Even Faster!

Also by T.J. Rohleder:

The Black Book of Marketing Secrets (Series)
The Ultimate Wealth-Maker
How to Get Super Rich in Opportunity Market
Ruthless Marketing
Four Magical Secrets to Building a Fabulous Fortune
The Ruthless Marketing Attack
$60,000.00 in 90 Days
How to Start Your Own Million Dollar Business
Fast Track to Riches
Five Secrets That Will Triple Your Profits
25 Direct Mail Success Secrets That Can Make You Rich
24 Simple and Easy Ways to Get Rich Quick
How to Create a Hot Selling Internet Product in One Day
Secrets of the Blue Jeans Millionaire
Shortcut Secrets to Creating High-Profit Products

SECOND EDITION

ISBN 1-933356-22-7

TABLE OF CONTENTS

Introduction:

Hi there! I'm T.J. Rohleder, co-founder of M.O.R.E., Incorporated in Goessel, Kansas. In this book, I'm going to share with you the 26 secrets that literally took me from $300 to over $10 million in *less than five years*. And that was followed up by tens of millions more in the years that followed — over $100 million in my first 18 years in business! I know that sounds incredible, but it's absolutely true — and I firmly believe that *you* can do even better.

I mean it. If you're willing to work hard and consistently practice the secrets I'll share in these pages, the potential is there. If you've got the ambition that it takes, the willingness, the desire — *and* if you're also willing to do everything I tell you to do — you could make well over $10 million in your first five years. Now, that's not a promise that you will, but I know you *can*.

Fair warning: I'm putting all this down without any filters whatsoever. I'm going to just bare my soul, and give you every single tip, trick, and strategy that's made me all this money, and break them all down for you. The first thing I want you to know is that there's absolutely nothing special about me, as I think you'll come to realize as you read this book. The more you learn about me, the more you'll tell yourself, "If *this* guy can make tens of millions of dollars, then I can make tens of millions of dollars too!" — and you'll be absolutely right. You really can. These are the 26 big secrets that have done it for me; they can do it for you too, and I want you to think very carefully about everything I'm going to share with you here.

I'll be telling you things that nobody else will tell you; and by the time you're done, you're going to know me in a very intimate way. I already believe I know a lot about you. I believe the reason you purchased this book is because you have the same desire to make millions of dollars that I had 30 years ago, when my wife and I started our business. I firmly believe I can help you make millions by combining your desire with my knowledge and experience to help you get off to a good, powerful start.

So with that in mind, let's begin.

SECRET ONE:

Develop a Deep Understanding of Your Target Market

Secret Number One is our greatest secret, the one I believe served us best when we first got started. You see, although we were new to the business itself, we were already very familiar with the market. I was 28 years old; my wife Eileen was 30. This was back in 1988, when we were just a couple of kids who had never made more than $26,000 a year combined. I had a little carpet-cleaning business at the time, and that's how I met Eileen: I stopped in at the filling station where she was working for minimum wage and asked for directions. I was looking for a street that was just two blocks long, and I thought it was in the area where her filling station was. As it turned out, it was on the other side of town, but I still got lucky: I met the woman who would become my wife of 22 years. We started dating, and she was the only girlfriend I'd ever had who actually wanted to come with me on my carpet-cleaning jobs. Even though she had multiple sclerosis, and still does, she would come along and do all the physically demanding work it took to do those jobs. I actually fell in love with her on one of those jobs!

By then, I'd had the carpet-cleaning business for about two years. All that time (and for years before) I'd also been sending away for all kinds of moneymaking plans and programs, and I had all these moneymaking ideas in my head. Luckily, Eileen was very ambitious; she was looking for an opportunity, too. When I told her about my plans for getting rich, her eyes just lit up. Even though I could barely afford a roof over my head at the time, she knew that it *was* possible to get rich — and so did I.

We had nothing going for us at all. I wasn't even a high school graduate. I went and got my G.E.D. because my dad insisted that I do so, but I didn't even have a real diploma. Eileen had graduated from high school, but she never went to college. We were dirt poor. And yet Eileen saw me sending away for all of these plans and opportunities, and she got excited about some of them. That was in 1987. We were trying different moneymaking plans, we were joining multilevel marketing companies, and I saw that she was the kind of woman that I could work side-by-side with. She wasn't one of those women who was always critical, cutting down all my ideas — and that was part of the key to our success. I think having a spouse who's supportive is vitally important.

Before we met, Eileen didn't know anything about the opportunity market. But when she started seeing all these crazy sales letters I was getting, and the fact that I was spending all my money on these programs, she got it in a big way. I remember her telling me, "T.J., the way to get rich is to be in this business. We need to come up with a plan of our own to sell." That was incredibly insightful of her. She saw all these plans and programs, and she saw that most of them were total crap; that was obvious because I lost money on most of them. Her telling me, "I think the way to get rich is to actually *sell* these plans and programs," was what changed our lives for the better.

About nine months after we got married, we took two programs we really liked, programs that we thought were a cut above the others, and combined them in a unique way to make a little booklet — more of a brochure, really. It was a terrible little thing, filled with typographical errors, that embarrasses me to look at to this day. It was called *Dialing for Dollars*. Then we took $300 that we'd earned from selling a beat-up old carpet-cleaning van and ran a one-sixth page ad in a moneymaking magazine to advertise our program. That was September 1988. Within less than five years, *Dialing for Dollars* had brought in over $10 million.

We had a lot of help along the way, and it took a lot of hard work, but one of the most important factors in our success was Secret Number One. We were familiar with the market, even if we didn't know it. Like I said, I'd been sending away for all these plans, programs, and opportunities for years. I was what we lovingly call an "opportunity junkie" — I couldn't get enough. Little did I know that there were millions of people out there just like me. This is a very lucrative market — and before we got started in the market, we already knew a lot about it.

That first little ad was the spark that started our mighty fire — and it took me a whole weekend to write it. I knew that we only had $300, and that we could only run a one-sixth page ad, which today will probably cost you $500 to 600. I knew we had a limited amount of space, and the ad had to be just right — because if we didn't get off to a good start, there went *that* idea. So, it took me a whole weekend to write this little, tiny ad. I laid it out like all the other little ads that I'd seen running forever, and I ran it. We used the profits from that ad to buy two more, and the profits from those two ads to buy four; then we built to eight and sixteen, and *then* we started running full-page ads. Eventually we started doing direct-mail and card-pack advertising, and we just kept expanding.

We got a lot of help from a lot of good people along the way. The first person who helped us in a big way was Russ von Hoelscher, a man I now consider one of our mentors. Now, Russ didn't help us out of the goodness of his heart! He started out as a consultant, and we had to pay him thousands of dollars for his help. This is a business, and time is the one element that is precious to us all. It's a limited resource we can never get back once it's spent.

The opportunity market is the best-kept secret out there, and we didn't even realize it at the time. It's such a lucrative market. There are millions of rabid buyers, people who are just like I was for years, people who are sending away for every single plan and program they can. I call it the second largest niche marketplace in the world. Now, let me explain that to you. First of all, a market is simply a group of people who have something in common. This commonality causes them to feel and act a certain way, which causes them to buy certain kinds of products and services — and to rebuy them. There are people in the opportunity market who are multi-millionaires. They're just looking for the next million-dollar deal, or they're bored, or they want to get into something new. Some of them are doctors and lawyers who are sick and tired of their professions, or now they're retired and they want to try something else. And on the other end of the scale, there are people who are illiterate. I'm not being judgmental; it's just a fact. They can't read or write and they're on welfare. I was somewhere in the middle of the field. I was dead broke, sending away for all these moneymaking plans and programs, and yet I had a small business and I was fully committed to being an entrepreneur. I was doing the best I knew how, even though I wasn't making very much money.

There are reasons why we were able to turn $300 into $10 million in our first four years. First of all, we were very familiar with the market — that's our Secret Number One. We also had a lot of help from a lot of people (as I'll explain in more detail in later sections of this book), and we were willing to do whatever it took to succeed. I like to call us the "Forrest Gumps." Remember the movie with Tom Hanks? Whatever you told Forrest Gump to do he did, and he ended up becoming a multi-millionaire and having a great life. He just did what he was told: He didn't question it. That's how it was for Eileen and me.

When Russ von Hoelscher first came along and started working with us, whatever Russ told us to do, we just did it. At the time he already had 20 years of experience. He'd already made millions of dollars and lost a few too, and we were just getting started. His experience became our experience, and he helped us take something that was already working for us and expand it. We already had a good solid foundation.

It also helped that we had some business experience under our belts. When you're in business, you realize that there's no such thing as a perfect world. You have good days, you have bad days. Just like a good marriage, it goes through droughts, hills, and valleys, but you know you're committed. People with business experience tend to do very, very well in this market — and not just because this market is so lucrative. You see, they're already used to the learning curve, and they realize that it's not a perfect world — that there's a price to pay for success. A lot of people who lack previous business experience just want everything handed to them, and they give up when the going gets tough. But a seasoned businessperson knows that there's no such thing as something for nothing, and they realize that if money is spent right, it's an investment towards future profits, not an expense.

There are two basic things here that can make you rich, and you need both. One is product knowledge: You've got to know everything about the product or service you're selling. This is so you can communicate it in the clearest way to all of your prospective customers and buyers, answer all their objections, and be 100% sold on it yourself. The second thing is market knowledge: a real understanding of the people to whom you're trying to sell and resell. Of those two things, the most important is market knowledge. The opportunity market can make you rich, because this market is so absolutely huge and so needy. Millions of people desperately want to find a way to make more money but they don't know how. They're scared, confused, and frustrated. There are rabid buyers out there spending all kinds of money looking for ways to make more money. They're more than happy to spend huge sums of money. We've had customers spend thousands and thousands of dollars with us on our various products and services — the kinds of things I'm going to tell you more about in this book, and show you how to create on your own. But that said, it's also a very skeptical marketplace, because there are so many scam artists out there in the opportunity market. Ironically, that's a great thing for you — because if you handle your business with complete honesty and integrity, you can win people over. They'll be more than happy to continue to do business with you once you earn their trust.

Another reason I love this marketplace is that there's an endless array of products and services that you can create. It never ends, and it's such a creative way to make money. Another great thing about this market is that most of the competitors in it are very easy to beat. Again, I don't mean to be disrespectful; that's just how it is. Now, I'm hoping that you, the reader, are going to get fired up about this market, get started in it, and make millions of dollars in it just like we have. I'm not worried about the competition; I *need* competitors. We need more good people in this marketplace. Since our company mails millions of pieces of direct-mail, if nothing else we need more companies that will put their lists up for rent — and I'm hoping to rent your list someday. I'll explain more about that when we get to our direct-mail secrets. Direct-mail is the exciting medium that's made us so many millions of dollars in this market — and I don't mean to brag. When I talk about all the millions we've made, it's to inspire you. I'm bragging on this marketplace; I'm bragging on the secrets that I'm trying to share with you in this book. I can't wait to talk to you in person about this at our free workshop; I'm itching to show you how to use these 26 secrets, and how you can get started with them.

The more familiar you are with this market, the better; and when I started, I was very familiar with it. I knew that the competitors who were really kicking ass and taking names were few and far between; and they still are. When you get right down to it, the competitors in this marketplace are very easy to beat, because there are so many fly-by-nighters out there. These fly-by-night companies don't understand what real business is all about — and I'll explain more about that. I'll make that crystal-clear for you by the time you finish this book.

Another reason I love this marketplace is the fact that the best years are still to come, and it won't be long now. The Baby Boomer generation is just starting to retire. Now, what happens when people retire, after they play golf for six months and gain twenty or thirty pounds and watch too much TV, they start looking for something else to do. They find out that retirement isn't all that it's cracked up to be; in fact, it's terrible for most people. They have too much time on their hands; for years they've lived a structured life, where they've had a job to go to and they had people they worked with and things to do and places to go and people to see. Now they're retired, and the phone stops ringing. The friends they worked with are busy doing the deal every day. This is one of the driving forces that causes people to start looking for business opportunities.

A lot of those bored retirees are going to be taking a closer look at the opportunity market. Millions of new people are going to be getting into this marketplace, year after year. Another thing about this marketplace — and I'll make this clearer to you as we go along — is that it's very easy to get started in. There are all kinds of ways to reach those millions of people who are desperately seeking a way to make more money, all kinds of magazines you can advertise in, plus direct-mail, card-packs, and the Internet. It's constantly evolving. The millions of people in this marketplace share something in common, even though they're from different demographic groups. They all have that same insatiable desire to get rich.

I'm the perfect example. Back when I first met my wife, when I was sending for all these plans and programs, I couldn't pay my bills. My electricity kept getting shut off. Why was that happening? Because I was using every last penny I had to buy all these get-rich-quick plans and programs. I was delusional — all my friends and family told me so. It's true; I was obsessed. A large percentage of the people who perpetually buy these plans and programs on a regular basis are overtaken with the same sense of delusion I had in the beginning. I don't mean to be judgmental about it; I was an opportunity junkie for years. That's part of what makes this market so lucrative. These people are rabid buyers.

Now, the way for you to get started is pretty simple, really. In fact, everything I have to share with you here is simple, and a lot of the ideas you're going to hear throughout this book are repetitive in nature. When you see the same things over and over again, though, you should feel good. Highlight those things. Write them down in a notebook. Each one is a common denominator in the business, and each is very important for you to know and remember. That's why I'll repeat them over and over.

Here is one example: Start building a swipe file. Send away for all the different plans and programs that you can find — they're everywhere. If you're not already on an opportunity mailing list, go to the nearest bookstore and find some opportunity magazines. Or go look in the back of *Popular Mechanics* or *Popular Science* — they've got great business opportunity sections. *USA Today* has a great biz-op section. Some of the most popular tabloids are good for business opportunity sellers, too. Do this, and send away for fifty or a hundred programs. Pretty soon your name will be traded; it'll go out to all the different mailing lists, and it won't be long before your mailbox will be jam-packed, stuffed with different opportunity offers. That's how you start building your swipe file — and then you have to start studying it.

When you start buying up these different moneymaking plans and programs, you'll see there's a lot of garbage in this market. That should make you feel very confident. Remember, the competitors in this market are very easy to beat.

This is the last point I'm going to make before we go on to our next secret: I want you to think carefully about all the unhappiness in this marketplace. You see, that's what causes people to buy. There are a lot of people who are frustrated when it comes to money. They want to get rich, they want to make more money, they're desperately seeking a way to do it; but they're so frustrated, and they're so confused. They're even desperate. A lot of them are fearful; they know that the window is closing. They know that they only have a couple of good decades left in them, and they're desperately searching for a way to make more money. Plus, they want some excitement. There are all these emotional factors, and I've already talked about one of the biggest ones, which nobody else will tell you about — the sense of delusion in this market.

There are millions of people like me who have never made any money. That's the way I was in the 1980s, just barely getting by, but spending every last dollar. In some cases, I was even saving it up. If I found a good plan or program I wanted, I'd save all my money for six or eight weeks, until I had a couple of thousand dollars, and I would spend it all at once. So don't think that just because a lot of people in this marketplace are broke right now that they can't get their hands on hundreds or even thousands of dollars. Because they can save it up, and they're willing to spend it once they do. It's a rabid marketplace. The marketplace is driven by emotional factors; the obsessions that people have, the insatiability. These folks are driven by a strong, overwhelming desire to make more money. They dream of getting rich. It's what they think of from the minute they get up to the minute they go to bed at night. As a result, there's a small group of people — I'm one of them — who are making millions and millions of dollars in this marketplace. You can be one of them too, and Secret Number One is so vitally important for you. It's just to become familiar with the marketplace.

So consider carefully about what I've said here; break it down and think about it. The opportunity market really can make you rich, and I'd like for you to start thinking carefully about this marketplace and start buying some of the available opportunities, and start building and studying your swipe file.

SECRET TWO:

Become Self-Employed Today... *and* _Never_ *Give Up!*

I've already mentioned the fact that Eileen and I had a little bit of business experience before we started M.O.R.E., Inc. At the time, I couldn't have told you just how important that previous experience was; it's only through reflection that I'm able grasp this principle. If you don't have any previous business experience, that's fine — just pay attention to what I'm going to tell you. If you *do* have some previous business experience, whether positive or negative, it can be a great asset for you. But it's only an asset if you recognize it, and I'm going to help you do that.

I started my first business in December 1985. It wasn't much, just a little carpet cleaning business, and I started it with a friend at the worst possible time of the year. Plus, it was a bad time for me personally. I didn't have a roof over my head; I was staying with friends and basically living in a sleeping bag on a floor. This is the real story; I was dead broke, and it was in the wintertime, right around Christmas. Nobody wanted their carpets cleaned; everybody wants to wait until after the snow melts in the springtime. But we had an idea... and it was my friend's idea, really. If it weren't for him, I never would have done it. I was cleaning carpets for another individual, and I was doing most of the work. I had a truck and equipment that he supplied, and I'd to go out and find all my own jobs. Then I'd to give this guy 40%. In a good week in the peak season, I was bringing in $1,000 a week. Then my friend came along, and I told him the kind of money I was bringing in. Of course, it was during the fall that I told him this.

Knowing what I know about business and marketing right now, I could have easily doubled or tripled what I was making with the other guy. But $1,000 a week was a lot of money back in the mid-1980s, so my friend talked me into going out and doing it ourselves. It wasn't much of a business, but it helped me get started, and it helped me learn some things I needed to learn. When I met my wife, she helped fill in all the gaps that were missing in my life; she's the Queen of Common Sense. I was a pretty good salesman, and I was confident I could do a good job cleaning carpets; if I knocked on your door, which is how I got a lot of my work, there was a one-in-three chance you'd let me come in and clean some carpets. That was how good I was. I just knocked on doors and I wasn't afraid, because I was confident and really focused on helping people. I learned a few things, and little did I know just how important all that was; but I realize how important it is now. I started figuring this out years later, when we were selling our *Dialing for Dollars* program and we had people who were making ten, twenty, thirty, fifty thousand dollars a month.

We even had one guy in Provo City, Utah, an ex-lawyer named Jay Peterson, who he was doing *$5 million* a year with our program. I know that because we were selling him our products at wholesale. They were just little booklets, but I know from the volume of business he was doing that that he was grossing about two-and-a-half times more than we were! Of course, he put a lot of his own ideas into it. When we were bringing in about $4,000 a week, he was bringing in about ten grand every week, using our secret, the principles that we'd laid out.

We tried to get a handle on our success, because at the same time we had so many people who were criticizing us. They were saying things like, "You guys are cheating us; we're not making any money off this program," and we'd get all these letters from people who wanted a refund on *Dialing for Dollars*. That used to really upset me. I would take it personally before I understood that refunds are a normal part of doing business. People would want their money back, and they would accuse us of selling them a program that was fraudulent or misleading, or that wouldn't work. Or they would tell us how terrible it was. And then we had other customers who bought that same, exact program who were jumping in their cars and driving in from four or five states away, or hopping on airplanes just so they could come and thank us, because it was the only program that had ever worked for them. It was so frustrating because I cared deeply, and I really wanted to help people. Even back then that was my goal; of course I wanted to get rich, but I also wanted to help people. I wanted to make a difference in their lives, so I took it personally when people accused me of cheating them, of selling them worthless programs that didn't stand a snowball chance in hell of working.

But they *did* work. In some cases, people were getting rich with these programs. I also knew that just like Jay Peterson, the guy in Provo who was doing five million a year, they were using a lot of their own ideas. Jay was very secretive; he was one of those business people who kept his cards close to his vest. I have friends and business partners like that; they try to be secretive about everything. I'm the exact opposite. You want to see my cards, I'll show you my cards; I don't care. You'd probably love to play poker with me, but I would *never* want to play poker, because I would give it all up! I love to be free with my ideas; I share my best secrets with people all the time. I hope they benefit from them. I believe in an abundant universe; I believe that you can make millions and I can make millions, too. That's especially true in a marketplace as big as the opportunity market, or the diet market, or the self-improvement market, or many other markets out there. They're so enormous that it doesn't matter; we can all make millions. Just because you make millions doesn't mean that you're making money that would otherwise be going to me. Now, it's true that there are competitors out there. Somebody's going to make these millions of dollars, so it might as well be you. But the market is so huge that you can reach people that I won't be reaching, and I can reach people that you won't be reaching, and together we can all make a fortune.

But back to my story. The unbalanced responses we kept getting in the mail really bothered me, month after month. We'd get letters in the mail where people would say, "Eileen and T.J., I love you guys! You're changing my whole life with this program of yours. I'm making $10,000 a month; thank you, God bless you, and God bless your family," and we would start feeling good about ourselves; we'd start patting ourselves on the back. We'd say to each other, "God, we're so good, we're helping people, we're achieving our dreams. We're not only making millions of dollars ourselves, we're helping other people achieve *their* dreams" — and it felt so damn good. But then we'd get another letter in the mail and it would say, "Dear Eileen and T.J. Rohleder: You scumbags! You cheated me! I spent thousands of dollars on your program, and it didn't work!" Imagine the frustration of *knowing* that you had a program that was tested, was proven, that other people were using to make thousands of dollars — and yet you had people who claimed that the program did *not* work, and that you had lied to or misled them. That bothered me so much so that I became determined to find out, what were the common denominators? What were the successful people doing that the rest of them weren't?

Take Jay Peterson; he's the perfect example. He was making more money than any of our other distributors — millions of dollars — before he cut us out and started doing it all

20

on his own. Incidentally, this is something all of our most successful distributors always do, and that we *encourage* them to do. In fact, I encourage you, the reader, to try that, if you like: To break out on your own, use our products and services as a way of getting started, learn what you have to learn, develop your knowledge and confidence and experience, and *then* start developing your own products and services. Eventually, cut us out. If you want to make the most money, you should be developing your own products and services; that should be your ultimate goal. We can still do business together.

Jay was our most successful distributor, and oddly enough he was doing everything exactly the *opposite* way we told all our distributors to do it in our book. He had his own theories, and he tested everything out himself. He was like most entrepreneurs: He was stubborn and independent, and wanted to do everything his own way. One of those things was the way he handled his scripts. You see, *Dialing for Dollars* used answering machines to replace a live salesperson to sell the products and services for you; it was a little ahead of its time that way. Incidentally, all the principles of *Dialing for Dollars* still work to this day; we use them on a daily basis, except that voicemail has replaced the answering machine.

Whereas we told people that their scripts should move quickly and shouldn't be too long, Jay's scripts were all very long, and they were boring. I once told him, "Jay, I can't even listen to one of your scripts," and he replied, "Look, T.J., the reason why you won't listen to one of my messages from start to finish is, you're not the prospect. You're not the person calling from these ads. A lot of those people hang up too, but I know that when they do hang up, they were just tire kickers anyway; they weren't that serious." He had his own theory — and he was making millions of dollars, so you can't argue with it. Other people were making money doing other things too. The neat thing about this business is you can do it your way, and I can do it my way, and we can still make millions of dollars.

The only real common denominator I found with all these successful customers was that they had some previous business experience. That's it. Case closed; look no further. That was the *only* thing. Now, that led us to some very interesting theories that I want to share with you. Keep in mind that these are generalizations. I want you to think about this: These people had some previous business experience, and so they tended to try things a little harder. Plus, they weren't expecting things to be perfect. They had more realistic expectations. They didn't just give up when things went wrong, because they'd been in business before. It's kind of like a guy and a gal living together. If you live together and there's no marriage contract there, what's to stop you from just saying "Adios," and packing up as soon as something goes wrong?

The people who had previous business experience were more committed; they were more persistent, had a greater level of confidence in themselves, and had broken through a lot of the fears that were holding the inexperienced businesspeople back. They had already suffered through some major setbacks; I know I have, and each time I've continued to move forward, I've always come back stronger. That's the way you develop your entrepreneurial skills and ability. These experienced people had the confidence that came from experience, and they also had a strong work ethic, because successful entrepreneurs are used to doing things on their own. They don't need somebody to tell them what to do, and they don't need somebody to constantly stay on their butt, keeping them busy all the time. Look, I love employees; I thank God for them. But I have to admit, a lot of employees — well, without supervision they're never going to work to their fullest capacity. Becoming successfully self-employed does require a new set of skills that must be developed.

Nobody told me that 20 years ago when I first got started, so I'm telling you now. Your awareness of that one principle is a skill. There's a new set of skills that you've got to develop, and your willingness to develop those qualities is all it takes. There will be some temporary pain and a learning curve; there will be struggle, adversity, and some challenges. The more money you want to make, the more pain you have to go through. But you see, you shouldn't even look at it as pain or problems; these are just part of the price you pay to get where you want to go. It's just like with a bodybuilder or a champion athlete. They know they've got to go through some pain. But the pain of discipline is far greater than the pain of regret — far, far less. Remember that. You've got to feel good about paying the price.

Again, the more money you want to make, the bigger the price you pay. If anybody tells you all that money's going to come out of nowhere, that you're going to make millions of dollars without learning a lot and developing new skills and facing challenges and adversity — well, then, you shouldn't do business with that person, because they're lying to you. They may be trying to tell you what they think you want to hear, but they're not telling you the truth, and why would you want to do business with somebody who's not going to tell you the truth? I'm trying to be honest with you here. And if you take advantage of the free workshop we're offering, where we're going to get together and focus in on these 26 different secrets that have made us millions of dollars, then maybe we'll take a good look at your past experience. If this is one of your weak areas, we can help you. You may be further along than you realize; if you've got some previous business experience, then this is an area you won't need any help with. You're already on the path. You've already experienced the challenges, and you're stronger than you think. That's what I want to share with you. It's a true advantage.

If you don't have the previous business experience, don't despair! You can develop these skills. When I ask myself the question, "What does it take to be a great entrepreneur?" I see that you must be disciplined, because you have to get yourself out of bed in the morning to do the work. Nobody's telling you what to do anymore, so you have to be self-motivated, you have to be focused, and you have to have a strong work ethic. You have to see things conceptually from the top down instead of the bottom up. You need the ability to work *on* your business, not *in* it, to pull back a little, to delegate your weaknesses. Before you delegate those weaknesses, you've got to face up to them. The more money you want to make, the more you're going to have to build a team of people to help. You can't do it by yourself, and you can't get bogged down in the details, although the details are important.

Now, part of what made us millions of dollars has to do with the fact that my wife and I had complementary skills and abilities. By her own admission, she's not a good sales person; she's not a good marketer either. She focuses on the details. She has a lot of common sense, and she's very conservative. I tend to be reckless and wild, and thank God I've picked up enough of her qualities over the years that some of her behavior, ideas, thoughts, and philosophies have rubbed off on me — so I now have the capacity to be a little more conservative. Getting older helps there too. With age, you do tend to mellow somewhat. I've faced up to my weaknesses, and many times the only way I've been able to do that is by suffering through the pain, going through the problems necessary to get to the place where I've said, "No more!" I did that several years ago with being a manager, when Eileen stepped down from the company because of health reasons, and I took over as President and CEO. Before that I'd just been doing the marketing. The first fourteen years, she had the company; I just focused on the marketing, selling, and product development, and I let her do everything else. Well,

I don't want to say, "I let her" — that would be wrong. She *took on* everything else. Then she stepped down eight years ago, and I tried to be a general manager. I tried to fill her shoes, and I beat myself up, and I really gave it my best. I wasn't making excuses. I found out that I'm a terrible manager. I found out that I just don't have the right skills and abilities.

So when I'm telling you to delegate all your weaknesses, it's because I've learned that I had to do that. I finally came to grips with the few things that I'm really good at, and I put all my focus there — and you've got to do that too. You're going to get a really good understanding of this by the end of this book. I'll give you a hint right now: Your focus needs to be marketing. That's the one area that will to make you millions and millions of dollars; and if you can't be a good marketer, then you have to find somebody who can help you. The more money you want to make, the more help you're going to need in this area; and if you're a natural marketer like I am, then you'll need to find people who can handle the day-to-day workings of the company.

You see, business is pretty simple. You've got to see it simpler and believe it bigger. There are a lot of details out there, a lot of different things you can think about when it comes to business. It's like a game of chess. The number of moves is endless, but the basics are pretty simple. You've got what I call the three M's: 1) You've got marketing, which is what makes you all the money; 2) You've got management, which keeps it all organized, keeps it all controlled; and 3) You've got margins. You've got to watch your profits. A business has to do just two things: Serve its customers and make money, and that's it. No matter what business you're in, every business in the world has those two objectives. We've got to serve our customers (which means different things to different businesses), and we have to make a profit.

Marketing is all about attracting and retaining customers.

25

Part of the secret of business is to study the successes of other companies. See yourself as an entrepreneur, subscribe to *Forbes* magazine, read some great biographies. There are some wonderful books on business that aren't "how to" books necessarily; they were never designed to be such. No, these are biographies of successful business people. Two of my favorites, both of which I would strongly encourage you to read, are *Behind the Golden Arches: The Story of McDonald's* and *Gates*, by Stephen Manes and Paul Andrews, respectively. That latter is a wonderful book about Bill Gates and the story of Microsoft. And then there's another great book that really influenced me earlier on: It's a book on Steve Jobs, the co-founder of Apple Computer, and it's called *The Journey is the Reward.*

I would just encourage you to think carefully about what I've said here. It sounds like common sense, in a way. If you do have some previous business experience, you should pat yourself on the back. If you don't, that's fine too, but you'll have to realize that it's a limitation you have. So just develop the awareness that you need to constantly develop some skills, and that you're never going to get there 100% — you're always growing. There's new knowledge to learn and experiences that you have to go through, but you can learn these things. You really, truly can do it. I know you can do it.

I've struggled so much to be an entrepreneur; it's been such a painful thing with me. Why? Because I wanted to make millions of dollars. If I'd only wanted to make a couple of hundred thousand a year, it would be no struggle at all. I can do that in my sleep right now. I don't mean to sound arrogant or cocky; it's simple fact. I can go out there and make $100,000 without even thinking about it, without even working. Why? Well, it's like that bodybuilder who goes to the gym every day. Year after year he pumps these massive weights; he's always adding to the bar, and he develops this very strong body, and eventually he can handle a massive workout. That's the way it is in business, too. These abilities and skills you develop as you go out there to make millions of dollars, to move forward in the direction of your dreams, to take on newer and better challenges, to learn more and more things will make you a very strong, very capable entrepreneur.

I'm here to tell you this: If I can do it, you can do it. But it's not going to come without a lot of challenge and pain and struggle. You have to be willing to go through it, to accept it. I hope that you do, and when I meet you at the free workshop, I'll help you through this area and the other twenty-five areas we're covering on this program. With that said, let's move to the next secret.

SECRET THREE:

Find the Right Business Partner

The third secret that helped us make millions and millions of dollars is the synergy between Eileen and me. Eileen and I formed a great partnership for the first 14 years of our company. She finally had to step down in 2001 because of health reasons, but it was the synergy of our abilities and the help of a lot of other people that made us millions. I was a good salesperson; Eileen is a natural manager. So, we have complementary skills.

As I told you earlier, when I met my wife I was sending away for all kinds of plans and programs. I was on every single opportunity mailing list, and everybody who was selling any kind of an opportunity was sending me stuff. The same thing will happen to you — we talked about how becoming familiar with the marketplace is Secret Number One. Part of getting familiar with the marketplace is sending away for a lot of different plans and programs. Do that, and soon your name will be on all the right mailing lists.

When I met Eileen, I had a tiny carpet-cleaning business, so I already had some previous business experience. I fell in love with Eileen while I was on a carpet-cleaning job. At the time she was just thirty years old, and I was twenty-eight. Although she had multiple sclerosis for seven years before I met her, she would go with me on these carpet-cleaning jobs and work right alongside me. She wanted to be with me. She had a strong work ethic — and I'd been with other girls who weren't like that, so I was able to recognize just how great that was. Something in me screamed very loudly at the time because I wasn't ready for the commitment of marriage. But there was a voice in my head that said, "T.J., don't let this woman go! This is a woman you can do something with, someone you can build something with. Here's a woman who can be right there by your side as you move forward, trying to go as far as you can and doing as many things as you can." And sure enough, I was right. Eileen didn't let multiple sclerosis stop her. I could tell that there was a fire inside her, that she wanted more out of life, just like I did. Together we did something great, and we built a tremendous partnership.

Eileen is determined, she's stubborn, she's independent, and she's very smart; she's also mature, very analytical and conservative. Me, I'm extremely ambitious and I'm also determined; I'm creative, I'm aggressive, and I'm very conceptual. I see things from the top down, and I'm able to see things more metaphorically and not get stuck in the details. But I'm also very immature; I realize that. I'm very impulsive, and I just don't have a good business sense about me. But Eileen does. Our first 14 years in business together, she ran the company as the President and CEO. I did all the marketing, and if it weren't for Eileen, there would have *been* no company. She kept me from destroying the company on more than one occasion, because I had a lot of learning to do. I wasn't able to see that back then. I thought I was better than I really was. I found out the hard way later, after Eileen stepped down and I stepped up as president and CEO, that I am *not* a manager. I found that out once and for all, and the only way I found it out was through hardship. You know, she made it look easy. All those years she ran the company, she picked the right staff; she worked with the accountants, the bankers, the lawyers; she paid close attention to all the details, and let me focus on the few things I was good at, so I could develop my skills as a marketer.

So for fourteen years, I didn't have to worry about running a company. Eileen kept everything organized. She let me spend all my time doing the things that helped us attract and retain customers. Without realizing it, we had stumbled onto a great secret for making millions of dollars. She ran the business; I ran the marketing. I got really good at what I do, and she got really good at what she did. This is the principle you should learn from our story here: You need a good partner to help you focus on your strengths, and to compensate for your weaknesses. That's what a good partnership can do. It can help you make much more money than you would have made had you not had the partnership.

Now, a lot of people don't want a partner, because they don't want to share the money with anybody — and they want to be 100% in control of everything. Some of the smartest people I know will never be rich because of that attitude; or if they do get rich, they'll never make nearly as much money as they should. They're never going to develop a team to help them, either. They're just too independent, too stubborn. I know people like this right now. Some of my closest friends, people I really admire and respect because of their intelligence and their knowledge, are never going to get rich, because they're trying to do everything themselves. A couple of them have personally helped me make millions of dollars — but they're not making nearly the money that they could and should be making. They could be worth millions of dollars themselves, but they're not; and they're not because they don't want to give up control. They think they can do everything themselves. One person in particular I know is so talented, so smart, that he really *can* do everything himself — but he's always broke because he does try to do it all.

If you want to make millions of dollars, you have to develop a talented team to help you. You've got to surround yourself with people who are smart in the areas that you're not smart in, who are strong in the areas that you're weak in. And remember, business is usually really simple. Now, it *can* get complicated, especially when you start running out of cash; and when you start building up your infrastructure, it can be very complicated indeed. But there's simplicity at its heart. As long as you always focus on that, you keep coming back to the simple things: marketing, management, and margins. Trying to keep your costs as low as possible while keeping the mark-ups of your products as high as possible: that's margin. It's like you're pouring water into a bucket with a bunch of holes in it, and you've got to plug as many of those holes as you can. You're trying to keep as much money as you can, without becoming pennywise and dollar-foolish; because sometimes spending more money, not less, is the secret to making big money.

I promise you, there's no better way to spend money than to develop a good, competent staff. Don't be chintzy in this area. The more money you want to make, the more important this is. A good partner will make you money that you couldn't have made without that partnership. The pie will be bigger, and you'll get off to a better start, too. That's another nice thing about partnerships, even if they're not long-term. A good partner can help you get something you want. They can provide the guidance, support and encouragement you need. When things really get bad, they can be there for you. They can help make the hard times easier, and help you enjoy the good times even more.

Now, should you work with your spouse like I did? Well... probably not, especially if you've been married for a while. But Eileen and I were working together from Day One, even before we ever got married. She was giving me business advice within days of meeting me, so our relationship was set that way from the very beginning. I know a lot of married couples who can't work together, and shouldn't; the only support from those types of partnerships should be things that aren't related to work.

That's important too. But I do know some great married couples who work together every single day. The secret is for each person in the relationship to focus on what they're best at. As long as those two things are separate enough, it can be a strength. It really has improved my marriage — even though it's also created plenty of friction.

After 1992, for example, Eileen and I didn't dare keep offices in the same building, so I moved my office out of our headquarters. One of the reasons I moved was because we were fighting, and it was all my fault; I was too immature. Why am I telling you this? Because among other things, you're never going to realize how badly you need a partner until you get honest about your limitations. If you're really as good a businessman as you think you are, why aren't you richer? I challenge you to think about that, because a lot of people who don't want partners completely miss that point.

I wish I could tell that to some of my friends, because I care deeply about them. If they'd listen, I'd tell them, "Look, you're too damn smart for your own good! You need some help!" Somebody's got to focus on the selling side of the business, and somebody *else* has to focus on the managing side. If you try to do both, you're going to fail; one is going to suffer as a result. If you focus too much on the selling side of the business, sure, you can bring in a ton of money, but it's all going to go out so fast it's not even funny. This has been one of the biggest mistakes we've made over the years: not putting enough emphasis on the management side. That's especially been true since Eileen stepped down in 2001. I honestly thought I could run that company as well as she did. I really believed that, because I'm willing to put in the time. I care deeply about the company. It's part of my life; part of who I am. It's more than just a way of making money; this is our baby.

But I found out that to be a manager requires a certain skill set. You have to be detail-oriented, very focused on the day-to-day operations. You have to be objective when it comes to people; you can't play favorites. You have to be somewhat mature and conservative, and can't be afraid to upset people or have people not like you. I'm sure that there are another four or five qualities that make for a good manager, but those are the basics. To be a salesperson, on the other hand, you have to be very emotional, because all selling is a transference of emotion. A good salesman believes so strongly in his product that he can sell that product to a prospective buyer. He can convince you, he can persuade you; it's an emotional, people-oriented kind of thing. The best salespeople love people. I'm not saying that the best managers don't, but they're more objective.

To do well in business, you have to know what you're good at — you have to know what your strengths are. Are they in sales or in management? That's it. Just focus on those two areas alone. If you're more of a salesperson, then you need to find somebody to be the Eileen in your life, the person who will help you with the management part of the business — managing your time, your numbers, your expenses, your people, and your projects. You need somebody to do the implementation, the day-to-day part of the business that I've always found extremely boring. That's not to minimize it, because I know how important it is for the day-to-day success of the company... but to me, it's just boring. If you're more of a management person, you've got to find somebody like me; somebody who can talk to customers, somebody who loves customers, somebody who will sell.

A great partner and a great team will make you money. Now, how much you make depends on how great those people are, since not all people are created equal — no matter how much we might want to believe otherwise. When it comes to running a company, some people contribute ten times more. Some people are much more capable when it comes to both selling and managing. Every employee in a company has value, of course, and as a human they have the ultimate value. So they do deserve all the respect in the world — but when I was a manager, I didn't treat people with respect. I ended up blowing up at people; I yelled and screamed at them. I just didn't have those skills needed to deal with people on a day-to-day basis. I wasn't a manager; and if you're not, then learn from my mistakes, please! Now, when I see you at the free workshop, we're going to talk about partnerships. This might be an area you're weak in, and I'll show you how simple and easy it can be to use this powerful principle.

Now, when it comes to your opinions on partnerships, I'm going to be very curious to learn whether you're more of a salesperson or a manager. I have to caution you that there's something I call the "Entrepreneurial Hero Myth" and it shows up all the time. There are certain entrepreneur heroes the press just loves to parade in front of you — the Donald Trumps, the Bill Gateses, the Michael Dells, the Ted Turners, the Ray Krocs — and you almost get the idea that these people are somehow better than you, that they're more talented, that they have all kinds of things going for them that you don't. But that's just the biggest lie there is. I want you erase that from your mind, because when you study these people's successes, you'll see that they *all* have great teams behind them. You'll find that, yes, they have certain common qualities, talents, and abilities that have enabled them to get where they are, but they have a whole lot of other people making them look good, too. It's always the people behind the scenes that matter; it's never the person out in front alone who's responsible for the success. I look at it like a band. Sometime ago, I wanted to play the piano, so I took music lessons for seven or eight years. My teacher stressed something very important to me. He said that in a band, a great rhythm section — the bass guitar, the drums and other accompaniments — can make a bad lead guitar player or lead singer appear to be much better than they actually are. Conversely, you can take the world's greatest singer or lead guitarist and put them in a band with a bad rhythm section, and they'll come across as terrible. The same thing goes with a company. You need people who are very, very strong behind the scenes, who can make up for your weak areas. Before that happens, you need to come face-to-face with what those weak areas are.

Let me repeat that. It's great to know what you're good at, but it's just as important, if not more so, to know what you're *bad* at. A big mistake a lot of entrepreneurs make is that they're too stubborn and independent, too cocky and rebellious. Now, those are good qualities, ones that are actually needed in the beginning, when you start your new company and you decide you're going to go out and make things happen. It requires a certain amount of ego and rebelliousness to flip off the whole world and say, "I'm going to go out there and do it on my own. Come hell or high water, I'm going to succeed and do all these wonderful things." There's a certain spirit of cockiness, egotism, and stubbornness that's required to rise above all the challenges, and all those people who are telling you that you can't do it. That has to be present in every great entrepreneur. If it wasn't, we would never start our own businesses. But after you get off to a good start, it's time to address some of these issues.

Part of the reason to start a business is to have control over your life — to do things your way, to call your own shots and not have somebody looking over your shoulder, to be independent and to be free. I understand and appreciate that, and it's vitally important — but you can't look at a partnership as something that's going to restrict you. You need to look at it as something that will actually give you greater freedom, because it'll let you focus on the areas you're best at, the ways that you can contribute to your company and your own financial future to the greatest degree. It's simple: Are you a better salesperson, or are you a better manager? If you're a better manager, don't try to be a salesperson; if you're a salesperson, don't try to be a manager. Find the best people you possibly can to do what you can't. Those people will help you focus on the few things you're really good at, and help you develop the skills you need.

The more money you want to make, the more important this principle is. If you want to make millions and millions of dollars, you have to go out there and find a great team of people who can help you, who can fill in for all your weak areas, who can complement your skills. There's nothing that's more important if you want to get rich.

I had a couple of other partners before Eileen, and those partnerships were very short-lived. They did help me get off to a good start, so they had value. If it weren't for the two partners that I had before Eileen, I would never have gotten to the point I was when I met her. But those former partners were exactly like I was: salespeople. They had no management skills or abilities whatsoever, and you'll require both. So think very, very carefully about this, and let this secret that's made us millions of dollars help *you* make millions of dollars. When I spend some personal time with you, we're going to talk about this, and I'm going to show you how you can use this powerful principle to make your own fortune.

SECRET FOUR:
Timing's Everything. Find Opportunities That Are Hot!

The fourth step that made us over $10 million in less than five years is *timing*. Now, I have many things to say about timing, so I want you to pay particularly close attention to this chapter. I suspect that in the past, you've been misled in some ways when it comes to this subject, and there are other things, besides what other people have told you, where timing is crucial. Everybody says you've got to find the right opportunity at the right time. Well, I'm going to show you how there's a little more to it than just that. I'm going to show you some other ways to cash in on this very important secret.

You have to understand that people who make millions of dollars are always searching for the right idea at the right time. There's a little more to it than that, but we're always looking for something that's hot, something that's new, something that's popular, something that's exciting, something that other people are already thinking about. We're looking for what's in the news, what's exciting or trendy that's changed the marketplace. The newer it is or the more exciting it sounds, the better. That's what creates the draw, the buzz, the excitement — and you need that. You've got to find some new angle all the time. This is especially true when you're selling business opportunities. Fortunately, with a little forethought, it's easy to take something that's old and put a new facelift on it.

People don't understand the secrets behind what we do. They don't even realize that the real secret is that we're constantly coming out with stuff that sounds new, but *isn't really new at all*. There's just a new angle to it; it's sort of like a Hollywood movie front, where there's nothing behind the buildings but a few braces, and all the equipment and the trailers where the actors go while they're waiting to shoot the next scene. The truth is that most of the things that are positioned as new often aren't new at all. And that's okay; it's actually a good thing, because it means you're working with something that's proven.

Let's say you're selling a proven business opportunity that's making other people money, but it's been out there for a while. Well, because everybody's already heard about it, people become apathetic. We've all heard the quote that says that familiarity breeds contempt. I think that that's true in some cases. But I think what's more true is that familiarity breeds *apathy*. People just become bored with it; they don't really care anymore. They've seen it before. It's not exciting, it's not new. And they're *all* looking for something new: They're like kids in a candy store, because they've been trained to be that way. We're just that way; you can be critical of it, or you can accept and embrace it.

When you embrace it, you start looking for things that are new, because that's what people really want. Consider this: When we talk to people that we haven't seen for a while, don't we always say, "What's new?" We don't want to hear the old stuff, even though it's probably the best stuff. It's boring. It's old. People want things that are new and exciting and different. Your job is to give them what they're searching for.

That said, there's a lot of sales resistance out there, and a lot of newcomers don't realize that. They're not in touch with it. They want to deny it. They want to take their heads and bury them in the sand. They want to ignore the fact that there are so many different companies and individuals fighting hard to get those same dollars that they're trying to get. That's where your focus really should be: You're trying to get people to give you money. As long as you sell something that's valuable and has a greater potential worth than the amount of money you're asking for, then don't be embarrassed about it. Instead, you should get very aggressive. Go for the jugular; get out there and get as many people to give you their money as possible, because you're doing them a disservice by not trying to do everything possible to get them to give you their money.

Remember, though, that you're looking for something that's proven. Now, by definition, something that's new isn't something that's proven. The very act of being new implies that somebody's got to be the guinea pig. When it comes to selling business opportunities, people like hearing about things that have a new twist to them, but are still a part of something old and established. That's what really gets people excited: to find out that there's a new way to do something old.

But you have to get people excited to get them to buy. People must be open and receptive to your marketing messages. They become open and receptive when they hear something that sounds different. That's what marketing is really about: differentiating yourself from everybody else. The best way to do this is to find something hot, something exciting. It doesn't matter what, "as long as it sounds good," as my good friend, the late, great George Douglas, used to say. Now, George was a very ethical businessman, and the richest man that I've ever personally spent a lot of time with. He was worth millions and millions of dollars when I had a rare opportunity to sit down with him for a few hours. For Eileen and I, that was a very important night of our lives — September 22, 1990.

At that time, George was very well established, while we were just getting started. He came to one of our seminars, and he was just sitting there in the crowd. George was an ordinary guy — you couldn't pick him out of a line-up. Some of the people I've met try to pretend like they have a lot of money; but the more I got to know them, the more I find out that it's just a façade. George wasn't like that, but he *was* straightforward. He used to say that a product or service will do well "as long as it sounds good."

Now, does that mean that he was cheating people, ripping them off? Absolutely not! It just meant he was a master marketer, and he understood that what people really want is something that's new and different and exciting, and it's got to sound good. There's a movie called *A Few Good Men*, with Tom Cruise, Kevin Bacon, Demi Moore, and the great Jack Nicholson. In that movie, Jack Nicholson uses a wonderful phrase in a scene with Tom Cruise: "You can't handle the truth!" We liked it so much that a few years back, we printed it on T-shirts that we handed out to seminar attendees.

A lot of people can't handle the truth — but just as many can, though not right away. They need to be eased into it a little bit. This is especially true where my expertise lies, in selling business and moneymaking opportunities. There's no such thing as a panacea in my field; there are no perfect moneymaking opportunities. They're all filled with certain challenges and obstacles and situations, and what some people call problems. And the more money you want to make, the more challenges or problems or situations you'll face. There are good sides and bad sides to everything in life. People can accept this, but usually not right away. Not in the beginning. They have to be eased into the whole thing. Then later, as they get into it, become committed, become dedicated — that's when they're ready to accept the not-so-perfect things. If you really think about it, it all makes sense. Your job is to ease people into the business. You can't tell them everything up front; that would just scare them away.

There are all kinds of other people out there who understand this principle I'm sharing with you. I want you to be one of them. *You've got to position things as if they're new.* Often you're offering the appearance of new, not true newness. So you're giving things a facelift — and I'll show you how we're doing this in a couple of different ways. The benefit of all of this is that if you cut through the clutter of the other marketing messages that are out there, people will become more open and receptive, and they'll be ready to buy — and that's the whole point here. Timing is everything.

Part of that timing is getting people in the mood for something — and this is something most gurus never tell you. Instead, they tell you to look for the right opportunity at the right time. Sure, that's important, but the truth is, timing is just as much about getting people hot for something you've already got. When somebody raises their hand and says, "Yes, send this to me, I'm interested," what they're really saying to you, if you understand the language, is, "I'm ready for it, I'm ready, I'M READY." You have to know just how important that timing is, because a lot of people don't.

Years ago, I was trying to help my sister get a business off the ground. Of course she's just as rebellious as I am, if not more so; and I'm her big brother and she's been fighting with me ever since we were kids. She was generating leads for her business. It was a local business, so she was smart enough to leave little boxes on countertops in places her prospective customers would frequent. She was selling a health service, so she was putting them into some of the upscale boutiques around Tucson, Arizona. I went out there to spend Thanksgiving with her, and while I was over at her house, she was telling me about her lead-generation process — and sure enough, she had thousands of leads from people who had raised their hands and said, "Yes I'm interested." I was really excited for her. But then I asked her one question: "How old are these leads? How long have you had them?"

That was the sticking point. She didn't know what to do with the leads she had. She knew she had to get leads, but then she spent too long trying to figure out what to do with them — and suddenly some of these leads were two and three months old. I told her something she didn't want to hear: that those leads were worthless, and she should just throw them away. Of course, she didn't understand that. The point is, when somebody's in the mood for something, when they raise their hands and express an interest in what you have, they're ready *then*. This is the purpose of two-step marketing, which I'll talk about in more detail later: to separate the smaller herd from the bigger one.

You're getting a group of people who raise their hand and say, "Yes I'm interested; send all of the secrets now!" What they're doing is saying, "I'm ready," and like the old quote says, "When the student is ready, the teacher will appear." When people are ready for something, you've got to get them while they're hot. In the restaurant business, they say that today's salad is tomorrow's garbage. Think about that: A beautiful salad that looks so delicious today is tomorrow's garbage. If it's not eaten today, it becomes worthless. It's the same way when it comes to the timing of the prospect. When the prospect is ready to buy, that's it — go for it! Timing is everything. Also, there are certain seasons in some markets. With the business-opportunity market, the very best season is the beginning of the year. People are focused on a belief that this is going to be year that everything changes. You've been there before. There's a certain spirit when it comes to the New Year. People are open and receptive, because they're determined that this is going to be the year that everything turns around for them. So they're ready, and you've got to hit them when they're ready.

Something happened a few years back that I thought was

interesting. Our accountant came over and we talked real estate. Two years before, he'd made a significant investment in some premium commercial real estate in downtown Newton, Kansas: He'd spent a lot of money and bought three buildings side-by-side. Of course, as a smart business person he was looking for somebody to help share the risk, and help share the opportunity. So he tried everything he could to get us excited about this — everything! But he might as well have been talking to a brick wall. We resisted him every step of the way. There was no way we were going to invest in commercial real estate then; no way. Fast forward to two years later, and we were starting to get into real estate. Our company was starting to interview all these real-estate experts, and our whole focus was starting to shift over in that direction. That's all we were thinking about. Eileen was, in fact, getting ready to make a strong move on another piece of real estate just a block from our accountant's property in downtown Newton. So I called him up and said, "Dwayne, are you still doing the real estate thing?" and he said, "Can I come over now?" He knew that we were ready.

After spending a couple of hours with us, as he was getting ready to leave Dwayne said to me, "T.J., I've known you now for eighteen years, and this is the most mellow I've ever seen you. What's wrong? Did you take a drink or something before I came over?" Well, he didn't know that I don't drink, so I said, "No, Dwayne; I'm just ready for this. I'm ready now, and that's it." I was open, I was receptive, I was eager to hear his pitch, and I was hanging on to his every word. In the past, I'd pretty much done everything I could to avoid spending much time with him. You see, I have a bad attitude when it comes to physicians, psychiatrists, lawyers, accountants, and bankers — so while Eileen ran the company, I avoided this guy. Well, now I was sitting there, and I was open and I was receptive to him. Why? The timing; it's all about the timing.

Again, one of the most popular — and trite — sales messages you'll hear is that you've got to be involved in the right opportunity at the right time. We ourselves us this sales message all the time to persuade our prospects and customers to buy and rebuy from us. But it's a little more complicated than that; you can be involved in the right opportunity at the right time and *still* lose everything. There are two more factors involved that most people never consider. First, you've got to be in business with the right people, because if you're not careful, some people will take advantage of you. They're going to try to use you; they're going to try to pull the wool over your eyes; they're going to try to mislead you. They're going to try to do everything possible to cheat you. So if you're involved in the right opportunity at the right time with the wrong people, you're never going to make the kind of money you could make, at best; and at worst you're going to lose everything. So you've got to have the right people on your side.

And then there's the other thing, which is vitally important: the execution has to be right. Even if you're involved in the right opportunity at the right time with the right people, if you don't do things right it could blow up in your face. All it takes is for you to make a few mistakes in the execution of whatever you're trying to do, and you're not going to make as much money as you could. That's the best-case scenario. At worst, it's going to all fall flat on you. You're never going to get the amount of money you could and should make, money that you would make if your execution were right.

So: what *is* execution? Basically, it's how you go out there to launch the new idea: how you promote it, how you attract new people, how you sell it, and how you package it. It's the entire implementation process, where you take a great idea and turn it into solid reality: how you're going to market it, how you're going to sell it, what your up-sells are going to be, what your additional back-end sales will be. What are you going to do to convert the largest amount of leads over to sales? What are you going to do to achieve maximum profit from every person you're trying to sell to? What are you going to do to keep people happy and wanting more? This is all simpler than you might imagine. You've just got to look for things that are hot and take advantage of them. That's what we've done, and that's a large part of what made us $10 million in our first five years.

We started with *Dialing for Dollars* back in 1988; that was when reasonable-sized answering machines were brand new. Remember, back in the early 1980s they were these huge coffee-table machines with big, clunky tapes and all that. Well, in the late 1980s, technology started shrinking the size of these machines; it also started shrinking the cost of the machines, and now that they were affordable, millions and millions of people had an answering machine for the first time in their lives — or they wanted to get one. All their friends were getting one. It seems funny now, because answering machines and voice mail are part of everyday life, but back in the late-1980s there was a tremendous buzz over them. Well, we came along with a way to make money with an answering machine. Because it was proven and exciting, we profited enormously.

Then, in 1993, we found computer bulletin boards. Nobody really knows what computer bulletin boards are anymore, but they were basically the precursors to the Internet. There was a small group of people who were advertising for free on thousands of computer bulletin boards. So we got started in that, helped our clients make money, and again we made millions of dollars. Then, in 1995, with the help of our good friend Alan R. Bechtold, we started selling websites. We made millions of dollars doing that, too, and we did it in a short period of time. The money came so easy and so effortlessly, and that's the whole thing I'm trying to point out here: When you've got something new, and really exciting, people will inundate you with orders. They'll Federal Express their orders to you. They'll use Western Union to wire their money to you. They'll jump in their car and drive across four or five states just so that they can get their package right away. Having something new and exciting creates a buzz. People want it now. That's what happened almost every time we've come out with something exciting and new — at least, when the timing has been right.

Now, when the timing *isn't* right, you may be in trouble. For instance, in 1999, we started promoting viral marketing. Alan R. Bechtold told us about this — he's a high-tech guy. There were a few people on the Internet at that time who were using viral marketing to get other people to help them make money, by passing out free things of value that contain embedded links that link back to whatever you're trying to sell. Well, for the time it was a little too high-tech. The name "viral" isn't a good name, really. It relates to viruses, a bad thing for either people or computers. The idea wasn't ready for the masses; it was too new, and we lost money on it. Five years later, we started promoting it again under the name Chain Reaction Marketing — and sure enough, people were ready for it. They were excited; it had a better name, and we'd had more time to develop it. Now people are embracing the whole idea of viral marketing.

In 2001, we found a way to help our clients make money with e-books. They were hot back then, and we sold a ton of e-books and e-book websites. In 2004 it was eBay, and we have our good friend Russ von Hoelscher to thank for that. Russ saw that everywhere you turned in the news, people were talking about the Internet; there was such an excitement in the air when it came to Internet marketing. eBay was everywhere in the news, and we cashed in on it; we found many ways to add that to things we already had going.

See, that's the point here. You're not necessarily coming up with something new. You're putting a new look and feel to it. That's one of the things we're going to talk about in our free workshop. We're going to show you how to put new facelifts on things and look for things that are new, add them to things that are old and proven, solid and established. Do that, and now you've got a way to ease into the marketplace.

Now we're doing it with real estate. I originally recorded the audio presentation this book is adapted from in 2006, when we were just getting into making money in real estate. You might ask yourself, what's new about that? Well, there's nothing terribly new about real estate at all, unless you're a person who's just now getting interested in it. That's where part of this timing comes in. Don't forget, this involves the timing of the prospect. When they're ready for something, people get excited, and we're finding new ways to put new twists into this. We're not real-estate experts, so we're interviewing real-estate experts, and then we're packaging it up in different kinds of ways, so that people get excited about it. People are ready for it; it's the important part of the timing here.

In this chapter, I've covered a number of different facets regarding the subject of timing, and how it's made us millions of dollars. You need to think these things through, because this is part of the secret that can also make you millions. Time things right, and you'll make super-easy money that you never would have made before. You'll cut through all the sales resistance and clutter with all these new messages. You'll create a buzz; you'll capture some of the excitement of offering new things at the right time. People will be more open and receptive to you — and the more open and receptive they are, the more willing they'll be to open up their wallets and freely start giving you their money, because they *want* things that are new and different and exciting.

SECRET FIVE:

Get Help from the Right Wealth-Making Experts

Our Secret Number Five is that we had the right moneymaking help along the way. That's a recurring theme throughout this book: Nobody ever gets rich by themselves. If it weren't for all the people who helped us, I wouldn't be a millionaire today. I've already mentioned that terrible myth that I call the "Entrepreneurial Hero Myth," where successful entrepreneurs want you to believe that somehow they made it all on their own. Nothing could be further from the truth. I needed a lot of help to get where I am today, and all the people who make the most money share that secret with me.

For me, it started with the people I met in multilevel marketing meetings. When I first got the idea that I wanted to make millions of dollars, I started getting hooked on all these multilevel marketing companies. With most of them I never stood any chance of making any money, and neither did any of the people I met at those meeting — but at least they were positive people. They weren't like all the other people I was running around with. These were people who really believed it was possible to get rich. They wanted to do something with their lives. They weren't happy; they had what I call "inspirational dissatisfaction." They wanted more out of life; and so they, like me, joined all these stupid multilevel marketing companies — and a lot of them *are* stupid, by the way; many are absolutely worthless. The only people who ever make any money with those are the heavy hitters and the companies themselves.

But you know what? That's okay, because they can be great places for you to get some support — and I would encourage you to join those companies for that, if for nothing else. Do the minimum it takes to become a distributor, just so you can go to their motivational rallies. Surround yourself with people who are moving forward, doing big things. Of course, there are also other groups that allow you to do that. Once you go into business for yourself, you can join the Chamber of Commerce. You may not feel like you fit in, but some of the people who belong to those organizations... well, don't let them fool you. Even though they have traditional businesses, most of them, they're still people who are doing something positive with their lives. There's also Toastmasters, and other independent, local groups you can join for inspiration. For me, that was so vital, having help from people who were positive. They were motivated, they were dreamers like I was, they wanted more out of life, and that's really what got me started. The more I hung around with those people, the less I hung around with people who seemed to be happy where they were, and didn't want anything more out of life.

My first two business partners also helped me a great deal, and by the time I met my wife Eileen in 1987, I'd already had 18 months of business experience. Of course, I burned through those first two partnerships very quickly. Those partners were exactly like I was, and when I met Eileen, little did I know that I'd stumbled on to that secret of synergy that I've already shared with you. She was very different than I was, and together we combined our talents and created something that was truly powerful. By the time I met her I was ready to succeed, and her help was vital. She had all the right skills to compliment mine.

Then, in 1989, we met Russ von Hoelscher — and from that point forward, our lives were changed forever. Now, we paid

Russ many thousands of dollars over the years, but he helped us make millions of dollars in return. It's not what something costs but what it will make you that counts, and that's the *only* thing that counts. I want to do the same thing for you. It's my sincerest goal to help you, just like Russ von Hoelscher helped us.

Our multimillion-dollar help didn't stop with Russ von Hoelscher. In 1992, we met the great copywriter Luther Brock, and we mailed millions of sales letters that Luther wrote for us. He's a great and experienced copywriter, and no matter how hard I tried back then to write advertising copy that did a great job of profitably attracting new customers, I just couldn't do it. I wasn't talented enough — and that used to bother me so much. I've always thought of my customers as friends, so when I wrote to my existing customers, I was writing to friends; but when it came time to write copy to new people who had never done business with us, I was dependent on these outside copywriters like Luther — and what they did was inspire me. Admittedly, it was mostly the kind of inspiration that comes from anger. I was so upset because these copywriters were able to bring in millions of dollars of business from new customers. They were able to write direct response marketing and advertising copy that was so compelling that it drew in people who had never had a relationship with us. Now, once those people were attracted to us, I could write from there and do all the promotion myself.

Of course, I've gotten better over the years: what used to take me three months now takes me three days, and what used to take me three days now takes me three hours. I'm better at drawing in new customers on my own today. But getting the right help from other people when we needed it has been very important in our success. I've had people like Russ von Hoelscher, Luther Brock, and Dan Kennedy, who came along in 1993 and wrote a lot of copy for us, helping me every step of the way. Watching them do what I couldn't do inspired me to do a better job. It inspired me to learn how to write copy. Of course, with Eileen running the company, I could focus all of my time and attention on marketing — coming up with great ideas for products and services to sell to our customers, developing promotions, learning the skills of writing copy. It's another reason why you need help, so that you can focus in on that one thing.

In 1996, we joined Dan Kennedy's Platinum Group, and again, that was crucial to helping me become a better marketer and to helping Eileen understand some of the principles of marketing. We met four times a year, and at that time I think we paid $6,000 annually. By the time we quit it was up to close to $10,000 a year, and I wouldn't be surprised now if it's up $15,000 or even $20,000 a year. Whatever it costs, it's worth it.

In 1993, we came across Alan R. Bechtold, whom I mentioned in the previous chapter. He's a living legend in electronic marketing. He was one of the very first people to started selling stuff online, a true expert who helped us make millions and millions of dollars. When the Internet came along and started taking over everything, it changed our entire business. But we had Alan, helping us profit from the changes.

That's the point of this particular secret. Russ, Dan, and Alan all helped us make millions of dollars — not just by profiting from their help, but also through various partnerships that we formed with them. The millions of dollars we made with them, and all our other joint-venture partners, was in the most part money that we would never have made without their help. That's an important principle that most people just don't get, because they're unwilling to make an investment. They see a coaching group that sells for $5,000 a year, $10,000 a year, $30,000 a year and they say, "No way am I going to pay out that kind of money!" They hear about a seminar that sells for $5,000 or $10,000 — or even $25,000, for some of Jay Abraham's seminars — and they say, "There's no way I'm going to pay out thousands of dollars to go to a seminar, or even to buy the tapes!" They don't realize that just a few ideas could turn everything around for them. That's all it takes: just a few well-implemented ideas, with the right help — and what costs you thousands of dollars can make you millions of dollars. Because they're unwilling to spend that money (they could get it, if they really wanted to) they always stay broke.

In 1995, we started our One Hundred Million Dollar Roundtable Group, where we get together with other marketers for product development and develop products as special partnerships, and it was the start of something that continues to this day. We have members coming and going constantly, but we're doing a lot of things as a group that we never would have done on our own — ever. It's been very profitable for us, these things that we've learned just by freely helping each other. You can never really reach out to try to help somebody without helping yourself, too. That's an important principle to remember; it's a spiritual principle, but it also applies to business and making money.

In 1992, we met Chris Lakey, who is now a vital part of our organization. Chris was just 15 years old when I met him, and he's 32 years old now. So he's been in and around our business for more than half of his life. He's very smart. He started out as an employee, but somewhere along the line a switch inside of him just flicked. He got interested in the business and I told him, when he decided to create his own company in 1996 or 1997, "Look, if you'll just do what I tell you to do, you can make $100,000 a year within your first three years, and you'll just work part time." He wanted one day a week where he could just focus on his business and come in four days a week, but I needed him to stay at M.O.R.E., Inc.! Well, he was open and he was receptive, just like we were when Russ von Hoelscher started working with us, and in his first year he made more than

$100,000. Again, it's all about the power of getting the right help, and learning the right shortcut secrets.

So let's talk about those secrets. Other people who have gone where you want to go have already figured out the problems that you need to figure out. They have experience, they know shortcuts, and they've done what you want to do, so they can shorten your learning curve by revealing their secrets to you. If you're open and receptive to those secrets, it can make all the difference in the world to your success.

We met Jeff Gardener in 1996. When he first got started, he was just 15 or 16 years old, still living at home in Dodge City, Kansas. He would come home every day and say, "Mom, how many orders did I get for today?" and his mom would say "Well, son, here's your mail," and he'd open it up, and there would be cash in the mail. That was his dream, even from the time he was very young. Of course, his parents told him to forget all this garbage about making money and direct response marketing, and they encouraged him to go to college and get a degree, which he did. But he never used his degree, and he's a millionaire now — probably a multi-millionaire. He learned it from the ground up, and he's been a vital part of our group. The same thing with Don Bice: we met him in 1999, and he's helped us make millions of dollars.

We've also had a great staff over the years, and I'm going to talk more about them in other parts of this book. In 1990 and 1991, Eileen hired Jeff McMannis and Randy Hamilton. Those two gentlemen are still with our company. Randy is a numbers genius; Jeff is an implementation guy. If you need anything done, there's Jeff. In 1997, I met Jeremy and Shelley Webster, and now Shelley's my general manager and Jeremy's a vital part of our organization. There are many others I could mention. These folks are the foundation of our group, and yes, they've helped us make millions of dollars. And I've got to mention our suppliers, like our mailing house printers.

I just cannot stress enough how finding the right people and sticking with them is a real secret here. It sounds like common sense: get all the help you can, and find the right people. But when it comes time to pay these people, a lot of entrepreneurs balk, because the right people don't come cheap. Russ von Hoelscher, as everybody knows, has been one of the key factors to our success — but over the years we've probably paid him about half a million dollars. So although he's helped us a great deal, that help has cost us. Even though he's a dear friend of ours, he has a business that has to make a profit. His time is money. That's a limited resource. So we pay him thousands of dollars an hour, in some cases, but it's worth it because it makes us so much more money than we pay him.

The people you surround yourself with, especially when it comes to finding people who are talented in the areas that you're weak in — those people will help you stay focused, and that's important in business. Too many business people spend their time doing what I call 'putting out the brushfires' every day. That's all they do. They come into the office, they've no real strategy, no real plan, they're not focused at all, they're trying to wear all the hats, they're trying to control every aspect of their business, and they refuse to delegate. I did this for several years when Eileen stepped down, so I can tell you what a waste of time and resources it really is. It's the worst thing you can do, and yet most businesspeople do it constantly. They have no agenda; they just walk in the door and solve problems, every day, that other people could be solving. They feel important; it strokes their ego, and they feel like they're getting something done. But the truth is, they're undisciplined and unfocused. They never get rich, and it's no wonder so many businesses go broke. They refuse to spend the kind of money you have to spend on the infrastructure. They refuse to spend the kind of money you have to spend to get the best experts, the best consultants. In some cases, these are people you're going to pay $10,000 a day to, but it's going to be worth that if you'll implement their ideas. No amount of consulting work, going to seminars, reading good books, or studying great programs is ever going to make you any money unless you implement the ideas. With the right implementation, you can make millions by learning shortcut strategies, by acquiring the important contacts that these people offer you, by learning the things they had to learn by going through a lot of pain and struggle themselves.

Eileen and I tell people that we were like little Forrest Gumps — you know, like in the Tom Hanks movie. Forrest just does whatever you tell him to, and he ends up becoming rich and having a very happy life even though he's mentally challenged. Well, see, I think in some ways *I'm* mentally challenged. I'm not the smartest guy out there, and I never really fooled myself about that much. Some part of me always knew that I needed help. I see people who are so much smarter than I am, people who are multi-talented; they can do lots of things, whereas I'm good at just a few things. I'm a great conceptual thinker, I can develop product ideas that make millions of dollars, and I'm a great copywriter to the market I serve; that's about it. But I have friends who are skilled in all areas and more — and it's a weakness. It's a curse, not a blessing, because they try to do everything themselves and they never stay focused on what's most important. Some of these guys are geniuses. They could be worth a whole lot more money than my wife and I are worth — and yet because they don't practice Secret Number Five, they're putting in 12 and 14 hours a day and are always broke.

So find people and lean on them. Find the very best people you can, and then grab ahold of them and don't let go. Pay them whatever money they ask for and let them become a vital part of your success; that's been our secret. The experts can give you the shortcuts that you need; they can help you do more with less, and they'll make you money, not cost you money, if they're the right people.

That's why paying consultants $1,000 an hour or more is usually worth the investment. I hope you can see that just a few of the ideas that they can provide you can make all the difference, turn everything around for you, and help you make the millions of dollars you want. Similarly, the more money you want to make, the more important your staff is, because you need that infrastructure. I'm going to talk a lot about that in this book, because it's extremely important. A great staff can free up your time and energies to allow you to focus on what you need to focus on. The good people you surround yourself with will help you do and be and have more of everything that you want.

And then there's the emotional element. Now, this is something that nobody talks about — and I don't know why, because it's such an important thing. It's something that will never show up on a profit/loss statement, but here it is: Good people will keep you in the game. They'll not only keep you playing at a higher level, but they'll keep you playing, period. You're going to go through some good times, but you'll go through some bad ones, too. The more you want to make, the more struggle and adversity you'll have to face. You're going to hit the peaks and you're going to hit the valleys, and to survive both you need good people that you really trust, who are capable and competent, who have the skills that you lack, who have the knowledge that you need, who can stay with you through thick and thin, through the ups and the downs. They'll take the lows and help smooth those out, so the pain will be less than if you were all alone; and in those times when everything is great, when the money's pouring in, the joy you'll feel will be intensified. They'll make the good times better and they'll make the bad times less painful. I'm so fortunate that I'm surrounded with people that I love and care about, who are also with me in the business.

Even though my wife Eileen officially stepped down as General Manager in 2001, she's still my business partner. We still talk about business all the time, and she helps me manage some of my joint-venture partnerships. Plus, she's my confidante. She understands the business and has helped me a great deal on a daily basis. But I also have Chris Lakey, who's worked his way up to the top of the company — he's also my son-in-law. And then I have my son Chris, who's only been with the company now for a few years, but he's coming around, and he's learning more and more all the time; and then I have staff members who are really more like honest-to-God family. The company could fall apart tomorrow, and I'd still be in touch with these people on a regular basis, and I'd always have a warm, loving, caring feeling about these people till the day I died, if I lived to be 100. This is something that doesn't show up on a profit/loss statement, but I know that it's been a vital part of my success, and the successful people I know who have opened up to me off the record (because nobody likes to talk about this) have said the same. It's the people you surround yourself with who make it all worthwhile, and they'll keep you in the game — even when you want to give up. But you won't quit; you don't want to let them down, and they'll inspire you. As they get excited about the business and as the business becomes more important to their lives, it'll help you.

Even your joint-venture partners help you, as you help them. Helping people like Eric Bechtold has been a wonderful experience for me, because I knew him for a few years before he broke away from his uncle Alan and started his own business. I've been part of helping him from Day One. He's 15 to 16 years younger than me, but he's exactly like I was back then — only he's so much smarter, and he's going to make so much more money by the time he's my age. He'll be worth ten or a hundred times more money than I'm worth, and that's okay — he's inspired me. Helping other people will help you at the same time; that's how you need to look at it. These aren't just people who are going to give you things; these are people who are going to play a role in your success. But you're also going to do everything you can to be there for them and to give them what they need, and that includes suppliers, staff members, joint-venture partners; that includes your customers too, your customers and your clients. You're going to do everything possible to reach out to help them, and you're going to benefit greatly in the process.

Nobody ever gets rich by themselves. It's the relationships that you develop with other people that are vitally important. When I meet you at our free workshop, we're going to talk about this. If this is a weak area of yours, if you're like some of my friends who are multi-talented and can do everything, I'm going to personally do everything possible to convince you that you need to surround yourself with those other people, so you can focus in on those few things that are going to be responsible for all the millions of dollars you want to make.

SECRET SIX:

Master the Art and Science of Direct-Mail

Secret Number Six: We leveraged the power of direct-mail to make our fortune. People who are familiar with our story know that when Russ von Hoelscher first started working with us, we were bringing in $16,000 a month. That was more money than we'd ever made in our entire lives. You see, Eileen and I had never made more than $26,000 a year, ever, and that was combined. Yet here we were, brand new in the mail-order business, getting rich. I'd already had a couple of years under my belt as a business owner, so there was some experience there, and we'd done a lot of different things. But once we got into mail order, that's when preparation met opportunity. We had the right opportunity at the right time with our *Dialing for Dollars* program. We were doing pretty well — but Russ von Hoelscher helped us take that income and turn it into almost $100,000 a *week*.

Everybody who knows us knows that story, and they all ask us the same question: "What exactly did Russ do to help you go from $16,000 a month to almost a $100,000 a week in just nine months?" The main thing that he did was to give us all his greatest tips, tricks, and strategies, and really help us to see what we had. We didn't realize just how many advantages we had, and what a great thing it was. You see, Russ von Hoelscher, back in 1988, was in some ways where I am right now. He was able to recognize a great thing when he saw it. That's the one advantage

I have now, with more than twenty years of experience under my belt. I can spot a great opportunity when I see one, and I can spot a winner when I meet one. I'm just smart enough now to quickly see when somebody's got a multimillion-dollar idea. When they're going in the wrong direction, I know that too. It just comes from years and years of experience. This is one of the greatest ways that I can help you, when I meet you at our workshop: I can help you spot the great opportunities and separate them from all the others, and help you focus in on the things that can help you make the maximum amount of money.

Direct-mail is the most powerful sales medium on Earth. It helps you instantly reach and sell to millions of people. It's fast, it's direct, and you're in total control. Direct-mail lets you do a complete job of selling from start to finish, and when you do it correctly, a thousand great direct-mail packages is the same thing as having a thousand of the best salespeople. I call it "direct salespeople in an envelope." But you don't have to put up with all the crap you normally have to put up with salespeople. I'm a salesman myself, and I can tell you that salespeople can be real pain in the butt. The best ones tend to be very egotistical. They're not team players, they want to do everything on their own, but hey, they're making you money, so you've got to put up with their crap.

But when you use direct-mail, you could have the best of the very best salespeople, the ones that go out there and bring back the money. They'll never call in sick, and you'll never have to pay them the big bucks. Direct-mail does a complete job of selling. This is a powerful medium, and it's a great way for you to build strong bonds of loyalty with your customers because you can stay in touch with them on a regular basis. You can separate out your best customers from the rest, and you can make special deals for them. You can do things for your best customers that you can't do for any other group of customers. I can't think of a better way to sell and resell customers. Remember, that's all marketing is: all the things you do to first attract new customers, and then to resell to them. There's no better way to do that than direct-mail. This is a vehicle that allows you to be in total control, unlike space advertising. We got started in space advertising, where you wait 6-8 weeks for your ad to run. If you run it in all the national magazines, you're at the mercy of the media ad departments. They can tell you if they don't want to run your ad. They can dictate the layout to you. But when you're using direct-mail, you're in total control. It's pretty simple, too, and it gets simpler the more you do it.

So what do you need to create a top-notch direct-mail product? First of all, you need a great offer. This consists of a great product or service, something that's designed for the exact people you're trying to reach. There are good profit margins in it, and some kind of a special deal for them. People always want some kind of a special deal. So when we talk about a great offer, we're talking about prices; we're talking about the value that you build up and establish in the minds of the prospect, and if it's the right product or service for the right market, then it'll have a high pursuit value. It also includes all the special things that make people want to give you their money right now — powerful, compelling offers, things that make people *excited* about giving you their money.

That's part and parcel of great advertising copy, which is also absolutely necessary. Writing great copy consistently is something that takes years to develop — but I want you to know that you can start learning how to write great copy immediately, by focusing in on your customers, attracting groups of them, and then writing to them like they're your friends. That's the one thing that every letter that you get in the mail has in common; it says, "Dear friend." So write to your customers as if they're your friends — and they *should* be your friends, because they support you. So you'd better think of them as friends, and you'd better treat them as friends. You learn how to write great copy over a period of time, and you do it by doing everything you can to serve your customers in the highest way possible.

You need a great graphic artist, somebody who's going to get your stuff ready to go to press. We have two graphic artists at M.O.R.E., Inc., and one of them, Mary Jones, has been with us since the very beginning. She used to design all the little fliers for the first business I started in 1985, and she's been with me right along the way, the whole time. Every great copywriter needs a great graphic artist to work with, to help them turn their copy ideas into powerful direct-mail packages and products. You also need a good list broker, and that was one of the things that Russ von Hoelscher helped us do. He introduced us to Stewart Kogan, who has been our list broker since 1989. A list broker's job is just like a bloodhound's, or like a detective's. They go out there and track down the very best mailing lists. They're constantly looking for mailing lists that are just right for whatever it is you're offering, so that you'll use those mailing lists and then keep using them. Every time a new quarterly hotline comes up, you re-rent that list through your list broker, and they get 15 or 17% — a nice little percentage. Now, with the best mailing lists you're always going to have to take 5,000 names, and the list is vitally important. In fact, the list you mail to is probably the most important thing when it comes to direct-mail. There are a lot of lists on the market; and there are a lot of sharks in the business who are going to take advantage of you by giving you bad mailing lists. So you've got to find a good list broker who'll give you the very best names.

Next, you need a great printer you can trust, somebody you can work with. Ideally you need someone who can give you the very best prices, the very best turnaround time, the very best quality. Sometimes you can't have all three; maybe you can only have two. If you want the best quality, it's going to cost you more money; if you want the best turnaround time, you're going to have to give up on some of your quality. So you've got to find the best printer possible who's going to give you all three of those things, and realize that sometimes you'll pay him a little bit more. We have a great relationship with our printer; his name is Steve Harshbarger, from CityPrint. We've been using him since the mid-1990s. Here's why: when I met him, I was so impressed. You see, earlier on, Eileen and I had started our own printing division — and it was the wrong idea. That department grew and grew, until we had all these huge presses and hundreds of thousands of dollars worth of printing equipment. It seems funny now, but that's the way it was, in the first five years of our business. In the beginning, no printer would take us seriously; we were small potatoes. But we were kingdom builders, so we built this huge printing department. The whole thing worked for a little while, and then it all caved in on us. I met my printer when it came time to sell all of that equipment, and he's been with us since that time. The first thing he said to me made a really deep impression, and told me that I was dealing with somebody who was very honest.

I was asking him about his prices, and he said, "I have a certain amount of equipment in my shop; it allows me to do some jobs and be very productive, as far as price and speed and quality go. There are other jobs you may have for me that I can make work on my equipment, but I can't make work for the best price. So you're better off using different printers to do those jobs for you — the ones whose equipment allows them to do it at the best price possible, the best turnaround time possible, and the best quality possible." Now, that really let me know I was dealing with someone who was telling me the truth. Because somebody who's lying to you says, "Oh, you bet, we can handle any job that you have! We'll always give you the best price at the best possible quality!" But that's not what Steve said; he told me the truth. What I've had him do since then is this: When they can use their equipment at the best price and give us the best turnaround quality, they do it right there in-house at CityPrint Printing in Wichita, Kansas. Whenever we have certain jobs that other printers can do faster and cheaper and at better quality than Steve can, then he's our broker: He goes out and negotiates for the very best prices, then adds a small percentage on for himself and makes a little extra money that way.

And then you have to find a good mailing house, a company that mails all your products out for you. We started with a company in Hutchinson, Kansas, and they cheated us every step of the way. They didn't mail the stuff they were supposed to, and so our responses all varied — that's how we found out they just were not honest. We switched over to another company in 1990 called CCI, and we've been with them ever since. Conservatively, they've mailed 200 to 300 million pieces for us, and they've done a fantastic job. That's one of the nice things about direct-mail. If you're mailing 50,000 pieces a week and you've got an offer that's just making you tons of money, all you have to do is pick up the phone, call your printer, and say, "Hey, instead of printing up 50,000, I want you to print up 100,000." Then you call your mailing house and say, "Look, I want you to mail 100,000 pieces a week instead of 50,000." Then you call up your list manager and say, "Get me 50,000 more good names." Pretty soon, you can double your business. If you've got an offer that's really working like gangbusters, that's causing people to drop everything to send you their checks, cash, money orders and credit card authorizations, all you've got to do to make it better is make a few phone calls. Suddenly you've got millions more dollars more coming in, and it's the most beautiful feeling on Earth.

I want you to experience that feeling. You *need* to experience that feeling. First of all, to get paid for other things than your time — to get paid for the products and services that are sold, rather than the hours that you have in a day — is just phenomenal. Most people make their money by selling their time. Even the highest paid people — models, brain surgeons, lawyers, doctors — they're getting paid for their time. Even though they may be making an enormous sum per hour, they're not getting the kind of money you could get when you're selling products and services that have nothing to do with the amount of time you're spending on those items. Personally, I can make more than $1,000 an hour by writing sales copy that sells thousands, tens of thousands or even hundreds of thousands of products and services. I don't mean to be egotistical; quite honestly you'll find, if you use these principles here, that *you* can make more than $1,000 an hour too. There have been times when we've had promotions that worked so well that when I take the time that I personally spent writing the sales letters and putting the whole thing together, and then you take the millions of dollars that we've made on the promotions, divided by the number of hours that I personally spent on the job — well, it's shocking. You wouldn't even believe how much money we make in an hour, but it's in the tens of thousands of dollars. That's God's honest truth.

You can make a lot more than that. That's the point I want to bring to your attention here: If you want to make millions of dollars like we have, all you have to do is the same things we've done. That's it; just do what we've done to make millions of dollars, and you can make millions of dollars too, and you can be in the same place that I'm in. If you know you have the ability to develop products and services and the sales materials that go with them, and you're using the power of direct-mail like I'm expressing here, you could make tens of thousands of dollars an hour when you get the right promotion out there working for you. This is a powerful way to make money.

I've talked about the printer, the mailing house, the list broker, the great copy. The last thing you need is an experienced staff to handle all the other things, because it's what you do with those orders that's going to help customers feel better about you. The secret to reselling to your customers again and again is to have a stable, competent staff of good people who know how to process orders quickly, and know how to handle all the customer service challenges, so the customers are happy. You're using direct-mail to attract thousands of new customers, and then using that same powerful medium of direct-mail, to resell to those customers, again and again. If you have a stable staff that's very capable and competent, they're going to help you make more money, because a happy customer is a customer who keeps buying from you again and again.

That sounds like common sense, but if it's really common sense, why aren't more people using the power of direct response marketing to build their fortunes? This is one of the greatest mysteries of the field, because even people I know who are very capable, very smart when it comes to marketing — they're still not doing enough. The reason that direct-mail worked so well for us in the beginning is because we were already on a good, solid foundation. We were already making a nice profit; then Russ came along and helped us take the sales promotion that was already working for us in space advertising, and expand it in this powerful new way. Going from space ads to direct-mail was like throwing a 55-gallon drum of jet fuel on a raging fire for us.

The bad news about direct-mail is it's expensive. We were already making a great profit, though, and that was the whole key for us. So my best advice is for you to start with space ads, just like we did; if you're going to get into direct-mail, you'd better be using some kind of a proven offer that's already made money for somebody else, and you'd better have the back-end of your business solved first. With those kinds of challenges, you need what we call a "slack adjuster." You need something expensive, or a series of things that are expensive, to sell to your best customers once you extract them, so you can make your profit. Direct-mail is expensive — make no bones about it. This is the reason why a lot of people lose their shirts with direct-mail. When we meet at the free workshop, I'm going to tell you more about this awesome, powerful medium. I'll show you how you can cash in with direct-mail, and the key is right here: You put 80% of your effort into reselling your best customers, and 20% of your effort into attracting new customers. If you'll do that, you'll do well. Believe me, a lot of people know that — that's not a secret. You'll find that concept in marketing books and seminars all over. If you go to an experienced marketer and tell them about the 80-20 rule, they'll nod their head. But I know people right now who are very, very good marketers, a lot better than me, and yet they don't practice that principle, and I don't know why. Again, it's one of the great mysteries. This is the golden secret to making huge sums of money.

When it comes to writing copy for direct-mail, to put that offer out to your best customers, it's so much easier because they trust you; they have a relationship with you, there's a bond, and they'll buy from you. Your copy doesn't have to be too good; you can even write bad copy. When I go back and look at copy that I wrote 15 years ago, I'm ashamed at how terrible it is — and yet it made us money. The reason it made us money is because those direct-mail packages that I was creating were going out to people who trusted us, even though I wasn't very good at any of this back then. They liked us, they liked what we were doing, they liked what we sold them the first time. So the copy didn't have to be as good, and the direct-mail didn't have to be as powerful. I cannot express this enough to you. It's powerful because it lets you develop your skills by writing to your best customers, by treating them as if they were friends —

and, again, they *should* be friends. The more you do this, the better you'll get, if you stay with it long enough.

We're grateful for Russ von Hoelscher for getting us started in this. We want to be to you, and your business, what Russ von Hoelscher was to our business. So when we get together at the workshop, let's put some real time and focus into direct-mail. I want you to stop calling it "junk mail" from here on out. Just get that idea out of your mind: This is not junk mail, because if it's done right it's the most powerful sales medium on earth. You can create money at will; when you do this right, you're never going to worry about money, ever again, for the rest of your life. You'll never have to worry about where your next $1,000 or your next $100,000 are going to come from, because you'll be able to take great ideas and turn them into direct-mail packages that go out to your best customers, who love you and appreciate you, who value you and have respect for you. Those people will buy from you so fast that it'll make your head spin, and the profits that result can just be absolutely phenomenal. I want you to think very, very hard about all this.

Direct-mail is really such a simple thing, once you master it. It may take you a little while to master it, but it's worth the time and effort, because the benefits are so great. It's out there for you right now. It's the same secret that we used to go from $16,000 a month to almost $100,000 a week in nine months. It can be the same secret that makes you millions of dollars. So go back and read this chapter once or twice more, and think very carefully as you read. Remember what I've told you: This is the greatest sales medium on earth. It can make you millions and millions of dollars in the fastest time, in the simplest way, as easily as possible.

SECRET SEVEN:
Put a Percentage of Every Dollar Back into Advertising

The seventh secret we've used to make millions of dollars is the fact that we constantly put a percentage of every dollar that we bring in back into advertising. In the beginning, we ran two different checkbooks at the company. We had one bank account that was just for advertising, and another that was for everything else; and every day, we made sure that we took 30% of every dollar that came in and put it into that advertising account. It required discipline, but it became one of the foundations of our company.

You need to have a way to constantly attract new customers to you, and to do that you've got to have money. It all takes money to make it happen. To make sure you have that money on hand, you need to discipline yourself and make sure you use our guideline here, our formula. Every day you *must* take a percentage of every dollar that comes in, and make sure that you put it right back into more advertising. Now, that may seem like common sense to you, and it *is* common sense to know where your next dollar's coming from. You've got to constantly ask yourself that, and yet most people really screw up in this area. I'm shocked at the number of marketers I know who are otherwise capable and competent but aren't doing this at all. They have no consistent message for attracting new customers and reselling to old customers again and again, and they don't bother to set the money aside to do it. It really confuses me, because this idea really does make sense if you think about it. I want you to really grasp this principle, because this has made us more money than anything else.

You've got to have a way to bring in new customers, and you've got to have a way to resell to those old customers again and again. This requires money. Now, I'm going to give you a very simple formula that we use. At first I thought, "This is too simple. I don't want to insult anyone's intelligence here," but then at the same time I know for a fact people I respect who are *not* following these principles — and they're not rich, either. That's one of my greatest personal mysteries: the fact that I know people who are smarter than I am, and yet they're not rich. There's no doubt in my mind, absolutely zero doubt, that these people have a lot more brainpower than I do. They were blessed with a higher IQ. They're more talented than I am. But I'll put my net worth up against theirs any day, and theirs will look pale by comparison to mine. That's not to brag — I know my weaknesses, and I know that I'm only really good at just a few things. But I'm here to tell you that if more people would just realize that the secret to getting rich is to consistently attract new customers, and then to consistently resell them, they would be rich, too.

The way to attract and resell to those customers is by advertising constantly. And it's got to be consistent; you've got to have a system. Now, what *is* a system? It's very simple. You build your business so that you constantly have some type of ad or direct-mail piece, some type of promotion, that's attracting new customers to you. Every week we send out 50,000 pieces of direct-mail, sometimes more, sometimes less; we've mailed as many as 100,000 pieces, and around Christmas we used to mail only about 20,000 pieces. Now, though, we're going full blast during Christmas — because we've noticed that our business doesn't slow down at all during the holiday season. There are too many people who are way too conservative about their mailings. For every reckless entrepreneur who blows their business up and goes bankrupt, there's got to be at least 10,000 who are playing it too safe. I'm going to tell you more about why that is, what the thinking behind that is, and why you shouldn't do that. It's all right here in this secret.

You've got to have a balance. A good 80% of your time and effort and attention must go to reselling to your old customers, but the remaining 20% should go to attracting new customers. Again, consistency is so important. One mistake that a lot of people make is that they're focused on bringing in new customers — and on one hand I applaud those people. We all need new customers; there's no question about it. We've got to do what I call constantly "replenishing the pond." Think about that. We've got a pond out in front of our house here, Eileen and I. It's a beautiful pond; it surrounds our house, and sometimes during the rainy season it'll be filled up to almost overflowing. We had to do some special construction, in fact, because the pond was actually running over the road outside our house. Then, at other times of the year, because we don't get any rain and the heat of the summer comes, it practically dries up.

Think about your business as a pond; it constantly has to be replenished, or it will dry up. The way you do that is, by having a constant front-end promotion out there that attracts new customers, and then you put a lot of emphasis on reselling to those customers, because that's where all your profits are. Most people put too much emphasis on the front-end, and that means they're constantly chasing new customers — constantly. Or they're so focused on reselling to their established customers where they're not replenishing the pond. Both of these strategies are a mistake; though if I had to choose one of the two, I think the better mistake is to focus on reselling to your established customers. However, even that strategy is wrong. The people who focus on the back-end constantly do it because they realize that's where the profits are; but if the pond isn't replenished, then the best customers you have today could be gone tomorrow. Life changes, people change, circumstances change. You've got to constantly ask yourself, always, "Where's my income for next month going to come from?" Now, if you understand residual income you might say, "Wait a minute — what about residual? Why can't I build that into my business, so I don't always have to worry about where my next dollar is going to come from?"

Well, residual income can be a nice safety net or buffer, and sure, it's wonderful to have products and services that you sell on a continuity basis, where every month you've got money coming in because of something that you sold once. I encourage you to go for that, to experience what it's like to bring in $100,000 a month automatically. But even that business will dry up if you don't replenish it. Because life changes, circumstances change, people change; for whatever reason you can't just do something once, kick back, and expect money to come in automatically forever. That's a fantasy. There are things you can do to bring in residual income, but what you really need to do is strive to develop a system for attracting new customers, converting the largest number of those new customers to sells, and then working constantly on your back-end.

That's what we're doing. Our system is more like a money machine; and that's what you've got to think about your business as — a money machine. We've been doing this for years, and it works well for us. I don't know why more people don't do it. We have one or two front-end promotions that constantly attract new customers to us. Like I said, every week we mail 50,000 pieces on average, just to bring in new customers, and then we have at least one new promotion every week to resell to our established customers. Almost all our marketing, both to attract new customers and to resell to old customers, is what we call two-step marketing. Now, don't let the term "two-step marketing" fool you, because it actually involves more than two steps in all, and I'll explain to you why it's more than two steps if it's done correctly. Oh, and by the way, you've been exposed to two-step marketing all your life, though maybe you just didn't have a name for it. Think about every single time that you've sent away for a free audio tape, a free CD, a free CD-ROM, a free report, free information; that's two-step marketing. You make it very easy for people; you're not trying to really sell them anything in the beginning, you're just trying to show that you're serious about what it is that you sell, and that they've an interest in it, and you're just trying to get them to raise their hand by sending in some kind of a form or requesting something for free.

We call it two-step marketing because here's what it's designed to do: 1) to get interested prospects to identify themselves and 2) to turn them into conversions. Now, what is a conversion? Simple. Your prospects raise their hand. They acquire something from you initially for a small amount of money, or for free; they request something, and now you're trying to sell them something, which is the second step. Your conversion rate is the percentage of the people who raised their hand initially who end up buying whatever it is that you sell. That's your conversion, and that's the second step. One of the reasons we do two-step marketing is because we're very sensitive about the fact that people love to buy things, but they hate to be sold to — and I know that sounds ironic. It's almost like a joke; but that's how it is.

People want to believe that they're coming to *you*. Their perception is that they're asking you to send them something, that they're the ones that took the first step, and they really did, of course, in their minds; but the truth is, you took the first step by making an offer to them. You either had an ad in a magazine or you sent them some piece of direct-mail; so you're the one that made it happen, but in their minds they don't think that way. People have the feeling that they're coming to you when you use two-step marketing, and that's one of the best reasons why you do it. You don't want people to feel that you're pressuring them to buy something, or that you're trying to get them to give you their money. On the contrary, the emotional feeling behind it all must be that they're the ones seeking *you* out, rather than you seeking *them* out.

You might think it's a small thing, but it's really not, and it becomes even more important when you're going to your established customers again and again. You always want people to raise their hands and send for something, so you can then separate the smaller herd of customers from the bigger herd. You get a small group of people that you know are qualified and serious, or else they wouldn't have raised their hands. They've expressed an interest, and now you're simply following up with them. So when I tell you that it's called two-step marketing, there really are two steps; but the second step is a series of follow-up mailings that go out to those people who raised their hands. Now you're able to focus your marketing efforts on that smaller group of people who raised their hands by saying, "Yes, send me that information package," or "Send me the portfolio or the report or the audio CD or the DVD," or whatever it is that sells the higher-ticket product or service. We've had two-step marketing where we asked for one or two hundred dollars on Step One, because what we were really trying to sell them was something for thousands. We've had two-step marketing where we even asked for $1,000 on Step One, because we were trying to sell them a $5,000 package on Step Two.

This process is just too simple for a lot of people. If you ask them, "Hey, what are you doing to constantly attract new customers?" you might as well be speaking a foreign language, because they just don't think like that. This is especially true for these super-smart people I know who are always broke. They're really sharp marketers, but they're focused on reselling to old customers. Now, they're not making the mistake that a lot of shallow marketers and fly-by-nighters make, where they're constantly trying to make a profit on the front-end. That's a terrible mistake, because all the real profits come from the back-end — from reselling to established customers who trust you, who respect you. They like you and what you're selling. They've already bought from you, so you've proven to them that you're a company they can depend on and that you're selling things they really want. That's where you're going to get rich, and the smart marketers all know it, so they put a lot of their emphasis on that — and they hate front-end marketing.

Look, I hate front-end marketing too, but it's an absolutely necessary evil if you want to keep your customer pool filled. It's not where the real profits come from, and in many cases we take an initial loss on the front-end, given the amount of money it costs to secure that initial sale or even just to get that customer to raise their hand. But it's an expense towards future profits, if you've got your back-end business together. If you have a wide range of products and services that you can sell to a customer once they raise their hand, and you've got a system in place that allows you to sell those things fast do that, then it may cost you $100, $500, or even $1,000 for every new prospect who sends for that free report — but what do you care, if you can immediately sell that person something on the back-end for a huge sum of money and make a quick profit? Who cares what it costs, if you can then go to that same prospect and resell them again and again? You want to keep customers for life.

Of course, you need to fill that gap between front-end and back-end immediately. The one time in my life when I really got into financial trouble was when I pushed the gap a little too far, and I didn't have other things going right with the business. Initially, we were asking people to raise their hands and send for a report: that was Step One. For Step Two, we were asking them to pay $49 a month for a continuity program. For Step Three, we had a package to sell them for $2,500 that was related to what they'd bought for $49 a month. So it was more of a three-step campaign, and it was working really well, and it was making us millions and millions of dollars — but the gap between our front-end expenditures and our back-end profits was wide, and it cost us a lot of money. We normally mail 50,000 pieces a week at M.O.R.E., Inc., but at that time we were mailing more like 75,000 to 100,000 pieces weekly. At 60 to 70 cents apiece... well, you do the math. It was expensive, and it took time.

We use two different sequences. When somebody raises their hand, you don't just send him one offer once and say, "Okay, here's the product or service I have for you." That would be foolish — and again, it's a mistake that most people are making. Most markets just don't follow up enough. When somebody raises their hand for a free report, the marketer will send them that report, which is really a sales letter — and maybe they'll include a CD or DVD, or whatever supports it and gives their customer more information about the product or service they're trying to sell. But then they just drop the ball. If they don't hear from the prospect, they assume the prospect isn't a serious buyer. The better marketers, the ones who are smarter, will go ahead and send him several packages. They'll send him a second notice, a third notice, a fourth notice. The really sharp marketers, the ones who are making millions, build a sequence where they'll send as many as 20 to 30 different follow-ups. They don't just give up on the people, which is something that's going to be more and more necessary in the future. You can't give up on people. Your job is to try to take those prospects who raised their hands initially and convert them into sales as fast as you can.

The one time when I almost took the company into bankruptcy, we had a promotion that was leveraged out too far and took too long. It took an average of 3 to 4 months from the time the prospect raised their hand to bring them through to the initial stage, which was to convert those $49-a-month service buyers over to a $2,500 sale for a related product-service combination we had. It took too long. I knew then what I want to teach you here, which is that the companies that make the most money are the ones that don't worry about how much money it costs to get somebody in on their front-end. They don't care about that, because they're in the business of converting those prospects into buyers and multi-buyers. But you see, a lot of these corporations had more money than we had, and we weren't watching all our numbers on the back-end, and the whole thing bombed on us. It was too aggressive, and just about took us into bankruptcy.

But most people are not aggressive *enough*. They have unrealistic expectations and they're trying to chase new customers constantly, which is not profitable at all. New customers don't know you, they don't like you, there's no trust built up, there's no relationship. It's terribly hard to make a profit selling to brand new customers once each. Even those who do it are never able to do it on a large scale. People who make millions of dollars are the people who have a consistent large-scale campaign, or several campaigns that attract the largest possible number of the most qualified new prospects they can find to some type of initial offer. It could be a free or low-price offer, something to make it for the most qualified people to raise their hands. Sometimes you have to ask for money, because that's the only way to really qualify a prospect and know they're serious — and to help offset some of your high costs. Most of the time, though, it's better to have a free offer. You give them something nice and you make a really good impression, and you show them how you're different than everybody else; you blow them away, you surprise them, in some cases you shock them, because of all the stuff that you send to them. You make a great favorable impression. Before a young man goes and knocks on his date's door, he'll go to the barber, he'll take a bath, he'll put on some cologne, he'll put on his best clothes, and he'll clean out his car. He wants to make a favorable impression; and that's exactly how you have to do marketing, too.

You have to winnow your larger group of potential prospects to a smaller group you can focus on, whether that's by having them send for something or by sending them to a 1-800 number or a website. Now you have a smaller group, but they're more qualified. They've proven that they're serious, so you can spend more money to market to them. You can afford to do that, if your profit margins are good and you're selling them something related to what they raised their hand on. And that's what it has to be: It has to be part of an integral campaign, so the front-end and back-end are closely tied together. Do that, and you're going to make a huge sum of money, because your conversion rates are going to be good. You've got to follow up on them more than two or three times. Stay on top of them. We'll send our prospects as many as two different follow-up packages every single week, and we'll do that for twelve weeks in some cases, especially when we're selling an upcoming seminar, or some other product where there's a real sense of urgency. The greater the pressure, the higher the conversion rates.

All this does take a good bit of time to think about and master, and you may have to go back and read this chapter a few times before you really get the essence of what I'm sharing with you. My best advice is to find the top companies in your market and study them closely. Look for the ones doing the best job of selling and reselling to their established customers, the ones who are doing the best job of attracting new customers because of the ads they're running or the direct-mail packages they're sending out. Find those companies, get on their mailing lists, see what they're doing, and start realizing the magic behind these tricks. If people are making millions and millions of dollars in direct response marketing, they're doing it for this reason; and the more you're aware of it, the better. So get on these customer lists and start thinking like a businessperson rather than a consumer; get on the other side of the cash register. When I meet you at our free workshop, I'm going to show you just how simple and how easy it is to have a front-end marketing campaign that constantly attracts new customers to you, and then a back-end marketing campaign that constantly resells those customers again and again — so that you can make the millions of dollars you want, and you can have a business that's basically a money machine that cranks out a continual stream of cash for you.

SECRET EIGHT:

Focus on Back-End Marketing

The eighth secret we used to make $10 million in less than five years is the fact that we focused on back-end marketing. In the previous chapter, I talked extensively about the difference between front-end and back-end marketing. On the front-end, you're trying to attract new customers; on the back-end, you're trying to resell those customers again and again, for the largest profit possible. As long as you make sure the value you're providing exceeds the dollar value of the money they're giving you, you can't go wrong. Then the question becomes, "How can I sell my customers more and more?"

I feel very strongly about this; you have to think this thing through, and realize that you absolutely have to develop long-term relationships with your customers if you want to profit. Far too many people are self-conscious on this point, including me; for years, I felt that I was going to upset my customers if I went back to them too much. I honestly feared that my best customers were going to become upset and quit me if I tried to sell them too much stuff. I didn't understand that both of us profited from that long-term relationship. I understand, now, that most people overthink this point, and that's one of the reasons they never get rich; they tend to complicate things a little too much. But it doesn't have to be complicated. I've always understood that business is mostly about retaining customers, because when I had my carpet-cleaning business, I depended on repeat business;

after all, I was operating in a small town. But a lot of people have never figured it out, so they don't have any kind of intimate relationships with their customers.

I've thought about why this is for years, and as far as I can tell, many of the people who are attracted to direct response marketing are simply people who want to hide out. They want to avoid contact with the entire world — and this is especially true for Internet marketers. I know that there are plenty of exceptions, and I'm really grateful that there are, but I see Internet marketers in general as people who just want to sit behind the computer screen every day. That's all they want to do, just as people who are attracted to traditional mail-order just want to get cash, checks, money orders, and credit card authorizations in the mail every day. They love the idea that they never have to speak to or meet with the customer, and that's part of what attracts them to the business. Hey, that's part of what attracted *me* to the business: the fact that you could get money in the mail, and you didn't have to deal with some of the things that other people have to deal with in traditional businesses.

My mother had a day-care center for 15 years, and every Sunday when I spoke to her on the phone, she would tell me about the pain and the adversities she had to go through with that day-care center. Twice a day, she had to see all her best customers — once when they came to drop their kids off, and once when they came to pick them up. There was still that constant contact with her customers, and that gave me a deep appreciation for direct-response marketing. This is a business where, in many cases, you'll never meet the people who give you the most money. But that shouldn't be your main reason for being in this business. We have regular seminars and workshops, and have for years — and I advise everyone to do that. We like to talk about the fact that you should view the direct response marketing business as if it were a restaurant: unless you're in a super-high traffic location you're going to go broke if you don't get the same clientele to come back again and again, month after month, year after year, and bring all their friends, family and associates, so their friends, family and associates can bring all their friends too. If you have a favorite restaurant, you know how that works. Eileen and I have a restaurant in Newton, Kansas, that we go to regularly; it's a Mexican restaurant, and when they opened up in 1988, Eileen and I were there. We were one of their very first customers. It was only a few blocks from our house, so we could actually walk over there. Their kids were just so cute and adorable; they used to bring us the chips and fill up our glasses and such — and now those little kids are running the place. We got to know the Mom and Dad and they got to know us, and there's a kinship there. Since then I've watched them carefully, because their business has grown and thrived and they're making so much money. I watch how they treat all their customers like they're special. They stop and talk to their customers, they get to know them, they make sure the food tastes good.

You know, they do that at Applebee's, too. One of the neat things about all those "neighborhood" chain restaurants, like Applebee's and Outback Steakhouse and Chili's, is that they try to focus on customer service and consistency. It's not the same thing as with a local restaurant that's owned by a family, where you get to know all the kids and aunts and uncles and cousins and brothers, but they try to instill that same attitude. They really focus hard on that, and that's one of the smartest things that they do with their marketing. It's also one of the smartest things you can do with *your* marketing. It's hard to be intimate with a mailing. It's easy to start thinking of your customers as numbers when all they are to you is a spreadsheet with some names on it. You lose that feeling that you had as a local businessperson, when you're face-to-face with your customers.

In the very beginning, when I started my carpet-cleaning business, I had customers who loved me and appreciated me; they looked forward to me coming, and they would have me inside their home to clean their carpets, just so that I could sit down and eat dinner with them, and they had cookies for me. I'm serious — milk and cookies. They just wanted a visit; their carpets weren't dirty. It's the same way old guys will go to the barbershop, even when they have no hair left, and spend a half-hour or 45 minutes in there. I'm thinking, "What is the barber doing? Using a tweezers for every hair?" But it's not about that. It has nothing to do with the haircut; it has everything to do with the relationship. So we think about all these old guys who go in constantly to the barbershop week after week to get their hair "cut." Their hair doesn't need to be cut anymore; there *is* no more hair. It's all about the routine; it's something they're comfortable with. They like doing business with that barber, they like going back; it makes them feel better about themselves. That's how it is, in general, for all of us. It's an emotional thing that has little to do with logic. There's no more hair to cut, but we keep going back to that same barber anyhow, because it's all about the emotional elements — and it's those same emotional elements that will keep your customers coming back. It's up to you to figure out what that those emotional elements are. In the market that we deal with, there are emotional reasons that cause people to become insatiable, to continue to buy the same things over and over again. There's no logical reason for this; it just fills an emotional void they have.

If you're going to sell to people again and again (which is what Secret Number Eight here tells you to do), you have to understand that it's all about the emotions; buying often has nothing to do with logic. To really comprehend this, you have to know your customers in the most intimate way. That was very easy for Eileen and me when we started in 1988. There are two basic reasons why we were able to turn our $300 investment into over $10 million in less than five years. The first reason is the most important one: We already intimately knew who our customers were, even if we weren't aware of it consciously. We were *exactly* like our target customer. For years I was what I affectionately call an "opportunity junkie." I just couldn't get enough of this stuff; I couldn't buy enough, and I was on every single mailing list. I had an insatiable appetite for getting rich, and I was sending away for all the plans and programs that promised miracles. The crazier the programs were, the more I liked them.

That's part of the insanity of it, because a lot of these programs didn't stand a snowball's chance in hell of making any money. Didn't matter to me; it was all about the emotions. I wanted to get rich, and I really believed that there was some secret out there that could make it happen. As it turns out, there *are* secrets — but they involve good, solid business practices and a lot of good, solid marketing. You know that cliché that says "it takes one to know one"? There's a lot of truth to that. The best advice I can give you is to do what they tell you when you take a creative writing course: Write what you know. Even a superstar like John Grisham was a lawyer first, so he started writing fiction books about the law. Then there's the late Michael Crichton, who was a medical doctor. You might have heard of him. He wrote a lot of books that had to do with medicine, and created a little TV show called *ER*.

So write about what you know; that's especially true if you're going to get rich in the information business, niche marketing, or direct-response marketing. Stay in that marketplace and try to figure out ways to attract the thousands, and in some cases millions, of people out there who have something in common with you and what you know about. When I started, I knew all about the opportunity market. When it came time to developing some of these ideas, I knew what was hot and what wasn't. I knew the places to advertise and I knew the companies whose ads were appearing over and over again, because those were the companies I was buying from. When it came time to decide on the first ad, I spent a whole weekend just looking at similar ads before coming up with something similar. We copied from proven stuff that I had an intimate knowledge of, without even realizing it at the time.

This was our Number One wealth secret for years, at all our seminars. Who shows up at these events? People on our mailing list, of course; and who are those people? They're opportunity junkies. They've been sending away for all the plans and programs, so they're on all the mailing lists; they have the insatiable appetite to continue to buy program after moneymaking program. For years, this was one of the things that I kept trying to beat into people's heads, because I feel so passionate about this, and I know it's true. I *know* it can help people make millions. I know without any doubt that the people who are already buying all these things are in heat for this kind of stuff. Heck, they should be the ones selling it to other people. But what do they want to do? They want to try all kinds of other ideas. It's always something else, some crazy, whacked-out idea that doesn't stand any chance of making any money. They all want to do something other what they should be doing, which is sticking with what they know.

The second secret is that we had a lot of help, of course. I've already gone over this one in detail. We had Russ von Hoelscher working with us from the time we were six months into the business, and that's what caused our income to really explode — because his shortcut secrets became our shortcut secrets, and we ended up getting a lot more done in a lot less time. That's how we went from $16,000 a month to almost $100,000 a week in our first nine months of working with him. If you don't have the intimate knowledge of your business that you need, you can get it.

Now, for those of you that don't understand the opportunity market, it's easy to figure out. All you've got to do is start sending away for some of the plans and programs that are for sale in the tabloids, *Popular Mechanics*, and *Popular Science*. Pretty soon you'll end up on every single mailing list out there. You'll go to your mailbox, and it will be overflowing with offers; and there'll be a little card in there that says, "Come to the front desk, we have more mail for you" or "We have packages for you." You'll see that this is a rabid market. There are a lot of people out there selling opportunities, and the good news for you is that most of them don't know what the hell they're doing. There are exceptions, but most marketers don't understand the concept of back-end marketing, so they're not doing a good job of following up with their customers.

They're not building relationships with their customers, either. All they're trying to do is make some money by selling one product one time. They're shallow marketers, and they're missing the point I want to emphasize here: People want to do more business with marketers they like and trust, and so the more you do to stay focused on reselling to your best customers, the more money you're going to make. People will want more of whatever they bought from you the first time — assuming they didn't ask for refund, and assuming it's a hot subject. It's all about variations on a theme; that's a lot of the secret, to continue to come up with something new over and over again. People will also re-buy a lot more than you think they will. People just can't seem to get enough; they're like I was.

When people get in heat, they buy like crazy. I used to worry that I was selling to the customers too much — that they were going to be upset and quit buying from me. Now the only thing I worry about is that I'm not selling enough to them. The key to making that conversion yourself is to know your customers in the most intimate way. We kept journals for years, and these journals were filled with customer comments from sheets that we sent out in all of our packages, where we offered a bonus, just some little free report, if they answered a few questions. At the bottom of the form we told them that they were giving up their rights if they accepted that report, so that we could use their comments in our promotional materials. This was a great way to develop testimonials, but more importantly, it was a great way to get inside the heads and hearts of our customers. We asked them for comments, and some people wrote the minimum, just chicken scratch that you could barely read. But about half of those comment sheets came back to us with some great stuff, and we typed it up and I studied it. I made it a science to know my customers better than they know themselves, and that made it so much easier.

I see a lot of people who are so confused and frustrated, constantly asking themselves, "What do I sell?" They can't seem to get beyond that one idea: "What do I sell to people?" Well, the one thing I want to say is, when you have a group of customers who have already bought something from you, the question of what to sell goes out the window. Now it just becomes, "What are the best things to sell?" That's because you know these people. You know what they like, since they've bought something from you already. Now you know that they'll continue to rebuy from you, if you just come up with variations on a theme. With our company, we're always coming up with new stuff, but people who don't understand how this works say, "My God! You guys are so prolific. How in the world do you keep coming up with all that new stuff?"

The truth is, most of it's just the same old stuff that's been given a new facelift, a new veneer. We keep finding new ways to recycle the same materials, and do you think our customers care? Absolutely not; they don't care at all. If they did, we wouldn't do it. We're in business to attract and retain customers, so why would we do something that our customers didn't like? We follow the money. Our customers like seeing new things — but they also want the elements behind those things to be established and proven. So we sell old, established moneymaking ideas, with a new exciting flavor or twist on top. Each product has that element of "new" which is the buzz, the draw, the jazz. It's this thing that gets them really excited, the "sizzle" that Elmer Wheeler, the great sales trainer, talked about; it attracts them to the deal. But if it's too new, people get freaked out. Nobody wants to be the guinea pig, so they love the idea that you've taken something that's proven and added this new twist to it; and the more exciting that twist is, the more they'll buy.

Product development is really the easiest thing for us opportunity marketers. I'm going to tell you more about product development later in this book, but for the moment I just wanted to share with you the fact that you're going to discover better ways to sell more products and services at higher profits to your customers as you move forward. With a little bit of knowledge and experience, that confusion about what to sell goes right out the window. The same things that confuse you now won't confuse you a month or a year from now, because you learn. You just keep moving forward, staying focused on your customers. When you stay focused on them and on how to give them more of what you know they already want, then all that confusion just goes right away.

Everybody wants to make millions of dollars, but most have never stopped and thought things through in even the simplest of ways. Here it is: All the profits that you'll ever need to run and build your business come from the back-end marketing. They come from being focused on that small group of your best customers, reselling to them again and again, constantly making them new offers. I want to share with you one of the greatest secrets that we've learned over the years, and if you'll master this secret, it's going to help you make a lot more money — and it's so simple. I'll try to express it to you in the possible clearest way. It's what I call the pre-publication product development strategy. Got to call it something, right? The pre-publication product development strategy involves using your best customers as the testing ground.

If you'll just dedicate yourself to spending a little time every day coming up with new ideas, you'll have the foundations of new products. You test them to your established customers first. You make an offer to them, and you tell them it's not even ready yet, that it's in the pre-publication phase. Then you have a deadline to meet. You've got a bunch of people who gave you money, so now you have pressure to perform; you've got a purpose. You've got a hundred or a thousand customers who just gave you big bucks and you don't want to disappoint them, so you'd better get off your ass and start working. The deadline helps keep you focused; it helps add purpose to your life, and you'll get a lot more done.

Once you've done all that, you take the things that sell well to your very best customers, and you start testing those to your new customers. Those products become part of your new customer acquisition. Your best, most established customers are the testing ground for your front-end customer-acquisition program. A lot of the secret to selling to your customers on the back-end has to do with constantly replenishing that supply of customers, so you need those new people. Put this secret into play, and you'll always have something on the front-end that attracts new customers on a continual basis, so that you'll always have customers on the back-end that you can resell to again and again.

You've got to think of your customers as if they really were your friends. You see this used all the time; every sales letter that you get says "Dear Friend," so maybe you're a little cynical about that. But your customers *should* be your friends, because they're the ones fueling your ambition. They're the ones helping your financial dreams come true. They're the ones who are really building your company; why shouldn't they be your friends? Think about all the elements it takes to be a good friend. First of all, there's some understanding. You feel that your friends understand you and you understand your friends; you have a shared interest in each other. There's some respect and trust; there's some appreciation. You look out for your friends; you try to do special things for them. If you try to treat your customers like that, you're going to end up head-and-shoulders ahead of all those direct-response marketers who want to hide out, who want to avoid the world.

I realize I'm speaking in generalities here, but it's almost impossible to feel any intimacy with names and addresses on a spreadsheet. This is why I honestly believe that you should produce seminars, tele-seminars, and workshops on a regular basis. You should talk to your customers; you should get to know them as more than just names and addresses on a list. The more you do to develop this intimacy with your customers, the more money you're going to make. When we meet at our free workshop, we're going to talk a lot about back-end. This is the key to profitability. We're going to talk at length about all of the ways that you can get huge profits by selling and reselling to the same people again and again.

Secret Nine:

Consistent New Customer Acquisition

The ninth secret that we used to make millions of dollars is this: We disciplined ourselves to do constant front-end marketing. I went over this to some extent in the previous chapter on back-end marketing, but I plan to hit it harder in this one.

Now, to discipline yourself means that you do something whether you feel like doing it or not. This is *not* the fun part of the business. You're lucky if you break even on the initial sale; you usually lose money to get those new customers. The people who make millions and millions of dollars don't even worry about breaking even on the front-end. It's not even a concern; nor should it be, since the back-end is where you make a profit. In fact, most companies go negative on the front-end. It may cost them $1,000 to bring in a customer who initially only spends $100 — and yes, some companies are willing to make that kind of sacrifice. Now, think about that; it's kind of scary. Admittedly, the people who are making the most money have the deepest pockets, and they can afford to do things that you can't afford to do; but you *can* be more aggressive. That's part of the secret to front-end marketing: to be aggressive. Do wild and crazy things; be bold and audacious, be outrageous, try to come up with things that wake people up and get them to pay attention.

The famous Tony Robbins has a wonderful story about this. He points out that you've got all these people who are so interested in the subject of meditation and self-hypnosis — and that's a joke, because most people are already hypnotized. They're already asleep at the wheel; they're already running around in an apathetic fog. Nothing could be truer in the world of advertising, where we're living in an overly competitive marketplace. There are all kinds of ads and marketing messages out there trying to lure customers in, all kinds of competition for the customers' dollar.

Now, that shouldn't be a negative thing. Some people use it as such, and it just ticks me off when I hear that. Here's an especially annoying example: the town of Hillsboro, Kansas is just six miles from where I'm writing this now. They had a store come into the marketplace called Alco; it's like a miniature Wal-Mart, which is about all the town can handle. Well, there was already a Ben Franklin store that had been doing business for 30 years in downtown Hillsboro, but when little Alco came in, suddenly the Ben Franklin store shut down. They just went out of business, because the owner decided they couldn't compete. That was it. I happen to think the owner of that company is a wimp; he's weak. I see other people who are so focused on the competition that they just let it scare the hell out of them, and that's not right. *Nothing* is more wrong then letting the competition scare you or make you nervous.

Sure, you should be aware of your competition — because if you're going to go out there to make millions of dollars you've got to be the lead dog. You've got to take that position right away. Even if you're not the lead dog, you've got to pretend that you *are*. You've got to be bold and aggressive; you've got to do things that attract customers to you. I don't care what it is, but you've got to do it on a consistent basis. It's got to be part of your routine. It has to be a systematic process of your business, so that every single week, every single month, you've got some kind of a new ad or direct-mail package out there, some type of offer that's designed to attract the very best customers possible. You want to repel everyone else. You've got to see your front-end marketing as a powerful magnetic force that attracts only the specific type of people you want.

Now, this won't happen overnight. It's a process; the more you do it, the better you'll get, and yes, some of these other marketers can be intimidating. They've been out there for a long time, they've got a lot of experience, they've tried a lot of things, they've got a lot of knowledge, and with that comes a tremendous amount of confidence or ego or both. There's a difference between egotism and real confidence, but it's hard to tell them apart because they look the same on the surface. It's easy to get intimidated by these experts who've been out there for 10, 20, 30 years. They've tested everything; they've got all these things figured out. Some of the things I'm going to talk about in this chapter they already know in the most intimate way. What you don't realize is they had to stumble and fall to get there; they had to go through some adversity to learn these secrets on their own. You're going to have to do the same thing. I wish somebody would've told me *that* 20 years ago! I wish somebody would have said, "Look, you can become great at this; you can become a master at marketing and making millions of dollars by selling and reselling to the same people over and over again within your marketplace — but it's going to take time, work, effort, energy, frustration, confusion, lots of anxiety, and lots of pain." I had to go through a lot of pain to get where I am right now, and I know I've got further to go, too, so it's a process. You keep moving forward, you keep figuring it out slowly but surely, and over a period of time as you do figure things out, the money does start flowing in; and the more money flows in, the greater the level of confidence you'll have. The greater the level of confidence, the more aggressive that you're going to be.

Being aggressive is very, very important when it comes to new customer acquisition. You've got to realize that your competitors are trying to get the same customers you're trying to get. They're trying to attract these people into their folds, just like you are. They're the enemy, they really are — though of course you can develop alliances with some of your best competitors. That's another thing we're going to talk about at our free workshop. I'll tell you how to do business with people who are attracting and re-attracting the same type of people you're after. Some of those people will end up becoming your best friends. But there has to be a certain attitude in the beginning — almost a cocky attitude, some real bravado. You're going to go out there to get these people and bring them into your fold, and if you really have something that's good for them, something that can really help them, something that can make a difference in their lives, if you're selling products and services that really do offer tremendous benefits — then you *should* be bolder, more aggressive, more outrageous, and do things that shock the living crap out of people. It makes them stand up and notice you and say, "Who the hell is this?" It breaks people out of that apathetic fog they live in.

Most people are running around in a daze. A lot of new marketers don't realize that, and neither do some old ones. They're so much in love with their stuff that they really do think, in their heart of hearts, that people are reading every word of their copy, that people really care about it — and they don't. Most prospects have built up an immunity to advertising. My best friend has a pest-control company, and so in the last six years, I've gotten a chance to get to know something about the pest-control business. It's an interesting business, by the way. She has customers who, for the last 27 years, have been paying a monthly fee to let service people come in. It's a great business from a money/profitability standpoint, because once somebody trusts you to come into their home and spray for insects, it takes a force of God to for them to switch companies. One of the things that I've learned from being around her and her business, something that I've used as a metaphor to apply towards marketing, is the way these insects become immune to poison. When her technicians go out on a regular account, they have to use a different poison than they used last month — because what happens is, those insects build up a tolerance for the poisons. If you try to shoot that same poison month after month, eventually it won't kill them — and then the customers get ticked off and you have to keep coming back for free, because it's part of the monthly contract. I believe the people within a marketplace respond the same way to advertising messages. It doesn't matter what you're offering, the customers still build a tolerance for it. So you need to constantly offer new things to your market and, most importantly, you must be sure you don't fall under the delusion that people really care about any of this stuff, because they don't.

The more you know about marketing, the more cynical you'll become about people in general. It's safe to say that people only buy for purely selfish emotions, and they buy the most when it comes to messages of total greed. Some fear messages work really well, too. The more you're aware of the fact that there are a lot of competitors out there who are trying to get the same people you're trying to get, the more you're going to be bigger and bolder; you're going to do things that are more aggressive, and you're going to do things that completely and totally separate you from everybody else out there.

I'm going to go over some important questions with you here, and your answers to these questions will help you continue to get better and better. Now, some of your first answers to these questions may be kind of uninspired, so you should keep some journals and keep thinking about all this. See yourself as the general at war; see yourself as the architect of your company; try to develop a higher image of who you are and what you're trying to accomplish here. The better you get at answering these questions and then implementing the right promotions based on the answers, the more money you're going to make, simple as that. Some of these questions sound like common sense, but then again, if they were, then everybody would be doing certain things, and they aren't.

One of the greatest things I can share with you, at the risk of sounding like an egomaniac, is that most marketers are weak. They're easy to beat if you'll just try. Most competitors never think through the kinds of things that I'm going to share with you here. Their marketing is very feeble and ineffective. They're not doing much at all to build strong bonds and relationships with their customers. They're not doing nearly enough to ensure that they can resell to the same people again and again. So you come along, and you just do the bare minimum sometimes, and that puts you out there in front right away. Here are some questions you need to ask yourself to do that: "Who are the best customers I'm trying to reach? What are they really searching for? How can I reach them in the best possible way? What could people in my marketplace want that they're not getting anywhere else?" That last is a particularly good question, by the way. Keep asking yourself that question. Keep asking them all; the answers will come to you! At first there might be just small answers, but be aware that answers — including some great ones — are waiting for you out there if you'll just keep asking the same questions. Who are the biggest and best companies selling to the people you want to sell to? What are these companies doing right? What are they doing wrong? Where are they running their ads to attract new customers? They're all doing some kind of lead-generation, front-end advertising, or they wouldn't be the biggest and best competitors in your marketplace.

So you're looking for that. You're constantly trying to get

on the other side of the cash register. Pay attention to your market, as if you were a consultant trying to help a client, and start thinking these things through for yourself — because you're always going to care more about your business than any consultant you can hire. Now, I believe in hiring consultants; I think they're very helpful, but they can't do it all for you, and that's what most people want consultants to do: everything. They hire consultants, and they want the consultants to run their companies for them. That's total nonsense. You've got to ask yourself: "What are these companies doing right, and what are they doing wrong? What are the top ten things that are most important to my market?" That's another great question, and the answer will evolve over time. You should keep journals filled with your answers, because I promise you that the top ten reasons why you think your customers buy things from you will change over of time. The answers will become clearer to you.

Remember, people buy for emotional reasons; they're insatiable. Often their reasons have very little to do with logic; and I expect that in the beginning, a lot of your answers to the questions I've mentioned will be logical ones. You've got to get beyond all that. I promise you that the emotional answers to those questions are more important than anything else, and once you understand the emotional reasons of why people buy and continue to buy, that's when you start becoming a great marketer. *That's* when you get to the point where you know things that other people don't know. Because, you see, most people are real "surfacy" about this. When I say that most marketers are weak, I mean it. They may be very good when it comes to product development; they may be very, very good at providing certain services, and they may be extremely knowledgeable. But when it comes to marketing, they're wimps. I don't mean to sound like some egomaniac here; I just want to tell you the truth. It's an advantage if you see it as one, and when we get together at our free workshop, I'm going to help make this clearer to you. It becomes very important when you want to make millions of dollars; all this does, because the more money you want to make, the more you have to turn up the volume. You've got to use these principles in the maximum way; the less money you want to make, the more you can be just like most marketers out there. You don't have to be that strong, and you certainly don't have to do anything in any aggressive way, if all you want to do is make a couple of hundred thousand a year.

But some of us want to make millions — and if that's what you want to do, you've got to turn up the volume. You need an appropriate balance between front-end and back-end. As I've mentioned before, front-end marketing is a necessary evil; that's all it is. Your real business is developing customers, getting them into the fold, doing things that establish relationships that cause them to think of you in a different way than they think about all the competitors. You've got to build a friendship with these people. A friendship is based on mutual understanding and respect, but it's also based on other things. For instance, the quickest way you can become somebody's friend is to get a mutual enemy. Find out who their enemies are, what problems they face, and get more in tune with that than anything else. It's about what they want — but it's also about what they *don't* want.

Part of the way you separate yourself in the marketplace is you speak directly to their pain and their frustration; you've got to know about these things in the most intimate way. It was easy for Eileen and me in the beginning. Little did I know that we'd stumbled onto a multimillion-dollar secret here. It's based on the idea of the unique selling position, or USP. I learned about USPs from Jay Abraham back in the late 1980s or early 1990s. You've got to have something about your company that completely separates it, in the minds and hearts of your prospects, from every other company out there; and when I heard that, I thought, "Man, that's a great idea!" So I spent a whole day just thinking it through: "What will be our USP?" I came up with a simple idea, and yet it's been the very foundation of our success. Our USP is the fact that for years, we were out there desperately seeking a way to make more money. *We* were the customers.

We established that as our USP, and decided we were going to be very upfront with the customer. We weren't going to play games with them. We were going to tell our story; we were going to let them know that we've been in their shoes before. We've traveled down that same road that they've traveled down, we've been lied to and misled, cheated and abused by all these other companies that promise all kinds of crazy plans and schemes that are based more on fiction than fact. We just decided, "No holds barred." We were going to remove all the filters and be totally honest with people.

Little did we know that we'd stumbled across an amazing secret. I would advise you to do the same thing with your customers: Be honest with them. Don't play games. Some of them are going to hate you, some of them are going to like you, some of them are going to love you. But even the people who don't like you, if they're good prospects in your marketplace they'll respect you, and that's the most important thing. They know that you're being real with them. People are so unbelievably skeptical in this day and age; even the people you think trust you probably don't. There's always something in the back of their heads that's saying, "Is that person for real? Are they telling it to me straight?"

With your new customer-acquisition marketing, what you're trying to do is to establish a relationship with somebody. I call the front-end marketing a necessary evil, because it's something you have to do on a consistent basis to constantly attract new people into the fold. You can't depend on your established customers being there forever. Life changes, people change, circumstances change. People get hot for something one year, and next they get hot for something else. Emotions rule most of these markets, and emotions tend to be unpredictable. If you had to describe the term "emotions" in ten words, one of those words would probably be "undependable." They are illogical by definition, and the most rabid markets, the ones that can make you millions of dollars, are the markets that tend to be most emotionally driven. So you've got to understand how to attract these people; you've got to look for things that are bold and audacious.

That's some of the best advice that I can give when it comes to planning and trying to think things through. Ask yourself, "How am I going to attract the best prospects, the ones I know everybody else is trying to attract too?" That's really what's important. The most aggressive competitors in your marketplace are consciously trying to attract the same small group of qualified prospects, the people who will end up buying the maximum number of products and services from them. Here's another great question to ask yourself: "What's the wildest, craziest, most compelling thing I could offer to these prospects, the people who have the greatest chance of buying the most stuff from me?" Just think about it; you don't have to do it. This is just a tool to help you jog your mind to come up with some creative ideas; to think bolder, think bigger. Everybody's afraid they're going to think too big, and the whole thing's going to come crumbling down. But the truth is, 99% of people don't think boldly *enough*. They're far too timid. Besides, you can test on a small level the boldest idea that you have. You can come up with the craziest, most outrageous idea ever to attract the best kind of people to you, and then test it on a smaller group of people.

If you're using direct-mail, that's perfect, because you can control it completely. But even if you're using space advertising, you can just run one ad; and if it bombs, if you lose your ass, if you get taken advantage of, if you're doing some outrageous no-risk kind of offer, at least you've learned something. That's what you have to keep doing: you have to keep learning by trying new things. The market will always change; it's constantly evolving. What's hot one year may not be hot the next year. Think of it as a game, and then you won't be so freaked out all the time. It's just a game you play; and if a lot of people saw it that way, they would have a lot more fun. Games are about challenging yourself; about having fun, about trying something new and then being so excited.

I love direct-mail, because with direct-mail you get a crazy, wild idea, and while you're in the heat of the excitement and the enthusiasm, you create some little campaign and you throw it out there — and within days from the time you got excited about it, you can see by the numbers whether or not it's something that resonates with your market. It becomes fun, and if you're constantly doing it, then your whole life is filled with fun. You think, "God, I can't wait to see what happens here!" Things move even quicker when you start using Internet marketing and start doing voice-blasting and tele-seminars. You can come up with an idea today, and by using voice-blasting to your best customers, you can have a tele-seminar two days from now — and you can make tens or hundreds of thousands of dollars within just a few days of the time you come up with the idea. Now, those kinds of things come with knowledge and experience. Some of what I am saying here just sounds like common sense, it really does — that you constantly have to have a way to re-attract new customers. But I'm surrounded by marketers that aren't doing it.

To me, that's one of the great mysteries of this business. People know they should be doing it and every time I spend time with them I ask, "What are you doing to attract new customers on a regular continuous basis?" And they mumble; they can't give me a straight answer because they're not doing it. We've strived to do this on a very regular basis. Every week we send out 50,000 pieces or more on a regular basis to attract new customers, to bring them into the fold. We also have at least one promotion every week that goes out to our established customers. It's so damn simple; I wish more people could get it. When we meet for our free workshop, I'm going to help you understand just how simple and how easy this is, so you can use this secret to make millions and millions of dollars for yourself.

SECRET TEN:

Form Alliances with the Right Suppliers

The tenth secret that made us millions of dollars is that we developed relationships with the very best suppliers we could find. Our suppliers really have helped us make millions of dollars. These are individuals and companies who are much more like partners than suppliers. We've continued to do business with the same people for many years, so they've developed a deep understanding of our business. They do all kinds of things to look out for us, all the time. They continue to find new ways to make us more money, and their success is tied to *our* success. They know that the more they can do to help us, the more money they're going to make. Some people might say it's a mistake to do business with the same small group of suppliers repeatedly. But in this chapter, I'm going to use examples to show you why it makes the most sense to do what we do.

First, we needed a company to produce our audio programs. From Day One we've been involved with audio. It's a great way to develop products; it's a great way to build relationships with customers. There's only so much you can do in print, so my best advice is that you create audio programs from Day One that speak to your customers. Audio is a great way to develop bonds with people that you can't get through print. Your customers will forgive you for not being perfect. They'll forgive you for not being a professional communicator. As long as they know that you really care about them, that you're trying to reach out to them, that you're trying to give them what you know they want — that's the most important part. People develop relationships with you when you produce audio.

We started working with a company called Stucky Audio in 1988, when we first got started. This was a company that was run by a husband-and-wife team. They were already fairly old when we started working with them; in 2000 they retired, and the Vice President of our company bought Stucky Audio. He saw an opportunity, and he knew we liked to do business with the same suppliers over and over again. He asked us this: If he bought them out, would we continue to do business with him? Of course we set some preliminary guidelines, but we've been doing business with McMannis Duplication now since 2000. Now Jeff is taking the company one step forward: Now we do audio CDs, and he also does our DVDs and a lot of our fulfillment. So what started out as being something very, very simple has now progressed because Jeff understands our business. He was Eileen's Vice President from 1990 until I took over the company in 2001, and he has the service mentality. He's somebody we trust, somebody we know we can depend on. He's helped us build our company. He's been involved with our company now since 1990, and so anything we need done, we simply ask him to do it. When it was audio CDs, he immediately took over that part of our business. When we wanted to start producing more DVDs, he took over that. And then, when we needed special fulfillment items done, because some of our other suppliers were charging us too much money for that, he took that part of our business on also. So your suppliers really do become your partners.

We've had the same mailing house since 1990. This is the company that mails all of our direct-mail pieces for us — at least the high-volume stuff. Direct-mail is such a powerful medium. When we get together at our free workshop, we're going to talk a lot about direct-mail, and I'm going to show you how you can use this powerful medium just like we've done to make millions of dollars. But for starters, you've got to have a mailing house. You've got to have a company that's going to take care of all this for you, so you can put all your time in developing the sales material. When you want to make more money you just make a few phone calls, and tell them to mail out more. You call your printer, you call your mailing house, you call your list broker or your list manager, and you tell them you want to do more.

I'm a firm believer that the only way you can truly know how good something is happens when you have something else to compare with it. We started out with a different mailing house, and they were ripping us off blind. When we realized they were cheating us, we started looking around for another mailing house. We found CCI in 1990, and we've been with them ever since. Our relationship with them is great; they do everything they can to help us. Now, they don't charge the least amount of money, I want to tell you that. One of the reasons we've started using McMannis Duplication to do a lot of what we call hand mailings — they can't be machine-inserted — is because CCI was charging us too much. All these companies have certain things that they specialize in, where they can be economical, and they have other areas where they can't.

We've had the same printer since 1994, Steve Harshbarger with CityPrint, and this was after a horrible experience of trying to be our own print shop. When it came time to get out of that business, when we just couldn't take it anymore, I called around and got ahold of Steve. To me it was a blessing that I got ahold of him. He ended up buying some of our printing equipment, and he ended up becoming our printer. Steve made a deep impression on me the very first time I met him, because I was asking him some specific questions, looking for the best prices on some projects. And I'll never forget what he told me: "Look,

T.J., because of the equipment we have at CityPrint, I can do some jobs cheaper and faster than anybody else. The other jobs I can still do them on my equipment, but you're not going to get the best price. I just can't do them as economically on my equipment as some other companies can." Well, that shocked me! There's a lot of dishonesty out there, and one of the reasons people have such bad attitudes when it comes to suppliers is because suppliers lie to them all the time. You can only be lied to by so many people before you develop a callous attitude. When you talk to most seasoned people about developing relationships with suppliers, they'll laugh at you. This whole concept is counter to the way most people teach, which is that you should have all kinds of different suppliers, and feed a little bit of work to all of them so you can always get the best prices. Most people are constantly beating up their suppliers. Well, that's no way to have a relationship with anybody, and a lot of suppliers you *can't* have a relationship with. They're not honest and they're not good people. Your job is to find the very best people you can, and then continue to do as much business with them as possible.

Steve is not only our printer, he's also our printing broker. All the printing that they can do at CityPrint at the most economical rates for their equipment — well, they go ahead and do that work. Then, with all the other jobs they can't run economically on their equipment, he works on our behalf; he negotiates the very best prices, and he takes a little percentage for himself. It's been a wonderful relationship. Both Steve Harshbarger and Pam Fleming of CCI come to our weekly meetings at M.O.R.E., Inc., where we plan new mailings and new promotions. They're constantly looking for ideas that can help us, and they're continuing to do things like invest in new equipment that gives us better turnaround time, lower costs and a higher-quality product. The reason they're constantly doing things like that is because we have a great relationship with them. There's a lot of trust there. They know they can invest money in specialized equipment just for us, because we're going to use it enough to make that investment pay off.

There are insiders in the business. There are always new things that are coming around. When you've got relationships with suppliers, you can ask them to do things for you that normally, if your supplier was just somebody off the street, you wouldn't get. A lot of people treat their suppliers as if they were commodities. It's all about price; and I'm here to tell you that while price is important — of course it is, you don't want to pay more than you have to — there are other things that are important, too. Sometimes, if you pay a little extra, you get a lot more for your money. All our suppliers know that we're trying to get the best price; we don't want to be taken advantage of. But we also want great service, and we want our suppliers to look out for us; we want them to care about our business, and we're trying to care about them, too. It's a two-way street. We're looking for more ways to do business with them, and they're looking for more ways to do business with us.

That's what relationships are all about, and it comes with a little bit of trust. If you're out there doing business with multiple printers and mailing houses, they're never going to have the same emotional connection to your business as they would if you'd just pick a good one and stick with them — because they know you really don't give a damn about them; all you care about is price. I'm here to tell you that there are other things that are just as important as price. In 1989, Russ von Hoelscher introduced us to our mailing list manager, who also is our mailing list broker — so he also gets us outside lists that he doesn't manage. His name is Stuart Kogan; he's one of the best in the business. We've been working with him since 1989. Although we've never met him face-to-face, we've got a great relationship with him.

My graphic artist, Mary Jones, started with me when I was in the carpet-cleaning business. She used to design my little carpet-cleaning fliers and brochures; then when Eileen and I started M.O.R.E., Inc., we needed a great graphic artist, and there she was. We have such a wonderful working relationship, Mary and I. We've been together since 1985. We've worked together on a daily basis, and just as in all good relationships — like if you've been married for a while, or if you've had someone who's been your friend for years — there are some interesting elements that come into play, because they know you and you know them. With Mary, I'm able to get a lot more work done in a faster period of time; she knows exactly what I want, she knows exactly what I like, and so she does everything exactly the way I want it. We communicate less and less every year, and we get more and more done. It's good work; it's stuff that makes our company money. Because of her and the relationship I've developed with her, I end up making a lot more money for our company than I would if we had half a dozen different graphic artists, and that goes the same with all the other suppliers too. The more comfortable you are, the more they understand your business and the more you understand theirs, the more you start to intimately know all the things they can do for you.

We have a company out of Toronto that's called AMS, Automated Marketing Systems, and we've been doing business with them since 1997. Every single year, the services they offer become a more intricate part of our operation. We start looking for more ways to make money with their services. We like them, we know that we can count on them; they make money for us, so why wouldn't we try to look for different ways to use their services? A lot of experienced businesspeople don't understand this. They don't get this whole relationship thing, so they're constantly price shopping all the time. They never establish any kind of long-term relationship with a supplier — and I think that's dollar-foolish, pennywise. If you're dealing with somebody honest who has integrity, somebody who's very knowledgeable, somebody who has a service-first attitude that you can really count on, then you're going to get a lot more done in a given period of time. You're going to make more money in the long run that you would by priceshopping. Long-term suppliers are going to work for you in a much greater way than one-time suppliers. It's in their best interest. They're going to look out for your business; they're going to do more things for you. You're going to find more ways to use their services, and they're going to find more ways to help you. They become your allies. As with all great long-term relationships, the most wonderful things can happen. Developing a long-term relationship with a supplier is an investment on your part. Most people just never figure this out; there's no loyalty to their suppliers, and their suppliers have no loyalty to them either. It really is a two-way street.

Now, a few more examples of how we've done this. In 2001, we developed a relationship with a company called Virtual Focus out of Wichita, Kansas. The owner of that company, Chris Morrison, is a kindred spirit. When we met him, he was only in his early 30s but he was already a millionaire, already deeply involved in Internet marketing and e-commerce. We started with them with just a few basic projects. We found out we could trust them; we found out that they were capable, that they were competent, that they were working far cheaper than any other company would work for, and they kept asking us every time they did something new for us: "What's next? What else can we do for you guys? What else can we do?" We would come up with all these wonderful ideas about developing interesting web-based products and services for our clients, and we'd call them in; and just like with all software, you can basically create it to do whatever you want it to do, within reason. So they started developing things for us. If it weren't for them, we would have never developed our Mall of the World, which is like a miniature

Amazon.com that we created for our clients. It lets them sell over a million different products via this huge mall that was built for us by Virtual Focus.

But see, that relationship started out small. It started out where they were just doing a few things for us. We found out that we could count on them, we liked their work, we liked their prices, they were dedicated, they were kindred spirits, and they happened to be within an hour's drive of our company, which is also very nice. You naturally want to do more business with people that you like. That's why we keep having the same joint-venture partners over and over again.

When I get to the chapter on joint venturing, I'm going to tell you the same thing there. Find people who are capable and competent; people who are honest and sincere; people who have integrity and have the knowledge and the experience and the track record to take you where you want to go. Hang on to those people and never let go of them; keep finding more and more ways to use their services, and they'll continue to find more and more services to offer you to help build your business. It's simple. It sounds like common sense, and yet most people just don't do it. That's the way a lot of these secrets are. To most people, suppliers are just people who offer some type of commodity, and because the whole metaphor of a partnership just isn't there, they can't even grasp that idea. At that point it's all just about price shopping — constantly about price, price, price. Again, prices are important, but other things are just as important, and there's no better example of what I'm describing here than Virtual Focus. They started out offering us the most basic of services and then it became, "What else can we do for you? What else, what else?" And we liked them. We wanted to do more business with them. Every idea we had we ran it by them, and they just kept taking on bigger and bigger things for us, and we kept developing better things. Who knows where it's all going to end up? Now we're an intricate part of their company; they like us, we like them. We want to do more business with them, and they want to do more business with us.

We also have a supplier in India, who we found when we were looking for someone to develop some special websites for us. We went onto eLance.com, which is a wonderful place to find good people at good prices, and we found this little company in Calcutta. They were one out of maybe 200 companies that bid on this special job for us. We loved their prices, so we gave them a try. At first we gave them just a few jobs; but they did such a great job on those small projects that they got our attention. The prices were phenomenal and the quality of the work was incredible, and so naturally we just started thinking, "Hey, what else can we give them?" And now every single time we came up with anything, we just sent it to them and said, "Can you handle it?" and they kept doing more and more things for us. Because the prices were so low and the service was so quick, we kept finding more and more ways to use this company. That's the point: you'll come up with ideas when you have real relationships with your suppliers, people you can count on, people you enjoy doing business with. You'll come up with more ideas for better products and services to offer your clients than you ever would have come up with if it was all just some sort of commodity deal.

I want you to think about this. Now, you're likely to get burnt while you're in the process of finding those good, solid suppliers. There are a lot of incompetent people out there; there are a lot of dishonest suppliers. There are a lot of suppliers where the idea of quality and service are just a foreign language. You may have to search around for a while; you may have to get ripped off before you find someone trustworthy, like we got ripped off when we dealt with our first mailing house. Then, when you do find the good people, you've got to grab hold of them. Look for many ways to do business with them; make them your partners. You know, the relationships we have with our mailing house and our printer are just so incredible. They come to our weekly meetings; they sit there even when we're doing all kinds of things that don't involve them. They're still there, eager to learn more about our business. That's really it. They've developed a great relationship with us because they understand what we're doing, and they're constantly looking out for new ways to reach out and help us.

I realize this is a novel idea to some people, but it's an idea that more people could benefit from, and I hope that you will. I hope you'll go out there and find these suppliers; I hope you'll continue to find more ways to use their services, and make money for yourself. You see, that's what it's all about. You'll develop the kind of relationships with them that we have with our suppliers; and you'll find it's more than just money, it's more than just business. To have people that you enjoy working with — it's such a great experience. It transcends the money alone, but it *will* actually help you make even more money, because you'll want to do more business with people you enjoy. Sure, it's centered around the business; but to me, that's a great thing.

Some cynics might look at that and say, "Aha! All you care about is the business!" Well, our business is our livelihood, and if we're the ones who started that business, it's like a child that we gave birth to. It's an extension of ourselves. It's our hopes and dreams personified. It's an extension of everything we long for, so it's not just something we do to make money. The more we enjoy the people we do business with, the more we want to do business. They feel the same way about us. Then it helps all of us to do what I call "bake a bigger pie." We all end up making a lot more money, but we also end up having a lot more fun too — so we get the best of both worlds.

When we meet for our free workshop, I'm going to express

this to you even more clearly. I'm going to help you understand how a good supplier won't cost you money; it'll make you money. I'm going to tell you more about how we've used our suppliers. We're going to talk about this, because I want to see you enjoying the same relationship with your suppliers that I have with ours. It can help you make more money. I'm going to make this very clear when we meet. Once again, it's a simple idea; it sounds like common sense, but if it were so common, more people would be doing it more, and they're *not*. But I want you to do it, and I'm going to do everything to stay on top of you and impress this upon you when we meet in person.

SECRET ELEVEN:

Become a Marketing Junkie!

The eleventh secret that we used to make millions of dollars? We became marketing junkies! Yes, that's right, we became marketing *junkies*. We became *addicted* to marketing. Hooked on it — hook, line, and sinker. We became obsessed with this whole wonderful subject of marketing; and it *is* a wonderful subject. It's something that can make you rich. When you learn how to master every aspect of marketing, you'll never have to worry about where your next million dollars is going to come from. This is the key. If I had to narrow this book down to one secret, just one, it would be Number Eleven, because it encompasses so much. I want you to think carefully about what I'm going to say in this chapter. This is your meal ticket for life. This is the answer to your highest ambitions. It's right here. It's simple; it's all about marketing.

Now, marketing is one of those things that takes a day to learn and a lifetime to master, because there are certain things that make it very complex. You can spend the rest of your life learning how to become a great marketer; there are certain skills necessary to do that, and most of these take some time to learn. I don't want to discourage you; what I *do* want is for you to understand just how complicated some of this can be. I'm going to reveal some specific secrets in this chapter that could change your life, so I encourage you to focus in on them as tightly as you can. Think carefully about what I'm saying here. The more money you want to make, the more complicated it's going to be — and the higher the price you're going to have to pay. Why more people don't tell you that is beyond me. They prefer to tell you that you those millions of dollars you want to make will all come raining out of the sky, that it's all going to be so easy and fast and simple.

That's nonsense, and there's a part of you that knows that. If you want to make millions and millions of dollars, especially if you have no knowledge, experience, or skills at the beginning, then you're going to have to work your butt off. You're going to have to sacrifice. It's going to take a lot of focus. You have to focus on the basics, and the basics of marketing are pretty simple. Marketing is all the things you do to attract and keep customers. In today's competitive world, that can get kind of complicated, especially if you want to be one of the dominant players in your market.

When you want to take over a substantial market share, the things you have to do can get pretty extensive. First of all, you need to set yourself apart in the minds and hearts of your best prospects and customers. What is it about you that's completely different from all your competitors? The answer is: nothing, really. There's really nothing different about you — so you have to create the differences. Then you have to make them real, and to do that, you have to know, first of all, what's most important to your best prospects. Forget about the rest. The smartest marketers in the world know how to attract the very best prospects, the customers who are most likely to do the maximum amount of business over the longest period of time, for the largest amount of profit in each transaction. They're the customers who are going to spend the most money; but not only that, they're going to spend the most money with the most frequency, and they're going to be the ones who are happy to spend that money, even *proud* to spend that money.

Marketing is about knowing what's most important to your best prospects and customers, and then developing products and services that give these things to them in ways that no one else is doing. Think about that; that's pretty complicated. It requires an intimate knowledge of the average customer in your marketplace. You've got to know them in an intimate way, deeper than they know themselves. You've got to know why they buy, and why they *re*buy. You have to understand the underlying emotional reasons that cause them to keep spending their money in an insatiable way. You look for markets that are rabid, markets where people just buy like crazy, and then keep rebuying and rebuying. Those markets are out there. I'm involved in one of them right now; it's called the opportunity market. When we get together for our free workshop, I'm going to stress this to you again and again: the opportunity market is the one to be in. It's a marketplace that can make you rich, because it's rabid; people just keep buying and buying.

Your marketing should give people all the reasons why they should do business with you, instead of all the other companies who sell similar products and services; and to do that, you have to understand your customers at a very deep level. This also requires knowing the biggest competitors in your market — knowing what they're doing right and, possibly even more importantly, what they're doing wrong. This is where marketing gets complicated; you've got to learn to see things from the other side of the cash register. Get away from this consumer mentality that most people are bogged down in.

You've got to start thinking like an entrepreneur, thinking like a marketer, looking at this as if you were a consultant who was hired to examine the marketplace. You're looking for the biggest competitors. Now, the biggest ones might also mean just the most profitable ones, the ones who have been around the longest. Sometimes they're kind of hidden, because great marketers love to stay hidden. We use things like direct-mail to make sure we're always flying under the radar, and the only people who really know what we're doing are the ones who know where to look. If your competitors are using stealth marketing methods like direct-mail, then you have to get on the company's mailing list and start buying from them on a regular basis — or you're never going to figure out what exactly they're doing. The very best competitors will always remain hidden because of the things that they do to resell to their very best customers, and you've got to be one of those very best customers, or you're never going to see it. You almost have to be an insider to really identify the people making the most money. But you *can* figure it out.

Once you've done that, start looking for all the things those companies are doing wrong, since that's one of the most powerful ways you can differentiate yourself from them. Marketing is about differentiation. What are *you* doing? Or, what *can* you be doing? Those are the most important questions. What can you be doing that's different from the rest of those companies out there, serving the same prospects and customers that you want to serve? Take a look at all the companies that are really doing well: the ones that are making money hand over fist, the ones that have been in the business the longest, the ones that are the most successful from a financial standpoint. Put those companies under a magnifying glass — through eyes of an entrepreneur, not the eyes of a consumer. Find all the things they're doing well, and develop products and services that have those qualities. Give people what they really want, without any negative side effects.

That's one of the most powerful ways you can communicate to customers. Marketing is about communication, it's about relationships, and it's about all the tools and the techniques, systems, and processes you have to use in order to maintain those relationships and make them even stronger. I want you to think about marketing in the simplest of ways. It's about developing thousands of relationships with people.

What is a relationship? It's a bond you have with someone. It's the bond, the feelings they have about you. They feel you're their friend; or at least they feel that you respect them and really understand them, and you're trying to serve them in the highest possible way. You have to do all you can to make sure that they *do* feel that. You've got to let your customers know that you do care about them. Everybody says they care about the customers, and you know that's nonsense. Customers don't even believe messages like that anymore. Everybody's saying it. But since marketing involves doing things that separate yourself from everybody else, show those customers, in the ways that are most important to them, that you really *do* care about them, that you understand them, that you respect them, that you know exactly what they want. You've got to make them feel that.

So when I say that marketing takes a day to learn and a lifetime to master, realize that the ones who have mastered it are the ones who know how to create and maintain deep relationships with hundreds and even thousands and, with some marketers, tens of thousands of people. Think about all the elements it takes to form and maintain a relationship. It takes communication; it takes understanding; it takes the ability to express how you feel. With marketing you do this with many people at once. It's also the creation and implementations of specific messages that attract the right people and repel the wrong ones. It's knowing exactly what to say to cause the best prospects to seek you out — and we suggest that you use as much two-step marketing as you possibly can. Use it in such a way that people are coming to you, or at least have the perception that they are.

And it really is just a perception, because you're actually

the one who ran the ads. You're who one that sent out the direct-mail package. You're the one who came to them first — but they don't even think about it that way. They buy in an emotional, unconscious vacuum. They see your ad, they get your direct-mail piece, and by their way of thinking and feeling, they're the ones who send in that reply card. They're the ones that come to you, seeking you out. That being the case, now they've given you permission to sell them, and to resell them again and again. They've also shown you by their actions that they're qualified. You want to create special offers, where you're only looking for the right type of people while getting rid of all the others. You want to make customers feel special; you know you can't be everything to everybody. The more you're able to communicate your unique selling position to your customers, the more you make them feel special, because they're part of an elite group. Now, all this takes years to learn how to do well, so I don't want you to be frustrated by what I'm saying. I want you to be *excited* about it. Once you learn how to do all this, you can make as much money as you want for the rest of your life. However much that might be, it's out there for you, and it's acquired by getting better and better at attracting and retaining the very best prospects and customers.

You're looking for prospects who stand the greatest chance of doing the most business with you over the longest period of time, so you need to know how to create ongoing systematic promotions that only attract these highly qualified prospects to you. The more you know who these people are, the more intimately you understand them, and the more you have the ability to create products and services that are just for them — then the more eager they are to give you their money in exchange for whatever you're selling. People are happy to give you their money, they're even proud to give you their money; if that sounds like a pipe dream or a fantasy, it's not. There are marketers out there doing it right now. I've seen it; I've done it.

This is the end goal: to get people who are overjoyed to be your customers, because they like your products and services. They know in their hearts that you're trying to do everything totally above the board, and you're trying to be the very best in your marketplace. You're trying to serve them at the highest level, whatever serving them means — because in each marketplace it means something a little bit different. Good marketing is made up of all the things you do to build solid relationships with your best customers. It's about bringing people into the fold, and then developing those relationships: building them, deepening them, just like you would with any other relationship you wanted to keep. Think of your best relationships. They came over a period of time, and time is the one element that does strengthen relationships.

If you break a relationship down to its essence, you'll see that there are a few things that are absolutely necessary: things like regular communication, understanding, respect, appreciation, and trust. The great marketers are wonderful about building all those things with thousands and thousands of their best customers. Do it right, and it turns them into raving fans for you and for your company. Make them feel bonded to you; make them feel they're understood and appreciated; make them feel great about their decision to keep giving you more of their money. All this is based on the creation and the implementation of certain systems and processes that automatically do this for you so that, on a regular basis, you're constantly attracting more of the people who are perfect for your company and the products and services you've developed. The better you know your best customers, the more you'll be able to create these crucial processes and systems that let you stay focused on the best prospects and forget the rest. Focus on the development of the systems that attract the very best, most-highly qualified prospects, then lead those first-time buyers through an orchestrated series of steps that causes them to rebuy the largest amount of products and services from you.

It does get complicated, much like the game of chess. When my son was nine, he taught me how to play chess. Now, I always thought you had to be genius to play chess — but the truth is, there are just 16 chess pieces on each side of the board, made up of six basic types. Each of those pieces can only move a certain number of ways. Within an hour after my son taught me how, we were playing chess. We were both feeling pretty good about ourselves, because he wasn't that good, and neither was I. We only knew the most basic strategies. Anybody who knew how to play chess could have come and beat us in about two simple moves. And it *is* simple. This piece can move this way, that piece can move this way and that way, and that's it. The end goal is very simple in chess, and yet there are chess masters who spend their entire lives studying every aspect of this game, keeping reams and reams of notes, thinking it all through very, very carefully.

My ancestors are German; my grandfather came off the boat. There were certain relatives who played chess with their friends and family back home, and they did it all through the mail, so they would have a way of staying in touch. Both sides would keep chess sets in their homes, and then they would think carefully about all their moves. The board is numbered, so when it was their turn they made their move, wrote it down on a piece of paper, and then mailed it back to their relatives back home; and then the relatives would put that move on their chess board, think through their moves very carefully, include it in a letter, and send it back to America. Sometimes it would take up to a year for one of them to come up with a move, because they would think it through so carefully. Every decision was weighed against all other possible decisions, so they'd spend months and months asking themselves, "If I moved it here, what would happen? What would they do?" They would try to think through all the various strategies that resulted, three or four steps in advance — so not only would they be considering each move, they would be thinking about the overall strategy of each. They would consider how it could affect everything else, and how they could ultimately win the game. That's the way good marketing is, too. The people who have mastered it are thinking things through, and they try to stay several steps ahead. Every decision is weighed against an overall philosophy — a deep understanding of their customers, and an intimate knowledge of who those people are. What do they want the most? What do they hate the most?

Eileen and I learned this by accident, really. It came as a result, first of all, of our desire to make millions of dollars. If it weren't for that desire, none of this would have happened. I became a salesman in 1984; that's how I learned to sell things. Some people think that marketing and selling are the same things, but they're really not. Selling is something that happens *within* marketing, but marketing is more about building relationships with customers, and then knowing and understanding the tools and the processes used to strengthen those relationships. Ultimately, you need to learn how to make people want to give you more and more of their money over the longest period of time for the largest amount of profit. Selling is something you do on a short-term basis; marketing is more about the long-term effects of what it takes to keep people coming back again and again. It's more about reselling them than selling them.

Eileen and I learned this by accident. Initially we were both trying to run the company at the same time, and then that simply didn't work anymore, and one of us had to go. It was a partnership that started creating problems. We would yell and scream at each other all day long, because I'm a control freak and she's a control freak, and I have my ideas that I'm very opinionated about and she has hers, and so I had to leave the office and start doing all my work from home. This was in 1992; four years into the business, and what did I do at home? Well, I learned how to work *on* the business rather than *in* it, and I learned how to become a good marketer; then for nine years, that's all I did. I simply focused on marketing: nothing more, nothing less. I became obsessed with it. I call it the "magnificent obsession." I bought thousands and thousands of dollars worth of seminars on tape. I bought newsletters; I studied this thing intensely. I ate it, slept it, breathed it. I thought about nothing but marketing. It was fascinating to me. It was the answer to all my ambitions. It became the thing I just couldn't get out of my head, and I surrounded myself with other people who were as crazy as I was, and we built this little group of like-minded entrepreneurs called the One Hundred Million Dollar Roundtable. Every year it's getting stronger and stronger, attracting like-minded marketers who are absolutely as obsessed about it as I am. I learn from them and they learn from me. I also spent six years with Eileen in Dan Kennedy's Platinum Group, where we met four times a year with the best marketers in the country, other people who were deeply committed to building companies that are solid and profitable. The idea was that by building relationships with as many customers as possible, and causing those people to feel so attuned to what we were doing, that would make them want to continue to give us more and more of their money. The more I subjected myself to this, the more I learned how to write copy, learned how to develop products, learned more about the customers and how to reach them in the deepest kind of way — well, the more money just started flowing in.

I'm assuming that you're the kind of person who wants to see that happen. You want to make millions of dollars — and I'm here to tell you that that money is out there for you *right now*. All you have to do is become a marketing master. You have to learn all the ways to attract and re-attract the very best customers within your marketplace, the ones who will continue to give you more and more of their money. You have to lose yourself in this "magnificent obsession" I love so much. I call it a magnificent obsession because it's actually so interesting. It's challenging, it's fun, it's exciting, there's a lot to learn, and the thrill of getting thousands of people to give you more and more of their money, every single year, is the greatest kind of thrill. It's the greatest kind of satisfaction you can have. It's the most wonderful feeling on Earth to have thousands of customers who love you; and if they don't love you, at least they respect you.

You know, some of my customers think I'm just a total jerk, period. That's okay; in some ways they're right. They think I'm egotistical; they criticize me for the way I repeat myself constantly; they criticize me for the fact that I fail to communicate in a professional way. But they still respect me, they still know in their hearts that I do give a damn about them, that in fact I really care deeply about them. They know that, because I've done everything possible to express that to them. I'm trying to reach out to my very best customers and give them more and more of what I know is most important to them. I understand them at a deep level, and so our profits continue to get bigger and bigger every single year. Our customers love us, they know us, they respect us, and they know we care about them. They know that we're striving to do everything possible to help them, and to separate ourselves from all those competitors in the marketplace who are basically ripping them off, lying to them, misleading them, and cheating them.

We've shared our story from Day One. We've reached out to the customers in a very intimate, personal way, just as I'm trying to do with you right now. I'm trying to reach out through the pages of the book you're reading. If I could, I would grab you and shake you a little and get you to see that all the millions of dollars you want are out there. It's up to you to recognize that.

THE BLUE JEANS MILLIONAIRE!

The day that you do, the day you finally wake up and really see the potential and know that all of the money that you want is out there, if only you'll learn these techniques I'm trying so hard to express to you — that's the day your life will change forever, and it can all happen by practicing this eleventh secret and becoming a marketing junkie.

SECRET TWELVE:
Develop Your Copywriting Skills

The twelfth secret that made us millions of dollars is the fact that we learned how to write copy that sells, and then how to implement it in our overall marketing strategy. Now, this is arguably the single greatest wealth-making skill you can learn. Knowing you can write a sales letter that causes thousands of people to give you millions of dollars is one of the greatest feelings on earth. I want you to experience this feeling. It's just an amazing thing: to get an idea, write a sales letter, send it out to your best customers — and if you have enough of those customers, you can make millions of dollars. Maybe there are greater feelings than that, but this is one of the top five you could ever experience.

So many people want to make millions of dollars... and they could, if only they'd just realize how simple it is to do it! You've got to have a group of customers who respect you, who feel great about you and who know you're out there to help them; and you've got to have the ability to communicate to them, simply by sending them a sales letter or a series of sales letters. You see, that's what it's really about. One sales letter can make you millions of dollars, but the key is having a group of customers that you can send a series of sales letters to on a regular basis, so you build a business, not just a promotion. That's what you're really after: a business, which is steady profits made over a period of time. That's the key to overall profitability.

Now, what is a great sales letter? A great sales letter is something that replaces a live salesperson. So if you have a thousand sales letters out there, you have a thousand sales people. It's a salesperson in an envelope. It does a complete job of selling for you. It answers every objection in the minds and hearts of the skeptical prospect, and the fearful prospect, and the prospect who feels overwhelmed. They're already getting a lot of solicitations, because the same people that are your best customers are also other peoples' best customers. Your sales letter answers all their objections, and it stands out from all of the other mail. It's interesting to read, it's targeted to a specific person, it establishes the value of whatever you're selling, and it proves to them that what you have to offer is worth far more than the money you're asking for in exchange. It makes people excited about giving you their money. That's what a great sales letter is. It's exciting, it's interesting, and it's persuasive.

It's the ultimate way for you to stay in touch with your customers and to continue to resell to them on a regular basis, to give them more of what you know they want the most. It's also the fastest way for you to make the largest amount of money. They don't call it direct-mail for no reason. This is a media that goes straight to the prospect or customer, and it delivers a very direct sales presentation to them. It compels them to send their money directly to you, and it's the fastest way for you to make millions of dollars. Direct-mail is a media that you have 100% control over, from start to finish. You write it; you design it; you choose your printer. You choose the mailing house that's going to mail out your sale letter; you schedule it; you pick all of the mailing lists; you analyze the numbers as they come in. You have total control and total power over every aspect of this. It's a media that you own, and that's the way I want you to think about direct-mail.

Think about it as if you had your own TV station — or

better still, think about it as if you had your own newspaper, and you control every aspect of that newspaper. You have regular subscribers who get it, and your job is to make sure that those subscribers stay subscribers. But even better, when you have direct-mail, your job is also to advertise in your own newspaper, and your job is to make sure that the largest number of your subscribers continue to give you money for all the advertising in your newspaper. It's a great metaphor; it'll help you think about this in the right way. Let's say you own your own newspaper, which you publish on a regular basis. It's a job; you just do it, and you send it out there on a regular basis to people that you know want it, because they subscribe. That's really what we're trying to explain here. This is a media that you control. You call all the shots. You have all the power; you have all of the freedom and flexibility to do whatever it is that you want to do with it.

That's the kind of control you don't have in other kinds of media, where you're totally dependent on the publication itself. They're the ones who set the deadlines; they're the ones to set the prices. If you want lower prices you have to negotiate, and it's often a painful thing. You're not in any position of power. But when you have a group of customers who have bought from you in the past, you know what they like and you know what they don't like; there's a trust that's built up between you and them. You can mail to them as often as you want, and you control exactly what you want them to see, every aspect of it; you're in charge. You don't have to ask permission from anybody. If you're not happy with the printers or the mailing house you're using, you can find new ones. If you're not happy with the mailing list broker, you can go out and find somebody else. You can mail as often as you want, as much as you want. If you've got a piece that's working and you know that there are more names out there, all you have to do is call your mailing list broker and say, "Hey! Give me another 50,000 names!" and then call your printer and say, "Print up another 50,000 pieces!" Then you call your mailing house and say, "Hey! We're going to mail another 50,000 pieces!" It's as simple as that.

You control it all, and it's a no-risk method if you use it correctly. Here's what I mean by that: You're constantly using direct-mail to test new ideas — and you can test *radical* new ideas, ideas that are totally bold and audacious. You can test them to small groups of your best customers first, and because the trust is established with those people, chances are they'll buy from you. You're looking for the things that make them most excited, the things that they buy the most. You'll never lose money, because these are people who will, in most cases, buy anything from you if you've done your job right. Then you take the things they buy the most of, the ones they're most excited about, and start testing them to other groups of customers. Then, if your numbers are still high, you start testing to outside mailing lists, the lists of prospects your customers all originated from. There are companies in your marketplace that sell the same types of products and services that you sell. If you're in a direct response marketing-friendly environment, those companies will be putting their mailing lists up for rent. At M.O.R.E., Inc., we rent our mailing lists out to all kinds of other companies. Our mailing-list manager picks the ones he wants; we're only renting our list out to companies he knows are honorable ones. Similarly, we rent names from other companies who have their mailing lists up for rent.

That's the way it is with the opportunity market; millions of names every year are available. These are proven buyers, folks who have bought other moneymaking plans and programs just like the ones we offer, so there's a buying history. We can go to the people we know are interested in what we sell, and we can offer them the kinds of programs that we sell to bring them into the fold; and now they become our customers. There are plenty of markets out there just like the opportunity market, where you can rent, in some cases, millions of names every year.

The big secret is that, by the time we get to the point of sending an offer to those outside names, we've already tested the product to our very small group of best customers. Think of your customer base as a pyramid: it gets smaller as it goes up. We test to the very best of our customers at the top of the pyramid. We take the offers that work the best there, the ones that produce the most sales and profits, and we slowly start testing to larger groups of customers, working our way down from there. Then, when we go through our entire customer base and the offer's still good, we take that offer and we start testing it to the outside mailing list. By the time we use it for our new customer acquisition, it's proven. We know it works. The only question now is, how well is it going to work with people who don't already have a relationship with us?

I just love direct-mail. Direct-mail and the ability to write copy: together, they're such a powerful thing. It's absorbing; it's interesting. You can spend hour after hour absorbed in this, and it becomes more a hobby or an art than anything else. That's the way I think about it. Sure, it's work; it's a lot of work. This is, again, one of the great things about it. I don't say this to dissuade or discourage you; I just want to say that it's taken me a lot of time and work to master my skills at writing copy that sells millions of dollars worth of products and services. To some extent it's been a labor of love, but in a whole other way it's just been an awful lot of work. There are parts that are more interesting than others. Some parts are very relaxing. Every night my wife and I sit on the couch, and I'm half-watching TV programs with her; but the other half of me is quietly editing sales copy I've already written. To me, that's the most relaxing way to spend an evening.

I'm always working on different sales letters, constantly. I always have different projects out there, and it's the most

137

wonderful feeling to create these things that produce revenue. It's almost like alchemy. If you study history, you'll see that up until about the sixteenth or seventeenth century, there were people called alchemists, and their job was to try to turn lead into gold — to try to take something of no value, basically, and turn it into high value. That's what we're doing here. The copywriters like myself, who know how to design and develop and create sales letters that cause thousands of people to willingly and gladly give their money to us — well, we're taking paper and ink, which has very little value, and making it high value. Of course you can do it on websites too, but basically it's the same thing concept. You're creating a complete sales story from top to bottom, and you're causing people to get so excited that they just can't wait to give you their money. We've had people wire their money to us through Western Union just to get our product quicker. We've had many people who Federal Expressed their orders to us. A few have jumped in their cars and driven from three or four states away, because they wanted to get the product even faster.

It's exciting to create millions of dollars worth of revenue where no revenue existed before, and to know that you're the one who did it. Now, I've had a lot of help over the years, learning how to write copy; and the best thing I can do is tell you that you have to just decide that you want to become a great copywriter. Make that decision. For years, I could write sales letters to my best customers. They trusted me; we had established relationships, and quite candidly my copy didn't have to be as good because of the relationship. It's just like when you have a friend — you'll do more for your friend. If you have two people who ask you to do something and one of them is your friend, you're going to go with your friend every time. Your friend hardly has to say anything. They just say, "Look, I've got this great deal," and you say "Hey! Stop, stop, I trust you. How much is it going to cost me?" Whereas any other person is going to have to work on you quite a bit. They're going to have to keep bugging you, over and over again.

If you just think about it like that, you'll realize that when you have an established group of customers, you don't have to be as good. Even a beginning copywriter can start sharpening their skills, creating new offers, writing new sales letters to those people who have shown a certain level of trust because they bought from you the first time. So for years, I would write these sales letters to our established customers. This is how I developed my skills as a copywriter. It was just to write sales letters to people who had already bought from us. They knew us; they liked us. There was some trust there, shown by the money they had given us. People vote with their checkbooks or their credit cards, and so for years I crafted all of these offers that went out to people who had already bought from us, and it was great to learn how to write copy and send it out there to people. When we wrote "Dear Friend," we really meant it. We were trying to be friends with our customers; we were trying to befriend them in every way, and that's what I'm asking you to do, too. Operate with complete integrity and complete honesty. Treat your customers very well and make all kinds of offers to them, and then take the best of those offers and use them for your new customer acquisition program. There are plenty of mailing lists out there, but only the very best offers and the very best sales copy will work for those people who don't know you. They don't trust you yet; they're still very skeptical. You're just another company showing up in their mailbox now.

For years I tried to write copy for new customer acquisition, and I simply couldn't do it; I wasn't good enough. That used to just tick me off! I used to get so angry because I was dependent on outside copywriters, and I wanted to learn how to do it myself. That anger and frustration emerged every single time we were forced to hire a copywriter because my copy wasn't good enough. I would take sales letters or variations that had worked great for our customers, and I tried to make them work to the outside list, and the profits were just never there. Then these outside copywriters came in who had a limited amount of knowledge and understanding of what we were selling and who we were selling it to — and yet they could go out there and make the copy work.

That just made me so angry — and I used that anger in a positive way. I became determined that I was going to be able to do this. I studied a lot of sales letters, I read a lot of books, I practiced a lot. This is one suggestion from Gary Halbert — arguably one of the best copywriters ever: a true legend according to many, including me. Gary said that the way to learn how to write copy is to take one of the best ads you can find, the long-form, full-page ads, or one of the best sales letters, and to write it longhand word for word, over and over, until you get so sick and tired of it you can't stand it anymore.

I did that; I took the *Lazy Man's Way to Riches*, a full-page ad that Joe Karbo used in the mid-1970s that made him millions and millions of dollars, and rewrote it in my own hand, day after day. I don't know how long I did it; at least for a couple of months, to the point where I just about had the whole thing memorized. I learned the language, the rhythm, the flow of writing good, persuasive, hard-hitting sales copy. That particular ad caused so many people to get excited that they sent in their money; and subconsciously, over a period of time, with the determination that I was going to learn how to write sales copy that really was capable of making millions of dollars, I became a good copywriter. It wasn't easy; it's still not easy. It's painful work at times, and don't let anybody kid you. There's a quote that I love: it says, "The secret of great writing is to re-write," and I'm famous for re-writing my sales letters a whole bunch of times. That's what I'm doing on the couch every single night.

So I want you to think about that tonight; think about me tonight. Whatever you're doing tonight, realize that if it's before ten-thirty in the evening Central Time, I'm on my couch next to my lovely wife Eileen, I've got a laptop in my lap, and I'm re-writing some sales letter. When I get up in the morning, I work on the copy. I work on sales letters all the time. I've always got about three or four of them going at once, because I get bored with them, and I want to keep shifting around. It's more like a job now than anything, but still there's moments when this is just the most wonderful feeling on Earth, and one of my secrets is, whenever I get really excited about an idea, I just start writing like crazy. Some of the sales letters that have worked the best have been those I wrote when I was higher than a kite on caffeine. I tend to drink a pot of coffee or two every day. So I get wound up, I get excited about ideas. The time to write copy is when you're in the heat of the moment, when you're really pumped up and excited. Now, that can change; over a period of time, your skill and knowledge will develop to the point where you can write powerful, persuasive copy whether you're excited or not. You can still make it look like you're excited, and that's the method used by freelance copywriters who charge many thousands of dollars. They don't really understand what your products are and who you're selling to, but they can create copy that's compelling. It looks like they were excited when they wrote it, when the truth is that they hardly understand anything about it.

This is a skill that can set you up for life. It's your meal ticket; it's the way to riches; it's the single greatest wealth building skill that you'll ever learn, when you think about the overall picture. That's what I want you to do: think beyond just writing one sales letter or whatever. Think about copywriting as a lifelong skill you can use to sell and resell to your customers again and again, and to attract new customers to you. Remember: the secret is to take your best promotions, work them through your customer base first, then send them out as part of your new customer acquisition process. That'll save you a lot of misery, because if your existing customers aren't excited, then you know that the people out there who don't know you won't be excited. There's no differentiation in their mind between you and all the other direct-mail they're getting.

These are the brutal realities we're dealing with here. There's a lot of competition, and people are sorting their mail over the trash can. When it comes to front-end, new customer acquisition, it's really tough to break through that shell of skepticism. But when you're mailing to existing customers, it's so much easier. You should have new offers going out to them all the time.

We've been doing this since 1988, and I used to worry that I was sending too much too often to our established customers. I don't worry about that anymore, and I don't think you should either. As long as you're making great offers that are altruistic in nature, that really offer tremendous value, that offer strong money-back guarantees if people aren't happy; that strive to give your customers special deals — then you're good. The perception is that other people aren't getting these things; you're offer's just for them. You should be in their mailbox constantly. The beautiful thing about it is, if you structure it right, and if your customer base is large enough, you don't need very many people to respond to an offer to make millions of dollars. The secret of making your customer base large enough is to have a steady stream of mail that goes out on a regular basis to attract new customers to you, so your customer base continues to grow bigger automatically.

We have one direct-mail offer out there all the time to new customers. Every single week, 52 weeks a year now; we used to stop around Christmas time, but we don't anymore. Fifty-two weeks of every year, we extend tens of thousands of direct-mail solicitations to new customers who have never done business with us before. We want to get them to buy once, or get them to take some minor action, so we can bring them into the fold. Nowadays, I'm way beyond that fear that I had for years, the fear that I would tick off my customers if I sent them too many offers. I realize now that I literally lost millions of dollars because I didn't market aggressively to our established customers, because I was always holding back, always afraid that we were doing too much to those customers. Now, we strive to have one new offer that goes out there to our established customers every single week. That's our goal. We don't hit it every week, but we try to, so we're in their mailbox 52 times a year. To make a profit on most promotions, we only need a small percentage of people to raise their hands and say "Yes."

The same can be true of your promotions, if you structure them correctly. You can make millions of dollars, and you'll always make more money by mailing more often to your very best customers. When we get together for our free workshop, we're going to talk about this in more detail. I'm going to try to persuade you to put in the necessary effort to develop these skills. I can't wait to get with you, to spend face-time with you, to talk about developing this very, very important wealth-making skill that can make you financially independent for the rest of your life.

Secret Thirteen:
Master the Skills of Information Marketing

The thirteen secret that we used to make millions of dollars is this: We honed our skills in product development. My entire life changed the day I created our first information product, *Dialing for Dollars*. I look at it now, and it looks like some kind of a joke. It was poorly written, filled with typos; it just wasn't a good program in any way. Yet that was product that got us started, and it was just a little booklet that we sold for $12.95. We ran a small ad in an opportunity magazine, using the last $300 we had.

But the program clicked with our prospects, because it was based on something that we had been using that was totally proven. That was the only great thing about *Dialing for Dollars*, and yet it got us started and the customers loved it. Then I started writing *Dialing for Dollars, Part II* just a few months later, and I started putting my heart and soul into a better program. The first one included some multilevel marketing aspects, and I just didn't like that; it was creating too many problems, and my wife was begging me to stop doing it. She wanted me to take all the multilevel marketing stuff out. So I started working on *Dialing for Dollars Part II*, which became our new and expanded *Dialing for Dollars* program, and with that program the multilevel stuff; it just went out of the window. It became a straight distributorship opportunity — and people loved the idea of making money with an answering machine. It resonated; people were absolutely crazy about it. This was in the late-1980s, when answering machines were brand new and technology was making them more affordable, even as they were shrinking in size and increasing in power — and people loved the idea that there was a way to make money with this new technology.

Ever since then we've continued to use that theme, as when we showed people how to make money with computer bulletin boards. When the Internet came around, we showed people how to make money with websites. People love the idea of new technology. They're just crazy over it, and they're always looking for some way to make money with new technology. It's exciting to them, it's interesting, and we really did *start* with our last $300. This was all the money we had at the time. We sold a beat-up van we'd used for our carpet-cleaning business to get that little bit of money, which gave us an opportunity to buy a tiny ad in one of the best moneymaking magazines of the time. Now, the first *Dialing for Dollars* was a glorified brochure! That's all it was. It wasn't anything that we would produce today, and yet the customers liked it, and it really worked for them. It really made them money. That was especially true after we came up with *Dialing for Dollars, Part II.* We got away from the multilevel marketing aspect. We showed people how to use their answering machine to sell the products we'd created, although we also showed them how they could use it for other things besides just our products. They found our honesty and integrity refreshing.

Once we came up with the idea of tiny manuals that were designed to sell in newspapers, we took a couple of different opportunities that were working for us and blended them together to create this whole *Dialing for Dollars* concept. The ideas are out there, folks; and we happened to hit on the right ideas at the right time. Little did we know it, but our idea resonated and it actually made people money, and that's a great thing. To be able to really, truly help people make money is wonderful. We had distributors who were making $10,000, $20,000, $50,000 a month. We had one guy in Utah who was making $5 million a year before he cut us out (as all of our successful distributors ultimately do), and that was back when our company was barely doing a couple of million dollars a year. So we had a distributor who was doing more than twice as well as us, and that's a great thing! It makes me really happy that we helped people. That's one of the things that a good information product can do: It can really make a difference in people's lives. This was the foundation of our success.

Within six months from the time we ran that $300 ad, we were bringing in $16,000 a month, and the strategy we used was very simple. It's one that you could use starting tomorrow. We ran that little ad; it did take about six weeks before it came out, but we used those six weeks as a way of gearing up and getting things ready to go. During the six weeks we were waiting for that ad to run, we were frantically creating that little booklet. The kind of product development that took me a month to do back then I can do in a couple of days now. That's not to brag; the fact is that you get better as you go along. I want you to think about that; you've got to get started, you've got to bloom where you're planted. So get started.

Within six months we were averaging $16,000 dollars a month, and Eileen and I were like two kids in a candy store. That was more money than we'd ever made in our whole lives. We didn't even know what to *do* with that money. Then we met Russ von Hoelscher, and Russ helped us go from $16,000 a month to almost $100,000 a week within the first nine months. In other chapters of this book, I've explained to you exactly what Russ did to help us achieve those phenomenal results. One of the things he did was help polish our product-development skills.

THE BLUE JEANS MILLIONAIRE!

Our first product with Russ von Hoelscher was called *The $2,500 Weekend*, and for us it was a major breakthrough. That was the first time we did over $1 million on just one product, and we did it *fast*. Now, that product took one weekend of our lives to create, but we're still using it. The sales letter took me three months to write, but we're still using parts of that sales letter *right now*. People loved the idea of *The $2,500 Weekend*. It was such a simple idea, just like *Dialing for Dollars* was a simple idea, but it resonated in the minds and hearts of the people who bought it. Here's where we got the name: We were paying Russ von Hoelscher $2,500 every single time he came down to spend a weekend with us, and the whole time he was there, we were working on ideas and brainstorming. He was sharing his greatest tips, tricks and strategies with us, and so I said, "Russ, why don't you come down here next time, and we'll a have a recorder set up. Let's ask you a million and one questions and get all your answers — ask you all kinds of questions that we know our customers have about mail order and making money, getting rich, and that type of thing. We'll go ahead and pay you your $2,500 plus your airfare, and then we'll be very honest and direct with the customers and let them know this is material that cost us $2,500." We sold the product at $295 — so our customers were getting $2,500 in real value for a little over a tenth of that price. This product was real and it was raw; it was honest. All we did was put a little tape player on our kitchen table. It was all unedited, unpolished, and genuine — and that's exactly what people want. They don't want anything fancy. The more you can create informational products that are just for them, products that are perceived as having been created just for them, the better.

You don't have to be professional; you don't have to be polished. In fact, it's better that you aren't. As you may or may not be aware, this book was adapted from an audio product, part of which I recorded in my basement studio. During that recording, I tried to express myself fully, honestly. I was surrounded with notes; I didn't just make all this up on a whim. I put a lot of concentrated thought into it, but at the same time, the original recording (and this book, too) is just me trying to reach out to you, trying to help you understand the secrets that made *us* millions of dollars so they can make *you* millions of dollars. When I'm producing an audio program or hosting a seminar, I'm not trying to be a professional speaker; I'm just trying to be me. And that's what people really want; they don't want you to play games with them. People want information that's going to help them. The *$2,500 Weekend* made us more than a million bucks because it was targeted; it was designed to help our customers get the information that they wanted and needed. It touched them emotionally, and they identified with us.

We gave people what they really wanted, and they rewarded us with very quickly with well over $1 million. It was a wonderful experience for us to realize that we could go down to a Radio Shack, buy a $50 cassette tape recorder, and record a product that brought us in a fortune. These days, I record on a computer, using equipment that cost thousands of dollars. Back then, I was using equipment that cost $50, and there was no real difference. The product was valuable in the minds and hearts of the customers who bought it. It resonated with them; it gave them what they wanted; it gave them what they needed. They loved it. When we get together in person, I'm going to stress the importance of this to you, and how simple and easy it is for you to develop your own informational products. You do have to think things through very carefully; you have to think about your customers. There are specific things you need to do, and yet it's very easy as long as your heart is in the right place — as long as you really do want to help people. Information products are an extension of you. They're a way for you to reach out to other people and try to make a difference in their lives, and try to share a part of who you are with them, and try to extend your hand and pull them up. In the process you pull yourself up; you make a lot of money. The profit margins are incredible on these types of products, which really do give people what they want.

In the opportunity market there are two basic types of products. There are what we call soft products and hard products. A soft product is just like this one: It gives your customers great ideas and shortcut secrets, proven strategies; it gives them personal stories from your own life that will help teach them the things that you want them to learn. It's an extension of you, and it lets you reach out and help people. A hard product is a product like our *Dialing for Dollars*. It gives customers something to sell, either a product or a service or some combination of both. It contains, number one, something to sell. Number two, it contains the sales material that you've developed for them that they can use to sell the product or service. Number three, it contains the marketing system you developed and put together for them, so they can use that sales material to go out and promote this product or service and sell it. It's some kind of a distributorship manual that puts it all together in one cohesive package. That's it! Just those three things.

Hard products are what sell the most in our marketplace. The fastest way to become a millionaire in the opportunity market is to develop hard products and turn-key distributorships. We have some of them, right now, which we make available for you to sell in this marketplace. That's what people really want: hard, turn-key products that let them go out and make money right away. All this gets easier as you go along, and your confidence and knowledge will develop. It's all about serving your customers.

Here are ten things that all great information products have in common. Number One: they speak to the person who buys them, just like I'm trying to speak to you right now; they're real, just like I told you about our *$2,500 Weekend* program. That program was real, and it was raw. Products like this give people something they really want. That's what I'm trying to do with you: I'm trying to show you how you can make millions of dollars. Number Two, these products are an extension of who you are. They communicate things about you. They let people know who you are, what you stand for, and what your company stands for. They let you express things to your customers, to help you bond with them; you tell your story, and you get a chance to reach out to people like I'm trying to do with you right now.

Number Three, they help to establish your credibility. In the beginning, we didn't really have any credibility — or so we thought. The whole idea behind our *$2,500 Weekend* product was to interview Russ and to let him share his tips, tricks and strategies with our listeners. Recently, we moved into the real-estate market. Did we know anything about real estate? Absolutely not, so we interviewed all kinds of experts, which helps make complicated things simple and easy. We went out there and found the experts, but we also established our credibility in the minds of the customers, because they knew we were trying to reach out, to give them the information they wanted, needed, valued, and appreciated.

Number Four: Because of all this, these products help you to create strong bonds with your customers. When I meet my best customers at seminars, they all feel like they know me and I feel like I know them. We share a lot in common. They've listened to me on these programs. They know my heart's in the right place, and I'm trying to serve them. Number Five: These information products are perfectly matched to the customers you serve. You're doing it for them, as I'm creating this product for you.

Number Six: They make people want to do more business with you. They separate you from the competition, and they really help bring people to you. People listen to you on your audio programs, they come to your seminars, they buy other kinds of information products from you, they like you; they know you're trying to help them, and they believe you really *can* help them, and naturally they want to do more business with you.

Number Seven: These products lead the prospect down the path you want them to take, just like I'm trying to lead you on the path right now to joining me for our free workshop here in Kansas. I'm trying to give you the basic ideas here, but I'm also trying to take you to the next step; I'm trying to get you to do more business with us, so we can help you get what you really, truly want. The things I'm trying to do right now with you, you can do with *your* customers. Establish your credibility or your authority. You can break the ice with them. Start introducing them to more of whatever it is that you have to offer. What I have to offer you is a workshop that would let us spent time together, and let me get to know you a little bit — but it won't end there. If you're afraid that I'm going to try to ask you to do more business with me, then don't even come to the workshop! Because I am; it's not going to end there, it's going to keep on going on and on; I'm going to keep continue to do everything possible to help you achieve your dream. Remember, Russ von Hoelscher helped us make millions of dollars, but we had to pay him hundreds of thousands to do it. However, for every dollar we paid to Russ, we probably made 50 to 100 dollars. What does it matter that we had to pay him hundreds of thousands of dollars? He made make us money, and that's what I want to do for you, too.

Number Eight: Your product helps the most qualified prospects and customers in the highest way. It gives them the shortcut secrets, and that's what I'm trying to give you right now: proven strategies, insider knowledge. How many people understand that the secret to getting rich in the opportunity market is to create hard products? That's just one of the strategies that I'm sharing with you in this book. I'm reaching out to you, right now, to try to give you the insider knowledge that I've learned over the last 20 years.

Number Nine: A good information product separates you from all your competitors. When it's done correctly, your information product has zero competition, because it's an extension of you. It's your unique thumbprint. It's also a great relationship-building tool that makes people feel that they know you. It deepens your bond with established customers, and makes new prospects want to do business with you.

And Number Ten: Product development is a highly creative activity that lets you clarify your thinking, lets you shape your thoughts, lets you learn as you teach. See, you can never really help somebody else without also helping yourself. So I'm trying to reach out for you on this product, I'm trying to give you some of my best ideas; but in the process, as I spent all this time writing and editing these chapters, thinking everything through very clearly, I'm learning things myself. To teach is to learn twice; one of the great philosophers said that thousands of years ago. So it helps you, but it's also something that's exciting; it's fun, it's creative. The profit margins are also incredibly high, and the perceived value is very high for what you're offering. In other words, developing products can make you millions of dollars. I told you about the $1 million we made with *The $2,500 Weekend*. That *Dialing for Dollars* program — it got us started, and eventually we made millions of dollars with it. But we've continued to develop more and more products, and that's the last thing I want to share with you on this section. You've got to do something every single day to develop products.

Ongoing product development is the secret to developing a ton of products, and you should discipline yourself to do a small amount of it every day. Every day, the first thing in the morning, my day starts out with product development. I'm spending one hour on product development each day, and it adds up to a huge arsenal of products. In doing this, you completely separate yourself from every other competitor, and it lets you attract and retain the largest number of best prospects and customers in your marketplace. Just do it a little every day. Think about your customers and what they really want the most, and what they hate the most. Think about what they're really seeking the most, and why they buy the things that they buy the most. Study the most successful companies in your marketplace and figure out what they're doing right, what they're doing wrong, where the gaps are in your market, and just start developing products. It doesn't have to be perfect. I've been doing this for 20 years now. I told you what a joke our first product was; it was just some thin little piece-of-crap booklet that we came out with. We give it away in our seminars now for free, just to show people what a humble beginning it was. It's a joke to look at it now, and yet the customers loved it. It was raw, it was real, it was genuine, it really worked, and it was based on something that excited them. That's all that matters!

You don't have to be perfect to produce products that connect with your customers and sell briskly. I do face-to-face seminars and create audio products all the time, but am I a professional speaker? Absolutely not. I am, however, trying to practice what I preach here. I'm very, very focused on you, the customers. I know what I'm talking about. My wife and I parlayed $300 into $120 million in our first 20 years, and these are the secrets that did it for us — and so what do you care if I'm not a professional speaker or writer? You want somebody who's going to be honest and straightforward with you, who's going to give you proven methods to take you from where you are now to where you want to go. You may be saying, "Well, I don't have any expertise," but I'm here to tell you that you *can* still create companies that provide all kinds of valuable information products.

I've told you that we're doing it in the real-estate world

right now. We're interviewing all these real-estate experts, and we ask each at the end, "Who else do you know that we should be interviewing?" One expert leads us to another. We did that in the world of eBay, and we've done that with computer bulletin boards for Internet marketing. Eventually, you *do* become an expert. But I just want to get you on the path; I want to tell you that it's more than just making money. This is a rewarding way of life that lets you develop products and services that truly can help people. The most qualified people out there, those who are willing to put in the effort to use the ideas you share with them — those people's lives will be transformed, just like my life was.

So I want to encourage you to think about everything I've said here. This thirteenth secret really is a secret, because most people just dream of it, no more. They would love to self-publish their stuff. They would love to produce books and audio programs, but they never do. They're always afraid, and part of that fear is that they've got to be perfect, that they aren't well qualified. None of that matters. I promise you, if you want to do this, you can. There are plenty of experts out there — as with the real-estate deal we're doing now — who have their own programs they want to promote. They want to develop clients and customer, so they're more than happy to spend 90 minutes or two hours with us on the phone, letting us interview them.

This is something that can make you millions and millions of dollars — and it can also provide a lot of joy and satisfaction. It can help you completely separate yourself from every other company that's out there, because the products that you create are a piece of you. They're an extension of who you are; they let people get to know you, and let you develop bonds with them so you can keep the same customers coming back and buying from you for many, many years. So when we meet at our free workshop, I'm going to stress this to you over and over again: Start getting into the routine of creating some type of information product on a daily basis. If you'll do that, ten years from now you can have a huge catalog of products that you've developed specifically for your customers, and it'll give you a high level of pride and satisfaction, the joy of accomplishment that you did something that was so productive and so creative. All you did was to discipline yourself to do a little every day and stayed focused on serving the customers. This can lead to a lifetime of wealth and great satisfaction for you.

SECRET FOURTEEN:

Constant Testing. What's Next?

The fourteenth secret that we used to make millions of dollars is: we tested as many different things as we could. We're always asking ourselves, "What's next?" It's not work in the traditional way that most people think of work; this is more like a game. It's more like a hobby, an activity that you do for total enjoyment. Work really does mix with pleasure if you do it the right way; you'll enjoy what you're doing and you'll make a lot more money. The secret is to treat work as if it were a game. What you're doing is searching for the ultimate way to make millions of dollars, and if you'll do that, you'll have a lot more fun; it won't just seem like work, and even the things that are difficult will become easier because you're totally focused on finding those one or two ideas. You can make a lot of money if you'll do this. It's simpler and easier than you can ever imagine. You'll see that it's just the way of life for you. It's about serving your customers in the highest possible way, and then going out there to new prospects and offering them the same types of things you offered to your best customers.

The secret to earning the biggest profit is just to stay focused on your best customers. Who are they? What do they want the most? What do they *buy* the most? The better you're able to answer those questions, the more money you'll make. That comes with experience and knowledge; it doesn't happen overnight, and the ideas you get today aren't going to be nearly as good as the ideas you'll get tomorrow. Sometimes it takes months or years to intimately know your customer. But once you do, you've got the golden key in your hand to making millions of dollars, and that's a great feeling. It's more than just the money and all the material things you're going to buy. That stuff is nice, but it has its limits. Money's a great thing to have, but you can only sleep in one bed at a time, eat one meal at a time, live in one home at a time, drive one great car at a time.

There's only so much joy and satisfaction that comes from money, and you need to get that out of your system. The joy is in the acquisition of it all; it's in the hunt, it's in the chase. That's what's going to give you the greatest pleasure when it comes to getting rich. It's looking for those ideas that are going to be your next golden winners. I think about it as a metaphor of a huge bank vault: we don't know what the combination is, so we're safecrackers in this metaphor. We're searching for that combination. We've got our stethoscope pressed against that two-foot-thick steel door. All the money we'll ever want and need is on the other side of that door, and so we're carefully trying different combinations, looking for just the right combination to cause the tumblers in that safe to come into complete alignment so the door will swing open and all that money is ours. I think about that often when we're testing new ideas; and you really do need to have that whole sporting attitude going, because when you find what works the best, when you have a promotion that's working and all of a sudden hundreds of thousands — and in some cases millions — of dollars are flowing in in a very short period of time, that's great fun; and that's the part I want you to focus on. It's nice to have all that money, but what's even nicer, and what will give you the most satisfaction, is knowing that you have the ability within yourself to create it anytime you want to. Anytime you want to make another fortune, you know exactly how to get it. The key is to go to your best customers first. Stay totally focused on them, and start testing from what I call the top down. Every new idea is tested to your very best customers first. Those are the people who know you, respect you, and trust you; and because of that, the selling resistance is lowered.

A few years back, we got involved in an interesting opportunity. This guy came to me with an outrageous idea; it almost sounded like some scam. He came at me with, "Hey, T.J., if I said I had a proven way to make $750,000 to $1 million this year and all you had to do was a work a little to get it, would you be interested?" If anybody else had said that to me, I would have said, "No thank you," or I would have sent them to one of my staff members. But because this is a guy I've known for a few years, and he's somebody I want to continue to do business with. Because I trust him and I like him, I was open and receptive. I want you to think about that. Your best customers will buy almost anything from you, especially if they know they can get their money back if they're not happy. Those are the people you should approach first; it's what I call your "warm market." And then, of course, you have other groups of customers within your customer base, because of the way that you pre-qualify them.

You can (and should) segment your customer base by the amount of money they spend, or how recently they spent things — because sometimes people get into emotional heat for a certain type of product or service. While they're in that mindset, you'd better sell them everything you can, because you never know when they're going to settle down. So you segment, sometimes by the frequency of their purchase; you know they're excited about your type of offer. You know that they're hot for it. You've got to use that knowledge to go after them in a more aggressive way than you would the rest of your customers. Or, you segment them by what it is they bought from you the first time. Remember the general answer to the question: "What do people want?" That's where a lot of marketers are confused. They run around in total bewilderment, thinking, "I don't know what to sell!" The answer is to sell people variations on the theme of whatever you sold them the first time. It's really very simple. When you look at everything in a holistic way and examine it from the top down instead of the bottom up, it becomes easier to figure out what's going to make you the most amount of money.

First of all, stay totally focused on your very best customers. Forget about all of those other people out there, and do what you have to do to make profits in the first place — which is serve your customers. Do very special things for them and create all kinds of opportunities for them, because you're using them as a testing ground; but you're also doing everything possible to serve them in the highest way, and to look for the things that excite them the most. You want more people like your best customers. That's the whole goal of your marketing. You want to attract the very best people and repel the worst people. I always run into these great customers at my seminars, and I know their buying history; I know that they've been with us for years, and they've spent thousands and thousands of dollars. Sometimes I'm able to build enough of a rapport with them enough where I'm able to ask them face-to-face, "Where do I find another thousand just like you?" If I don't have enough rapport built with them, I at least think it. That's the question you should be asking too.

You're looking for people who will spend a huge sum of money with you over a long period of time, because they have such a deep interest in what you're selling. It causes them to buy and rebuy because they trust you and like you, you've built a real rapport with them, and you've expressed yourself enough to them where they know that you care for them. Your best customers will forgive you for not being perfect, because they know you're striving to reach out to them, to give them more of what they want the most. You end up knowing your best customers better than they know themselves.

For years I kept journals, and every time I learned something new about a customer, I would write it down. Those journals got filled with all kinds of things, and we had testimonial sheets that went out disguised as surveys. We would reward the customer with a free bonus if they filled out a survey and sent it back to us. They'd give us permission to use their comments in any way we wanted to, and we'd give them a free gift. Well, I had those transcribed, and I saved all the best ones. Sometimes people just wanted to fill out the bare minimum so they could get the free gift, but about one out of three was really good. I transcribed them and took notes and did a lot of careful thinking, until I got to the place where I am today, which is a high level of confidence that I understand my customers better than they understand themselves. I know why they buy. Ninety percent of the time, it's for emotional reasons. I've also done a lot of heavy reflection on all of the reasons that I personally used to buy those moneymaking programs, because that was our entry into the marketplace.

Little did we know it at the time, but we had a lot of insider knowledge — because I was buying them all. I was obsessed with buying the same kinds of plans and programs that we sell now, and when I say obsessed, I mean it. Now, succeeding with most of these plans involves a lot of work — unfortunately or fortunately. It's unfortunate because people want to delude themselves that they can make millions of dollars with no effort. It's a fantasy. It's what I call lottery mentality: you just know you're going to buy a ticket and win the grand prize. The fortunate part for you is that because there's a good bit of time, work and effort involved in succeeding with these programs, it levels the playing field. The desire to make millions of dollars is the most important thing, because through that desire, you'll hopefully be willing to do whatever it takes — and there are a lot of people who aren't. The good news is, yes, all this *does* take some time, work, and effort to learn; but if you're willing to go through what you must and do whatever it takes, then you're going to be part of a small minority. This makes it all that much easier for you. When you develop the skills and abilities of all 26 of the areas I discuss in this book, it does become easier; and there's the irony right there.

People are looking for a simple, easy way to make millions of dollars. That way does exist, but *only* after you develop these skills. Then it becomes quite easy. When we first met Russ von Hoelscher, one of the first things he said to us was vital. I'll never forget; we'd known him for a little while by then, and had talked on the phone a bunch of times. He's a likeable, friendly guy who really does care about other people, and he had more than 20 years of experience at the time. In the course of a conversation as I was driving him home from the airport one day, he said the words that stuck in my mind and have dominated my thoughts ever since. He said, "All it really takes to make millions of dollars in this business is just one idea." I just about drove the car off the road, I was so excited. I was so thrilled at that, and I still am, and since then we've proven it to be true. It's not just some concept that I'm throwing out because it sounds good. It's true. All you need is just one idea. That's one of the reasons why you should continue to experiment with as many new ideas as possible, so you can find that one idea. Or it may be some combination of ideas, because sometimes the ideas that make you the most money are the ones you mix together with other things you've tried. That's been a large part of the secret to our success. You continue to find new ways to mix different ideas together.

Often the secret you're looking for is a combination of other things that have worked for you in the past. One of things we do is continue to find new ways to repackage the same, successful ideas that have already made us huge sums of money. Why not? You're there to serve your customers. You're there to give them more of what they bought from you before. Now, customers always want new stuff. New, new, new; everybody loves it. It's part of our thinking. If you don't offer your customers new stuff, someone else will. Either you get the money, or one of your competitors gets the money.

You've got to do it, if for no other reason than that you recognize and accept the fact that marketing is about attracting and re-attracting customers, retaining customers, continuing to do business with the same people again and again — as long as your customers don't get the idea that you're just trying to slam them all the time. No matter what you do, some customers are always going to feel you're just trying to take advantage of them, that you're just trying to get their money. So your messages have to be altruistic, and you really must have a desire to serve the customers and offer strong money-back guarantees. Let your customers know that if they're ever unhappy, they can get their money back. That way, you're dealing with a lot of integrity.

The second reason you have to continue to test new ideas all the time is because you never know where your next multimillion-dollar idea is going to come from. Your biggest breakthrough could be right around the corner, and unless you're testing new ideas you're never going to find it. Make a game of it; have fun with it. The next reason to test is that the secret to getting great ideas is to get *many* ideas. More ideas lead to better ideas, and the more things you test, the more power you'll have. The very best, most profitable ideas are often a combination of many ideas — the themes, formats, and models that you've used before. The best ideas for you will often be a combination of many different things that you've done, the years that you've spent intimately getting to know who your customers are, what they want the most and why they continue to rebuy, and how to give those things to them.

Your biggest breakthrough is out there right now. One idea really does lead to another. It's an evolutionary process, and your biggest breakthroughs will be a new combination of different ideas that you've used before. The more ideas you test, the more wealth-making power you have. Again, it's all about selling to your very best customers, because you're doing what I call testing from the top down instead of the bottom up. You're constantly thinking about that smaller group of people who buy and rebuy from you the most. I recommend that you have seminars and workshops just so you can get face-to-face with these customers.

Too many direct response marketers, especially this new breed of Internet marketers out there, want to hide out from the customers. They're attracted to direct response marketing because they don't want to be face-to-face with people. One of things that really turned me on the most about this business in the beginning was that I could do everything from home. I was in love with the idea that I could do business with hundreds, thousands, even hundreds of thousands of people without ever meeting most of them. But you can't really hide out from your best customers. If for no other reason than that, have seminars constantly so that you can get up-close and personal with them. You can get to know them that way. The most rabid markets out there, the ones where you can make the largest amount of money in the fastest period, are 100% emotional driven.

You also have to think conceptually. See the absolute simplicity of even the most complicated ideas; find the hidden secrets behind the ideas that are making other people money right now. See it simpler, believe it bigger. Go to your best customers first, and then test through the rest of your customer base. Take the ideas that make you the most money and use them for new acquisitions. It's the most risk-free way to make money.

I also recommend that you schedule meetings on a regular basis. We've been having regular weekly meetings now for well over ten years. We're always asking ourselves what's next, and we're planning different mailings, and we number all of them, and we schedule them, and we make commitments to do new things before we have all the answers figured out. Remember, your best customers will gladly buy almost an unlimited number of products and services from you. I used to worry that I was trying to sell to my best customers way too often, and I was always afraid that those customers were going to leave me; and what I found is that nothing could be further from the truth. They're going to buy and rebuy from other companies unless I'm selling to them. Now I just worry whether I'm selling enough to them, and I'm trying to stay out there in front of my best customers all the time, offering them other products and services.

You'll do well as long as the products and services you're offering help them get more of what you know they want, as long as you're striving to serve them in the highest way, as long as you're not just trying to suck money out of people for no value. You're trying to offer value for value; actually, you're trying to offer greater value than what you're getting. So you're giving them more and more of what you know that they want. As long as you're providing tremendous value and running your business in an ethical way — where they can get their money back without any game-playing, if they want it — you'll build their trust, and they'll end up buying more stuff from you.

Then, last but not least, keep finding new ways to recycle and repackage the same products and services; the same models that you tried before, the same ideas, the same themes, everything that's worked great for you in the past. Keep trying to find new ways to give products a facelift, a new theme. Try to come up with something that looks new but is actually just repackaged; and again, the more you do it, the easier it'll get. People love new stuff, and they want new stuff; but if it's too new, it won't fly. Nobody wants to be the guinea pig; and so what you do is find new stuff for your customers. But then you let them know that it's not *entirely* new. It's still based on something that's solid and proven and tested, and there's still that conservative element present; because if it's too new, people are going to freak out. If it's too new, it will arouse their skepticism. So you're constantly coming out with variations on a theme. The car companies do it all the time. The best movies are just variations on a theme of all the other best movies. People want proven models, again and again.

This is a secret that most markets never put enough time and effort into. They'll never go through the painful learning curve of testing new things and working all this out. But if you'll do it, you'll become part of a small group that's making huge amounts of money.

SECRET FIFTEEN:

Fall in Love with Your Business!

The fifteenth secret that made us millions of dollars is the simple but powerful fact that we fell in love with this business. Now, when I say "we," I'm talking about my wife Eileen and me. But I can really only speak for myself; she has her own opinions, and to her it was always more like a business. It was an exciting business; it was a good business but to me, it was more than that. It really, truly became an obsession for me, and I believe that in my contribution as the marketing arm of the company, I was able to contribute at a higher level, and I know that I made the company millions of dollars. Now, it would never have happened without Eileen; I just want you to be very clear about that. I'm not a businessperson, I'm a marketer. I became very, very good at developing information products that the customers loved, and they showed their love because they continued to rebuy from us, again and again.

That's how you know that people love you in this business. They vote with their checkbooks, their credit cards. Customers stay with you year in and year out, and continue to buy from you. That's the whole secret to making millions of dollars: Just get enough people to rebuy from you enough times with enough profit margin on every transaction, and the question isn't, "Will you get rich?" The only questions are, "How rich will you get?" and, "When will you make that money?" Think about that: Business can be complicated, there's no question about it, especially when you go through some hard times, when you make mistakes. There are hard lessons to learn; and the more money you want to make, the more of those things you'll have to learn. But you also have to stay focused on the basics, because no matter how complicated it gets, if you always go back to the fundamentals and see the simplicity in all this, it will help you. It will give you greater confidence, and help you through some of the hard times that I know you're going to have to go through. That becomes truer with the more money you want to make.

If you want to make $10 million in less than five years like we did, or if you want to do twice that, three times that, that's fine — you *can* do it, and I'm going to show you why I believe that this is the best business on Earth. It's the ultimate way to make money, and you can use some of these ideas within any business that you choose — these ideas of developing information products that go out to the prospects and customers, attract them to you, and keep them coming back for more and more. Any business can benefit from this. It's a business that's worthy of falling in love with. It's highly creative, it's fun, it's interesting, it's challenging, and it's stimulating. There's always something new, and you get good at it. The better you get at it, the more confidence you develop, and the greater feelings that you have for it. I just can't stress that enough. I want you to fall in love with this business; if you do, you'll not only achieve a greater level of satisfaction, you'll end up making more money.

I became absolutely obsessed and possessed by this business. I fell in love with developing and selling information products, and I still love it. In fact, I love it even more now than ever before. It's this intense love that I feel for this business that's caused me to do many things that other people would never be willing to do. I worked harder, I put in more hours, and I've gladly taken on newer and bigger projects that would have scared others to death. They do scare others to death; they just won't do some of the things we've done. We've taken on all kinds of major projects, based only on the smallest, haziest concept of how we were going to put it all together; and then we *did* put it all together. It's the fact that I've been literally consumed with this business, and totally absorbed by it, that has caused me to come up with some of the ideas I've come up with, that have helped to contribute to this whole thing. The result hasn't always been perfect; it hasn't satisfied all the customers. We do have customers who don't like us, and that's fine! We're looking for perfect matches; and the longer we're doing what we do, the more willing we are to tell certain customers, "Look, I'm sorry, you're not right for us and we're not right for you," and send them off on their own way. I don't want to pretend we're perfect for everyone.

If it wasn't for Eileen, the whole thing would have been destroyed in the first 14 years. She was smarter than me; she ran the company, but I absolutely fell in love with developing products and services for our customers. I absolutely became obsessed with marketing, maybe to the point that sometimes, I took it way too far — putting in far too many hours, working way too hard, being too absorbed by the business, living it, sleeping it, dreaming it, eating it, all of those things. It's because of this passion that I had, this obsession and the willingness to try new things and take on new challenges, that finally I developed some very specific skills that helped us make millions of dollars. Now, we also had a great team of people in place. Eileen had a great staff, because we needed an infrastructure to help us attract and retain our customers. You have to have that; you can't get away from it. For every 1,000 customers you bring in, you'd better add some staff to support those people, or those customers will go away. There must be people there to take care of them, after they buy things. The bigger you want to get, the more money you want to make, the more infrastructure you need. Nothing takes the place of that.

But you also have to have products and services that people really, really want; you need products and services that they want so badly, they'll continue to come back for more and more of the same. There's an art to it, remember — an art to creating products that look and appear to be new and different, and have unique slants or angles or themes to them, and yet are just basically variations on everything else you've done. There's that level of familiarity that you must have with the products and services you create, no matter how many of them you create. There's enough of the familiar to make people feel comfortable and secure, and enough of the new to captivate their imaginations, to keep them moving forward. Selling information products can make you much more money than the highest-paid doctors and lawyers are making right now. That's one of the things that captivated me about the business then, and it still captivates me today.

Think about that: you have people who go to law school for 6 or 8 years, like my Dad did, going through this tremendous learning curve just so they can go out there and make enough money to live in the nice areas of town. Now, I have a business that's made me millions of dollars. I can safely say that it can make you millions too, if you're just willing to put in some time and effort. The secret of our success is in large part due to this tremendous obsession, this hunger that I had, to learn everything possible about how to develop information products that would keep people coming back for more, and keep those customers spending more money, and keep them happy and continue to give them everything I know they want the most. It's been painful; I've spent a lot of hours working very hard to try to understand all of this stuff — and it's been worth it.

Now, you want to make millions of dollars too — or so I assume. Why else would you buy a book like this? The only people who would spend what I'm charging for this product, simply to read it and not take it seriously, are foolish. I'm going to assume that you're *not* foolish. Clearly, you really do want to make the money. Now, here's a perplexing thing: why would people go and spend 6 or 8 years of their life, or in some cases 12 or 15 years of their life, learning how to be doctors, brain surgeons, lawyers, nuclear physicists or whatever? I realize that it's about more than just the money for them. But come on, let's face it — nobody spends all that time in college without the understanding that once they arrive, they're going to live in the nicest areas in town, they're going to drive the nicest cars, and they're going to have the kinds of things most people don't have. I'm sure there are exceptions, but most people are more than willing to go through 6 to 15 years of putting up with all kinds of pressures and challenges, and the discipline of being a good student, passing all the tests and learning all they have to — if behind it all is the knowledge that no matter how hard they're working right now, there's going to come a time when, because of what they're doing right now, they can spend the rest of their life living the good life, having all the wonderful things that money can buy.

That's why they're willing to put in those long hours. That's why they're willing to work so hard, to learn how to become professionals in their chosen crafts or professions. Yet this is a business that can do the same thing for you. You can actually earn money while you learn — unlike going to college, where you've got to pay to put in all that time, so that you'll eventually get out of school and the money will start flowing in. This is a business where you're making great money, as long as you have a group of customers who bought something from you once, and your total focus is on reselling to those people again and again, then taking the very best ideas that come from that process and using those to help you attract new customers who are similar to your best customers. In some cases, you're making huge sums of money, and you're still learning. You don't have to be as good a marketer, copywriter, or information producer to sell stuff to your best customers. They love you; they respect you. When I say love, I'm using the term very loosely; at the very least, they appreciate what you're trying to do for them. Selling information products is a great way to reach out to people and develop strong bonds with them, so they get a sense of who you are. They can feel you, especially if you're using a medium like audio or video, where they can actually hear or see you, or if you're doing seminars, where they can get up close to you and spend time with you. This is the chance for you to build huge profits, to serve people in the highest way, and still make more money than most doctors or lawyers can ever dream of — but there's a learning curve.

You've got to go through some pain to learn all this, unless you're just a whole lot smarter than I am — and you may very well be. I don't doubt that, but you're still going to have to learn some new skills. I want you to think of the benefits, just like those college students that'll spend all those years in college, and their eyes are bloodshot, and they're putting in all that time to cram for those finals. They know that on the other side of that, a whole new life waits for them. Most people are more than happy to put in the time — but it's tough! Every time they call home to their parents they say, "Mom and Dad, I just can't take it anymore! I'm studying 12, 14, 16 hours a day, and I'm just barely making it!"

There's a lot of pressure on those young, ambitious, beautiful children who are trying to do big things with their life, and yet their parents are always saying, "Now look, you're only 25, 26 years old. After this, you're going to be a top doctor; you can work in Boston, you can work in New York City, you can pick your own salary." The parents are telling them these things; they're helping them hang in there, and pushing them to expend all the time, work, effort, and energy needed. There are times when your brain is just so tired, you feel like your head's going to explode. I've gone through all that to learn what I've learned, too. And I'm still trying to learn more, because the problem is that when you learn all of these things, you start making money, and now the money just comes effortlessly — and you get bored.

There's nothing worse for an entrepreneur than boredom. We need new challenges; we need to take on bigger and bigger things, try to do more with our lives, and make more money and see how high is high. How high can we go, and what are we capable of doing? This is a business where there are always new challenges and new horizons, if you're willing to take on bigger and better things. Certainly, you'll have to undergo struggles and adversity to get there, but you might just be a whole lot more talented than I am. Your capacity may be greater than mine, and therefore you'll do it all even faster. If so, I envy you; I respect you if you can do it. If you can make millions of dollars without going through a painful learning curve, then God bless you. I had to go through a lot of pain, but I've been willing to go through it, and the longer I do it, the more I appreciate this business and think that it's a perfect way to make money.

When we get together at our free workshop, I'm going to stress this to you, again and again. I'm going to challenge you to get involved in this business. We're going to spend some good, quality time together (hopefully just you and me) and the best thing I can do is tell you to get involved in the information business. So many of our clients, our best customers, are people who habitually buy all kinds of information products. They're spending thousands of dollars every year — in some cases, tens of thousands of dollars — on information. The kind of people who buy these types of products, we're constantly in their faces, telling them, "Hey, look, you're already spending tons of money on all this other stuff; why don't you get into the business of producing it yourself? You've got an intimate feel for the type of person who buys this material, and you need that if you're going to be a great marketer and you're going to sell information products. So what better person to get involved in the market than someone who already has that knowledge?"

And yet so often, our advice falls on deaf ears. We stress this over and over again at our seminars. If I could grab people and throw them against the wall, slap them and stress this to them that way, I would. If only I could just drill it into their heads that they need to get on the other side of the cash register, and start serving the kinds of people out there who buy this stuff. If I could just wake them up out of their trance, get them to think about the other side of the cash register, so they would get into this business, so they'd learn some of the things they need to learn, so they'd go on to make a fortune in this business — then I'd do it. I see that so many people have the potential, and yet *they* don't see it. That's the problem: they don't see what I see. I think if you're already a customer and you're buying lots of different information products and you have a hunger for them, and you have the knowledge for this type of thing, you ought to get involved in the market yourself. It's a great way to make money, and here's why. First of all, the demand for information products is absolutely huge, and it's growing all the time. There are millions of people out there right now who want, need and are happy to pay for the benefits that a good information product can give to them.

What does that mean? It's simple; the general premise is that the amount of money you're charged for these products has nothing to do with the actual cost to reproduce the product, because the costs are low. That's becoming truer all the time. We're able now to take an audio program, like the one this book is based on, and compress 12 hours of audio onto a single CD-ROM that can be played in any computer, or that can be downloaded into any mp3 player, or even played in many cars. When you're able to take 12 hours of good audio or programming that really helps people and teaches them and tries to reach out and give them the things they need to get whatever they want — why, you can make a fortune. Look at all the information products out there: there are many, many different information producers selling a wide variety of things, and when (for example) you're able to take 12 hours of audio and put it onto one thin little piece of plastic that costs you just over a buck, that's amazing. But do people care if it cost you a dollar? No! Not the people who really matter. The people who want and need the benefits of what you're selling are more than happy to pay for those benefits; what do they care if it cost you a buck? Do you think it matters to them? I don't. Not the people who really matter, who are in your market, who are hungry and have the need for whatever you sell. They couldn't care less about what it cost *you*.

So look closely at that huge demand and the low cost to produce these products, which very often is just your time. Now, you've got to value that time, of course, and you've got to structure it and discipline yourself. But when you've got a demand that's so powerful here, and when the absolute cost for the products and services that you create to fill that demand is so low, but the perception of value is so high — then you've got a recipe for making millions and millions of dollars. If that was all there was to it, that would be enough. I promise you, that alone spells major success: the fact that there's a huge demand, there's a rabid market, there are millions of people that are constantly buying these information products. The perceived value is enormous, and the cost to produce these products is very low. That alone would be perfect. We could stop right here, and that would be enough. But there's so much more to this business than that!

THE BLUE JEANS MILLIONAIRE!

This is a fun, creative, challenging, and extremely lucrative way to get rich. It's rewarding in every way. When it comes to packaging and selling information, the number of markets out there is almost endless, because within every niche market, there are sub-niches. If you're producing these products out of your home, you're producing them for almost no money at all, except for the time needed to develop them. That means you can serve small markets and still get wealthy. You need fewer people, because you're able to sell things for high prices. You're able to take something that takes you a small amount of your time, put it into a product that you can sell, and make money with it for the rest of your life. Think about how exciting that is! To take something that you do once, and leverage it for the rest of your life. If you choose your market correctly, it'll mean a lifetime of profits for you — enormous sums of money. This is a very personal medium where you're able to express yourself fully; and I don't mean to sound overly-dramatic about this, but when I hand someone an information product I've poured my heart into, I'm giving him a little piece of me. It's a piece of my entire soul, the essence of who I am.

That's what a great information product is: it's an extension of who you are, what you stand for, what you believe in, what's most important to you. You're sharing your best ideas; you're reaching out to the people you're producing that product for, just like I'm trying to reach out to you right now. You bought this book to learn these secrets that made us millions of dollars in just a few years, and I'm trying to express those in the fullest way that I can possibly can. I'm trying to reach out for you, reach out *to* you. If I could crawl through those pages right now and come into your home, and we could sit down and drink a cup of coffee, and we could talk for hours — I would. I hope to meet you in person someday. I hope you come to our free workshop, spend some time with me, get to know me better. Your goal is to help people in the highest sort of way; not everybody, but at least those who really want it the most, who are willing to take your ideas and use them. You're able to develop relationships with those people, and that's another reason why I believe that this is a business that's worthy of falling in love with.

The ideal in this business is to develop good information products that reach out to people, that form strong bonds with them — a strong connection that helps them get whatever they want. That's what you're really trying to do. You're not just trying to make money for yourself: you're trying to make money through serving people. You're helping them get what they want. The better you know your customers, the better you're able to help them. That's how you develop customers who respect and appreciate you.

Fair warning: it doesn't always work. If you're like me, trying to express everything in the fullest way with your heart in the right place, without thinking about what you're saying... well, you'll have a few people who can't stand you. They can barely listen to you. You drive them crazy, like in that movie *Jaws*, when the captain runs his fingernails along the chalkboard. I have customers who hate my communication style. I upset them, because I say things that aren't politically correct. They wish I'd be more professional, polished. They hate listening to me, but they know that my heart's in the right place, and they know I have things that can help them get what they really want — and they have a desire to learn those things. So they come to our seminars, put up with the things about me they can't stand, and they learn what I have to teach. They move on, and take this information and change their lives with it — and that's what's important.

So even if your customers don't love you, they *will* appreciate and respect you. When you do it correctly, there's no real competition. You're producing products that are uniquely you. They're a piece of you; they're your ideas. If you're not the expert, find the experts. Right now, we're moving into the whole new area of helping our clients make money in real estate. What do we know about making money in real estate? Absolutely nothing! But that's not stopping us. We're developing products where we go out and interview all these real-estate experts — and there are a huge number of them, because the market is enormous. They're more than willing to let us interview them and capture their best ideas during the process, because they're looking for customers for their products and services. You have that in every single market. If you want to get involved in the health market (another multibillion-dollar market), you can create an information company that's uniquely positioned. You don't claim to be an expert, you just go out there and find all the experts and do business with them.

You can put on seminars, workshops, tele-seminars, or create all kinds of programs based on interviews where people freely share their greatest secrets, because they're trying to sell their own books and tapes. You become a toll road. You can develop many information products without really knowing much about the subject, simply by finding other people who do understand it; and then you simply work on developing new customers and create proprietary-based programs based on the interviews you do with these experts. We're doing it now with real estate; we did it with eBay. When it came to making money on eBay, which is a really popular subject, we didn't know anything at first. But there are experts out there, and this time we decided to interview them; and that led us to other things.

You could do this with anything, and I would encourage you to try. This is a business where you really can separate yourself from every other customer, because you're creating products that are uniquely you. You own them. They're proprietary, and you can keep customers excited and wanting to do more and more business with you. We've had customers who have been with us for 10 or 15 years; even a few who've been there almost from Day 1. They like us and what we're trying to do. They know we're trying to operate with integrity, and they're very skeptical of all these other companies, so they continue to favor us rather than try to do business with a new company. People develop relationships with you as they get exposed to you through the products you create. What that means for you is that, if you're using the marketing systems I'm talking about in this book, you end up with a huge customer base that keeps you motivated and excited about developing newer and better products.

Once you get this huge customer base, stay in touch with them on a regular basis. You know they're going to buy more stuff, if not from you from somebody else, so it might as well be you. You'll find yourself developing all kinds of new products and services just for your best customers, because you know they'll continue to buy, and you want to serve them in the highest way. When we get together for our free workshop, let's talk about this. We can talk about the information-publishing business, and how you can reach these marketplaces, and how you can make money for the rest of your life — an endless stream of money, and in many cases far more money than any of your local doctors and lawyers make. You can be right there next to those people. I don't care how broke you are, you can't be much broker than I was when we first started. This is the business that can do all that for you, and besides the money, it can give you a great level of joy and satisfaction; it's so rewarding. I can't wait to spend time with you, so I can help you get involved in this tremendous business.

SECRET SIXTEEN:

Hold Seminars and Other Special Events for Your Customers

Secret Number Sixteen is simple: We held seminars, workshops, and tele-seminars, and created many different audio and video programs that bonded with our customers. This has been very important to our success. Now, if the secret to getting rich is to get the largest number of people to rebuy from you on a regular basis, then you've got to ask yourself, "What are the best ways to do it?" The answer is actually about ten different things here, and I'm going to go through them pretty quickly.

You have to get personal with your customers: Let them get to know you. You have to tell your story; you have to try to reach out to them and help them, whatever that means to your market. Every market is different; every market has needs or desires that require fulfillment. It's up to you to figure out what they are, but then you have to extend your hand to your customers in as many ways as you possibly can. Just like I'm trying to extend my hand to you right now; I really *am* trying to help you. I'm assuming you want to get rich, and I'm trying to show you exactly how I've made millions of dollars with a lot of help from people like my wife, my staff and my joint-venture partners.

You've got to do these things I'm revealing here; you've got to strive to show your customers that you understand their problems, their frustrations. People want to feel understood, and they want to feel important, and they'll gladly spend more money with you, as long as you're providing them the things that they really want. To put it simply, what they want is products and services that fill some demand they have. It's up to you to figure out want that demand is; they can't figure it out. Don't think you can just ask your customers what they want and they'll tell you; that's not always true. Any answers they give you will be surface answers. It's up to you to figure out the real emotional reasons why people buy and continue to buy on a regular basis, and for every market it's a little different. If you want to make money in the opportunity market, which is the market I'm in, you develop products and services that offer people the opportunity to get very, very rich with the minimum amount of time, work, effort, and energy.

I'll never forget the first time we had a major seminar where we charged a huge sum of money — close to $5,000. We were upstairs before the event, and we were trying to get a game plan going; we had a couple of hundred people downstairs waiting for us, and we said, "Look, let's tell people that the secret to getting rich" — which happens to be true, by the way — "is that you do it as a series of steps." First, you make $100,000 a year, learning everything you can, and keep building to the point where eventually, your knowledge and experience let you take the ideas that made you $100,000 a year, and you're able to make $1,000,000 or $10,000,000 a year. It's a gradual process for most people. But our problem was, we were thinking logically about a subject that's extremely emotional. It sounds perfectly rational to tell people that, first, you've got to focus on making $100,000 a year; then you focus on doubling and doubling until, finally, millions of dollars are pouring in, and you have the skills and experience to handle it all, and you're making all the money you want. So we went downstairs, and that's how we opened up the seminar. I said, "I know you all want to get rich, but how many people here would be happy if you had an extra $50,000 or $100,000 a year, and you barely had to work for it?" We were expecting everyone to raise their hands.

Guess what? *Nobody* raised their hands. We were a little shocked. So quickly, just impulsively, I said, "Well then, how many people here want to make millions of dollars right away?" and everybody raised their hands — *everybody*. People jumped up and danced, and they started shouting. It was funny; but it also taught me something very important that I want to teach you. There are emotional elements underlying this desire for riches, and emotions are mostly irrational, so rational thinking goes out the window. Sure, taking it all in steps makes a lot of sense from a purely rational standpoint — and yet we're dealing with people who are influenced chiefly by their emotions. They buy things for emotional reasons, not logical ones.

So your messages need to be as emotional as possible, to the point where you're pushing the envelope — and, of course you have to watch your legal issues. There are *serious* legal issues here. If you're selling a business opportunity, for example, you don't want to *guarantee* that anybody will make serious money. As long as the potential is there, though, you can talk about it. You talk about possibilities, you disclaim yourself on regular basis — but you still realize what's behind the market. And that's the fact that people want to get as rich as they can by doing the minimum possible — and in some cases they want to get rich by doing nothing. I know that may sound cynical, but it's not; you sell people what they want, and then you give them want they need. What they want and need are often two entirely different things. What they want is instant cures, miracle solutions, fast, easy answers, shortcut secrets — and that you'll do everything for them.

One of the greatest copywriters who ever lived was named Gene Schwartz. He was a brilliant man, and he said that what people want is a miracle. And Gene was right; people really *do* want a miracle. Every seminar we have, people come expecting easy answers and quick solutions, and we do have systems in place for them. However, when they get there, that's when we're able to give them heavy doses of reality. If you try to tell them everything in the beginning, you're going to chase them away. How do I know? Because back in the 1980s, I got this crazy idea in my head that I wanted to become a multimillionaire. I had no experience, no knowledge, no IQ, no talent, nothing — absolutely nothing — and all my friends and family told me, "You're an idiot, T.J., for thinking you can get rich." I heard that over and over again; they laughed at me. Looking back at it all... you know, back then I was very offended, but now I can see exactly where they were coming from; hell, I would have laughed too. I started buying all these crazy plans, programs, schemes and scams; and the crazier and goofier they were, the more attracted to them I was. It's an emotional thing, and that's the way rabid buyers are in all markets. Look at the diet market. People are attracted to the schemes where they lay down on the couch, eat a few pills, and all of a sudden these pills are going to speed up their metabolism and they're going to lose all kinds of weight. That's what people want. It's the child in us — that's what I really, firmly believe. You've got to understand all the reasons why your prospects buy, and then you have to develop all kinds of products and services designed to give them what you know that they want the most — which is, oftentimes, irrational, emotional stuff. It's going to be fun, it's going to be exciting, it's going to be easy. Look for areas of need that your competitors aren't filling.

I think a lot of marketers never think this through, so on the surface, this idea sounds really bad to them. They want to be honest with people. Well, you can be and you should be, just not right away; you've got to sneak things up on your prospects. Like I said, my suggestion is that you sell people what they want and give them what they need. That point was taught to me by Dan Kennedy, and I want you to take note of it and think about it. Serving customers in the highest way, developing products and services that fill the gaps the competitors aren't filling, and striving to understand your customers at a deep level — all this sounds like common sense, but again there are a lot of people who just aren't doing it, so you have to ask yourself: is it *really* common sense?

Most business people don't have a plan for making their customers feel special or understood. They don't know what to do to reach out to their customers and let them know that they care about them deeply and that they're trying to serve them. Secret Number Sixteen is a powerful way to do it. You hold seminars; you hold workshops for your customers; you set up tele-seminars. You create events that let you extend your hand to your customers, to show them you care. Prove to them that you really do care about them, and you're separating yourself from all the competitors who never will. You can stay in touch with your customers on a regular basis, as long as you're inviting them to all of these events, especially if the events are free.

We hold a lot of free tele-seminars, where people sit on the phone and listen to us. Yeah, they get pitched, but they also learn some stuff. We try to be altruistic about it. We try to reach out and let them know that we care. That's something you can do through audio that you can't do quite as well through print. People can listen to audio on their downtime. They don't have to work at it. Their time for wading through information, for learning, is limited; they only have so much capacity, and audio products can fill the gaps when they're doing other things that don't require all their attention. Audio products are an awesome way to build connections, to give people a sense of who you are and what you're all about. So record all of the events that you have. You create these events for your special customers, and later you make them available to all the rest of your customer base. So you're holding an event once, but you're getting paid for many years.

It's a great way to get leverage; and even simple tele-seminars are powerful. They offer the perception of value in the minds of the prospects. They can get some of the benefits of coming to a seminar, without the hassles of attending a live event. You can have some of those same advantages of reaching out to your customers. I like doing tele-seminars, because people can sit at home and still reap some great benefits. I like the fact that you can take recorded excerpts from these events and make them available to the rest of your customers.

Part of the secret to getting people to come to these events is, you've got to make them all kinds of big, bold promises. Now you've got a deadline, and you've got to put all this stuff together before the event. What happens is, you end up getting more done in a week then you normally get done in a month. So you keep having these events over and over again, and you keep promising bigger and better things to your customers if they'll come, and you continue to develop new materials that, in most cases, you would never have developed had you tried to do it another way. You only develop them in the process of trying to serve your best customers and giving them more of what you know that they want. What we do just to challenge ourselves is, we make promises that we have only sketchy ideas of how we're going to fulfill. We have enough confidence in ourselves through experience to know that we can pull it off somehow.

I think it's fun, when you have only the vaguest of ideas of how you're going to pull something off, to go ahead and invite people to come to a seminar, telling them in advance that you've got it all figured out. Now, maybe just to protect yourself a little bit you tell them that it's all still brand-new and you're still putting the pieces together, but you promise them by the time of the seminar all the answers will be solved. Just in case you don't have it all put together, you give yourself a little wiggle room.

You have until the time of the event to figure out how to fulfill on those promises. As the deadlines draw near, you start worrying a little. Not in a negative way, but you know you're there to serve your customers and you make a game out of it. It's a fun and creative, if somewhat stressful, kind of thing. Whoever said stress is bad was totally wrong! We need stress, we need challenges. What's wrong is strain, when you don't get time to pull back a little, and you're trying to burn the candle at both ends. We constantly need to challenge ourselves and look for better and better ways to serve our customers.

There is nothing that works, in my opinion, better than to hold events for your customers. Free events, low-cost events, even expensive events. Our most expensive seminars to date have cost $7,000; that was for a three-day seminar. Well, the magic is in the marketplace; the magic is knowing what the people in your market want, which things are the most important to them, and how you can then take that knowledge and give them what they want. It sounds simple, but a lot of people are overcomplicating it. Yes, of course there are a lot of things to learn; there are details, and you know you've got to get it all right, but the more you stay focused on all those details and the ways you're going handle all those different complexities, the more you're going to be what my good friend Ken Peterson calls "vapor-locked". The way to get things done is to stay focused on the simple. Every time you do get frustrated or confused, keep going right back to the simplicity of it all.

There's nothing that can replace an intimate knowledge of what the people in your marketplace really want. Every market has hidden secrets that only the insiders know, because only the insiders have penetrated the surface to see what's the beneath the shell. At the outset, for example, you might think that the opportunity market is made up of people who want to make more money. It sounds right, and yes, there's some truth to that.

187

But as you penetrate that surface, you'll discover that what people really, *really* want is a way to make huge sums of money in the fastest time possible in the easiest possible way, where they have to do very little — even next to nothing. All that, and they still want the potential to get filthy rich. I'm not being sarcastic here; it's just how things are. There are exceptions. There are people who enter the marketplace and fall in love with it. Once they become committed, once they understand more and you're able to teach them more, they learn what it really takes, and they get serious. That's another benefit of charging high prices to let people come to seminars. We value what we spend money on; and the more money we spend, the more we value something, as long as it really is worthwhile.

One of the reasons people remain in the opportunity market, going from opportunity to opportunity like a bee that flies from flower to flower, never doing anything with it, is because of the low barrier of entry for many of these programs. Most sell for $500 to $5,000; that's not a lot of money to most people, so they don't have much invested in it, and so they just drop it. There's no high level of commitment or responsibility on their part; they just keep buying all this stuff, because the very act of buying it makes them feel like they're doing something. If you start charging more money, you get people who are more serious, and they express their seriousness by the money they spend. Those people will also tend to get more of whatever it is that you're trying to give them, in terms of the information, the materials, and the turn-key systems. So it's a two-way street; the door swings both ways. That's one of the reasons why I'm charging premium prices for most of my products and services now.

I really do want to help you; I want to get you to understand and internalize the secrets in this book. I want you to start using them, to be willing to go through the necessary learning curve. The more money you want to make, the greater the learning curve you'll have to go through — but I would encourage you to go through it. The first seminars you do are going to scare you; but the more of them you do, the more you're going to learn. You're going to gain experience, you're going to gain confidence, and you're going to see all of the benefits when it comes to building solid relationships with the largest number of people. That's the secret to getting rich. The whole thing then becomes not, "Will I get rich?" but "How rich will I get?" and "How fast will I get rich?" Because you *will* get rich by practicing these things. Think carefully about what I've had to say here. When we meet for our free workshop, I'm going to try to drill this into you in a very positive way. I'm going to try to encourage you to practice this principle right here, as well as the others we've talked about on this program, so you can start making millions of dollars with these secrets.

Maintain a Stable Staff and Invest in Infrastructure

The seventeenth secret that made us millions of dollars is that we invested heavily in the infrastructure of our business. What we wanted to do from Day One was build an empire — and we took a lot of crap from a lot of people who constantly criticized us as kingdom builders. There's a philosophy out there, a certain belief system that most entrepreneurs share, which says that employees are bad. It comes from some of the teachers we all respect and admire; *they* believe that having employees is bad. They point out all these negative things about employees in general, and I've been around this game long enough now to know that some of it's true. Now, I'm not slamming my employees here, I've got nothing but good things to say about them. But here's the real deal: Entrepreneurs and employees tend to be two entirely different kinds of people. That's not to say that one is better than the other. Employees are just different than entrepreneurs, and some days I really admire them; I wish I could be more like them, because employees are able to go home at night and not think about the business. They have a life that's aside from the business, whereas entrepreneurs tend to be so focused on the business that they have no life outside it. It just absorbs them, takes over and possesses them.

I wish sometimes, when I'm going through a bad patch, that I could just punch a time clock, go home, and forget about it all. But I can't. I'm way beyond that point. If you're a true entrepreneur, you're going to be way beyond that point too. The business takes over your life. It possesses you; it obsesses you. Right or wrong, good or bad, that's just the way most entrepreneurs are. I admire people who can stay balanced, and that's how employees tend to be. They have things besides work that are important to them.

Entrepreneurs tend to be driven people; the work completely takes over every aspect of their life. That's wonderful when things are going well. It's exhilarating when you're doing what you love, when business is going great, when the money's flowing in, when you're doing all these exciting projects; and that's what you need to try for. This is one of the reasons why having a staff is such a great thing, because when you have a set of employees who know what they're doing, who are capable and competent, then you let them do what they do best and you do what *you* do best. As long as what you do best are things that contribute to your company in the highest way, then focus all your time, energy, talents, skills and abilities on the bottom line profits. Let your staff do the rest.

One of the popular business philosophies that really bothers me is that if you do what you love, the money will follow. I think nothing could be further from the truth — because most people love to be *lazy*. They love to do as little as possible. Instead I think you should find those few things that make you the most money, fall in love with those things, and *then* spend your entire time doing what you love to do. Now, it takes a while to become a good marketer — unless you're much smarter and more talented than I am, which you very well may be. It may take you years, but once you go through the learning curve, you're fine. It's somewhat painful, and it's a good thing that it's painful; I'm telling you, the more pain involved in learning some of the things that you have to learn to make millions of dollars, the more you can pat yourself on the back, because you'll realize that so few other people out there are willing to do those kinds of things. For me, I had to pay a tremendous price. It was a struggle. But now that I've developed the skills, it really, truly feels good. There's just no greater thrill. It does take work, but it becomes fun after you master it, after you go through the long journey, the tremendous number of hours, the total dedication and focus; when you get to the other side of all that, and you learn the things you have to learn so that you can make money at will. There's nothing I know of personally that feels better than that.

Part of that is the seventeenth secret here; it's having a team of people who are right there, taking care of all the aspects of the business that you don't want to do so that you can focus on those few things that bring you the most money. You're able to take all the time and energy, talent and skills that you've developed, all the knowledge and experience, put it into the things that attract more customers to you, and get more of your existing customers to continue to do more business with you. Remember, that's the whole secret to wealth. Just get a large enough group of customers to rebuy from you as often as possible. All the money you want is out there right now, and the more you're able to focus your time and energy and attention on the activities that produce the largest profits and let everybody else do everything else, the more money you're going to make.

Secret Number Seventeen is the key to retaining customers. A great staff is an investment towards future profits. You've got to realize that. These are people who can make you money; and you're making them money too, even though a lot of them don't realize that. They suffer from the delusion that they're the ones making *you* money, which is true; but you're providing for them at the same time. At M.O.R.E., Inc., we've built a nice foundation for attracting and retaining customers. Our business is designed to operate like a well-oiled moneymaking machine, and I want you to think about that, because that's really what you want. You don't want to just own a business. What you want is to own a moneymaking machine that will crank out the largest amount of money over the longest period of time. Having a good staff is the key to that.

Each week we have one promotion that's designed to bring in a steady flow of new prospects. It's usually some type of two-step marketing campaign that gets people who have never done business with our company to raise their hands and send for some type of information package or portfolio. We also have some type of back-end promotion that brings us more business from our established customers. That's it; that's our business. Remember, it's all about attracting and retaining customers. It takes a staff of knowledgeable, capable and competent people to pull this off. You can't do it on your own. You shouldn't *try*. Don't fall for that "Entrepreneurial Hero Myth" — the idea that these entrepreneurs are heroes. The Bill Gateses, the Ted Turners, the Michael Dells: these guys are the superstars of business, and it's easy to imagine that they accomplished it all alone. Yet nothing could be further from the truth. It's always the people behind the scenes that make it happen; these are the people who make the CEOs the heroes of all the stories the media loves, and those people never get the recognition they deserve. A lot of these entrepreneurs just go along with it; they never give their staff the credit that they deserve.

I believe you have to find people who are strong in the areas you're weak in. That's what we've strived to do at M.O.R.E., Inc. My wife Eileen first built this company; she ran it for 14 years. I did the marketing, because she has all those skills I don't have. She's got all the common sense, and she pays attention to details, and she's very focused on the day-to-day aspects of the business. Then, when she stepped down in 2001, I stepped up. Here I am: I'm a marketer, a person who thinks conceptually. I don't focus on details, I just focus on the big picture; I hate the day-to-day part of the business. Here I was trying to fill Eileen's shoes, and it was a total disaster. I found out fast that I'm the world's worst manager. If you want to make millions of dollars, I'd recommend that you *not* try to manage your business. Find other people who can. Once again, there's only one thing in your business that will make you money and contribute to your cash flow, and that's marketing: all the things you do to attract and re-attract customers, to get them to buy the maximum amount of your products and services at the largest amount of profit.

Everything else is just an expense. That's not to say it's a bad thing, because it's necessary. I believe you have to find good people and train them, and that's what we've done at M.O.R.E., Inc. We have a good staff that understands our business in an intimate way. Many of them have been with us for years; they understand what we do and how we do it, and there's a system in place that all started with my wife. My big achievement after Eileen stepped down was that I retained nearly all her staff; I didn't run them off. For years, though, I *would* have run them off; I wasn't mature enough to handle managing my company. You have to have a certain level of maturity if you're going to find good people and keep them. You can't expect too much from them; you have to give them a break sometimes. You have to realize that they have their strengths and weaknesses too.

You have to look at the long-term. You can't fire people every time you want to fire them, and you can't expect them to feel the same way about your business as you do. They're not as driven as you are. I believe that you really have to accept them for what they are, and try to understand them for what they are. They're employees; they're not entrepreneurs, though they may be entrepreneurial. There's a distinction. A lot of the employees at M.O.R.E., Inc., have entrepreneurial tendencies, and that's one of the reasons they love working there. Unlike a lot of established companies, where the job is always the same year after year, we're in a marketplace that's constantly evolving, and we're constantly doing new things and practicing what I'm preaching to you in this book. So, our employees tend to be entrepreneurial, and yet they're not entrepreneurs. They like having a steady paycheck and they like the security, and they've got a life beyond M.O.R.E., Inc. I envy them many days, when things go bad — and things *will* go bad.

I'd be doing you a disservice if I didn't tell you straight out that you're going to have days when you wish you never would have started your business. You're going to have hard times. If that's a turn-off for you, then maybe you shouldn't be in the game. I'm just telling you it's not a panacea. This isn't a perfect world. There will be problems that you'll have to solve, every step of the way, as you go higher and higher, and try to make more money and try to develop all your skills and get more knowledge and gain more experience. You're going to have to continue to challenge yourself. There are going to be new problems and new obstacles that are going to have to be surmounted, and anyone who tells you different is lying to you. If you want to do business with people who are willing to lie to you, then fine, go for it. But I'm not going to do that. You want to make millions of dollars? That's great; you can do it, and I'm assuming that's why you invested in this book — but you're going to have to learn new things. You're going to have to go through some adversity, some pain, some pressure, some long hours. A lot of employees aren't willing to do that, and a lot of entrepreneurs aren't either.

I feel sorry for entrepreneurs who don't know the seventeenth secret, because they're trying to wear every hat in their business. They're trying to be everything, and they scatter their energies, and they never have any focus. When you develop a good staff of capable, competent people, you get the power of focus working in your life, where your whole life can be dedicated to those few things that make you the largest amount of money. That's the kind of power you need, the kind that can turn everything around for you. Your staff will keep your happy customers happy. They'll free you up, they'll let you focus on your strong areas, they'll fill in the gaps for all your weak areas, and you've got to think long-term with people. If you find really good people, hang on to them.

In the beginning it's going to be a struggle; it always is. Expect it and embrace it, and just move on with it; every time you go through some adversity, realize it's part of the price you'll have to pay. You'll be happy to pay the price if you realize that challenges are an important part of this process. I'd suggest that you find a few good employees in the beginning, and as business gets busier and you have a demand for more people, use temporary help services to fill in the gaps. So you have your core group of staff that you're deeply committed to; and you're trying to do everything possible to make sure that they know it, that they stay with you, and that they're happy. Then you start looking for temporary employees. We've found some really good employees that way. You can hire them as you need them; you may have to go through a dozen temps to find a good one, but then once their contract expires with the temp agency, hire them.

Once you have a staff in place, you have stability; that's what you really want. And that's what a lot of entrepreneurs just don't have. Many entrepreneurs are very creative, very ambitious, extremely driven, and they have a huge capacity to work and put in a lot of hours. I pride myself on the number of hours I put into my business — and yet I'm constantly running into people who are outdoing me. It's a bit of a macho thing, but it's also something that happens when you're deeply committed — and you know what? I hate this concept of workaholics.

THE BLUE JEANS MILLIONAIRE!

Entrepreneurs are often misunderstood, because most people in this world are employees. The employees of the world look at us and scratch their heads; they don't understand us. They even feel sorry for us, because, after all, we're workaholics — or so they've labeled us. Well, I don't think there's any such thing. If you see famous artists, musicians, actors, and writers interviewed, it's okay for them to talk about how dedicated, passionate, committed and involved they are with their art; but then when you find a business owner or an entrepreneur who does that, "Oh no!" That person is self-absorbed, greedy, a workaholic, obsessed with their business. We feel sorry for them; we call them workaholics. Nothing could be further from the truth.

I believe that happiness really is a positive cash flow. Rachelle Callahan, one of my staff members, found a little plaque that says just that in an antique store and she gave it to me: "Happiness is a positive cash flow." When business is good, I'm good. When the money's flowing in, it's great. When I'm doing work I love and building projects I really enjoy, like the one I'm doing right now — man, I'm in entrepreneurial heaven. The secret to happiness is to make sure your business is always bringing in tons of profits, and that you're always involved in projects that keep you motivated and excited, things that get you up in the mornings so you don't have to drag yourself out of bed. You're *excited* to get up, because you're doing things that you really love. When you've got a great staff, they can give you the foundation to do more of the things that you really love.

Here's one last thing I want to say about this before I move on to the next secret. It's something most entrepreneurs will never discover, because they're anti-employees. They're constantly looking for cheaper people, and want to pay people less; they see every dollar they pay their staff as a dollar that should be theirs. That's a shortsighted way of thinking about it. I know in my heart that a great staff of dedicated, competent, capable employees who understand your business and are strong in the areas you're weak in are an investment you make towards future profits. If you think about it like that, you're not going to be so unhappy about paying out the big bucks to your employees. You're going to be happy to do it, because you know that's one secret to long-term wealth.

A lot of entrepreneurs don't build the infrastructure because they don't want the pressure that comes from constantly trying to make your payroll every week — the pressure that comes from those obligations where you've got to pay those people. I'm here to tell you that these pressures can be a damned good thing. Doing things that other people run from can serve you in the greatest way. Having infrastructure in place, so that you've made commitments and you've made obligations, is good. You're asking your employees to make an obligation to you, to stay with you; well, if you'll do the same thing with them, to try to keep them, you're going to be deeply committed to your business. You're going to do more than most people do — and a lot of people will scratch their heads and try to figure out what it is that's your driving force.

Simply put, part of it's those things that most people think are negative. Commitments, obligations, pressures, and responsibilities: those things can help you stay motivated and keep you moving forward, and you can get a lot of joy from working with the same people year after year. These are people you like, people you respect, people who understand your business and are out to help you — and you're out to help them. It not only makes you a lot of money, but it gives you a huge amount of joy and satisfaction. So think very carefully about this. Once you accept the ideas that I'm sharing with you, you'll have a solid foundation for attracting and retaining customers, and your business can be set up and run like a well-oiled moneymaking machine!

SECRET EIGHTEEN:
Schedule Weekly Planning Sessions

The eighteenth secret that we used to make millions of dollars is that we hold weekly meetings where we plan all our marketing strategies. These meetings are a form of discipline that keep us focused on where our next dollar is coming from. They keep us moving forward; and this is something you need to do if you're going to make the largest amount of money possible. You always have to ask yourself, "Where's my next dollar going to come from?" I'm shocked at the number of talented entrepreneurs I know who aren't using these strategies.

Even if you don't have staff yet, you've got to hold those meetings with yourself. I know that sounds funny, but it just means disciplining yourself, making the time to ask yourself, "Where's all of the money I want to make going to come from?" You see, many entrepreneurs get so lost in the promotions they're working on today that they never spend quality time thinking about two months from now. Now, you probably don't have to think much more in advance than two or three months. I never think more than a few months out at any given time — so forget all this long-term planning about where you're going to be a year from now, where you're going to be five years from now. All that's too confusing, so just stay on the path here.

Think about it as if you're jumping into your car in the middle of the darkest night of the year, where there's absolutely no moon; and now, you want to drive somewhere that's three or four hundred miles away. If you're a fairly competent driver and the roads are in good shape and the weather is okay, you can drive 300 to 400 miles in one evening, in pitch-black dark, and you'll never really need to see more than 150 or 200 yards ahead at any time. This is metaphor that I've thought a lot about over the years. As long as you're able to see ahead 150 to 200 yards, what do you care? Just don't outrun your headlights. It's the same thing with running a business. You don't have to worry about next year; you don't have to worry about two or three years from now. Sure, you should generally figure out your direction; you need to know where you want to go long term, and what your company stands for. Those kinds of ideas and general concepts about the marketplace you serve and your long-term commitment to that marketplace are important. But otherwise, you just have to think about what you're going to do in the next month or two months, and that's it.

Most entrepreneurs are lazy and undisciplined. A lot of the people I've gotten to know — very talented, super-creative people who really understand marketing — could be making so much more money than they're making right now. I even know some really smart people who are always struggling financially. They're great marketers, they intimately understand a lot of the secrets that I'm sharing with you in this book... and yet they're broke all the time. If they just applied some of these secrets to their businesses, they wouldn't have to be broke. They could make all kinds of money, but they're lazy, they're undisciplined, and they love to get lost in their projects. They love the work, but they hate all the planning and the organization; they hate going to meetings.

Many entrepreneurs are also very independent, so they don't work well as part of a team. They're very undisciplined, and they don't like all the planning that's necessary to keep the ball rolling, to keep moving forward. I can relate to that. You see, for years I absolutely hated meetings. I'm not going to tell you I love them now; I do one a week and that's it. It only lasts ninety minutes to two hours, and in that meeting we plan the new mailings, we come up with ideas for new promotions, and we keep the whole thing rolling. I'm going to explain to you just how simple it is before this chapter's over. But many entrepreneurs aren't doing this; they're not thinking ahead.

The money you want to make next month must be put into action *today*. It sounds simple, and you would think that this is just common sense, but most people have no method or no system to put this into play, so they're always disorganized. They're always frantically busy, and they're tired and they're too working hard, but they're never making the kind of money that should and could be theirs.

Remember, what you want to do is try to turn your business into a moneymaking machine. Get it systematized, so the money just keeps rolling in. Here's how to do it: You simply develop a marketing plan like ours, and our marketing plan is so simple that a twelve-year-old child can understand it. First of all, during our regular weekly meeting, we plan mailings that go out on a weekly basis to attract new customers. There are 52 of those mailings every year. We only schedule them about a month in advance, so we're watching the numbers constantly; we're not foolish about all this, we're looking at the numbers and making sure we're still profitable. We're constantly testing new things on the front-end, so in case one new customer acquisition promotion goes flat, we've got something to replace it with. Every week we have a new marketing campaign, which is a series of direct-mail letters. About 50,000 pieces a week go out on a regular basis; sometimes the number's 35,000, sometimes it's 75,000, and we're always experimenting to see what we can do to attract new customers who have never done business with us.

During our weekly meetings we look at all of this. How are our regular mailings working out? What's going on? What do our numbers look like? Our printer is at every one of these meetings, because he's looking for new printing business, and our mailing house representative is there at every meeting because *she's* looking for more business. These people are paid on commission. My goal is to always make sure the presses keep rolling, to always make sure that there are mailings going out — because as long as we're watching the numbers and doing everything right, the more we mail, the more money we make. For years we just weren't aggressive enough with our mailings. Now we're deeply committed to doing more and more mailings, so we watch our front-end, our new-customer acquisition mailings, and we make sure we've got something out there all the time, and it's working well for us. We're testing new things on the front-end. Next, we have regular new mailings that go out to our established customers to get them coming back. All these mailings, and all the implementation of the products and services that these mailings or promotions sell, must be planned and kept organized. All it takes is an hour to an hour and a half a week; that's it. You can do this even if you don't have a staff.

If you want to make millions of dollars, you have to get a big enough group of customers to rebuy from you repeatedly. Do it long enough, at a large enough profit margin, and you'll get rich. You've always got to ask yourself, "Where is that next dollar coming from?" Well, I'll tell you where's it's coming from: established customers to whom you make some type of an offer. Those customers give you their money in exchange for your offers, but you've got to plan these mailings. It has to be done in a disciplined, organized, regular way. Consistency is so important. I can't stress this enough, and I'm shocked at the number of talented entrepreneurs who never figure it out.

I was talking to a good friend of mine recently, and we

were sharing the secrets that I'm sharing with you now. He's new to the business, and he asked me a great question: "Why don't more people do this? Because it really is simple." Develop a staff of employees who understand your business in an intimate way, have a regular promotion that goes out to attract new customers to you to buy from you the first time, and then have a series of systematic follow-up offers that go out to resell to your established customers. It's so very easy. You have a regular weekly meeting that keeps it all organized, that keeps the blade sharp; that's the way I think about it. But when my good friend Ray asked me why more people don't do this, I thought about it, and I could come up with only a few reasons.

First of all, I think they're really shortsighted; they're too focused on the moment. They get so caught up in what they're doing that they forget that the money they want to make next month and the month after that has to be thought through in advance. There has to be some planning there, some organization. But they never think it through in any long-term way. The second reason is what I shared before: They're undisciplined, lazy, disorganized, too rebellious and too immature. How do I know? Because that was me. For a number of years, that was exactly who I was. I hated meetings, just as entrepreneurs just hate meetings in general. We look at the way some of these big corporations are run, where all they do is go to one meeting after another, and it's the *appearance* of work. They feel important because they're going to all these meetings, but they're never getting anything done; and we know this. Non-lazy entrepreneurs are people of action; we like to be out there *doing* it, not sitting in some meeting talking about how we're going to do it.

But it's an absolute necessity to have regular meetings where you're planning and organizing things. This is a secret that can make you so much money, and it's so simple; and the benefits come from working with a staff who show up for these meetings once a week, who understand your business in a deep, intimate, way, and who can remind you of things and keep you centered. They can say, "Look, why aren't we doing this? Why aren't we doing that? Are we doing this? Are we doing that? What's going to happen here? What are we doing about that?" They help you stay sharp.

Number Three: most entrepreneurs just don't want to have an infrastructure. I talked about that in the last secret: They want to do it solo. They want to make millions and millions of dollars all by themselves. I think that's so wrongheaded. Of course, my friends have called me a kingdom builder, an empire builder, and have told me that I have a huge ego because I need such a large staff. But I believe that the key to good customer service is making sure that for every thousand customers, you'd better have some staff there to support them. It just makes sense to me, but granted, my critics have been sort of right about me over the years, too. We've had a hard time with this; often we've either been understaffed or overstaffed. Either we've had too few people, or too many people. It's been a constant struggle. There are so many people who claim that they want to make millions of dollars, but want to do it all by themselves, and to me that's a recipe for disaster. You need to delegate your weak areas to people who are strong in those areas you're weak in, and you need to get good at the few things that it takes to make the largest amount of money, and put all of your time and all of your effort into those things.

Nothing could be more important than that. If you're trying to wear all the hats, trying to do it solo without any infrastructure, you're never going to make the kind of money that you could and should make. So get rid of that idea. You need a good staff of competent people; if you have one, they can be a great asset, especially if they've been in your business for a number of years. They can make you money, not cost you money. Everything these people do to help you make more money will more than compensate the amount of money you're paying them. It's true, I promise.

It may not be simple or easy, but that's the secret to my success, and that can be the secret of your success too. It only becomes something negative when business gets bad, or you start going through cash flow problems; and if you'll use this secret, you don't have to go through those cash flow problems. For years, we lost millions of dollars by not marketing more aggressively to our established customers. Now, I couldn't have told you that then. Wisdom comes from hindsight; there's the old quote that "hindsight is 20-20," when after a number of years you're able to look back and see your mistakes. I clearly see that this was a mistake, and I'm asking you to not make it. You don't have to lose money.

You see, there are only two real ways to make money. Number One: everybody knows about this one. You look at all the areas you can cut. "Oh! We're spending too much here, let's cut this, let's cut that!" That's important, sure; you should always look for ways where you can cut expenses by doing something more efficiently, assuming you can still get the same quality with less effort or cost. But what's just as important — and in some cases more important — is to look at all the things you could be doing to make more money. These are things you should start fixing right now. When we meet face-to-face for our free workshop, I'm going to drill this into you. You need to make more offers to your established customers, people who have already shown that they trust you and like what you're doing. If you'll do that, you're not going to have the cash flow problems that we've had occasionally. See, I used to worry so much that I was being too aggressive with my customers. My fears were that I was going to wake up some morning and all my customers were going to be upset because we were trying to sell to them too aggressively, and they were going to start thinking that they were nothing but walking walls, and they were all just going to go away. It was a completely irrational fear, as most fears are.

The truth is that if you're making your customers offers for products and services that really can help them, they'll respond positively. This is a service where, if you'll use my ideas and my personal help, you can make a ton of money. By the time you're done reading this book, and you know that I can really help you with these things, you'd be crazy not to use me as a personal coach and mentor. As long as you've got the same kinds of products and services you're offering to your customers, where what you have to give is worth far more money than you're asking them to give you in return, go out there and make them a ton of different offers. Go out there very aggressively, and offer them more and more of the things that you know in your heart can really help them make money.

Another reason I came up why so many entrepreneurs don't want to have meetings goes back to that laziness factor. They're terrified of all the hard work. They don't want to plan things because they're afraid of commitment, responsibilities, and deadlines. They don't want to put themselves under all the pressure it takes to achieve the maximum level of productivity. You see, that's what comes out of these meetings. Every single week, as we plan out our next mailings, we're always asking ourselves, "What can we do? What can we do? What can we do?" The printer's there — he wants more business, he wants to keep those printing presses rolling. The mailing house is there — they want to mail more stuff out, and we know that's the key to making more money. Our business isn't there to serve our printer or mailing house or our employees, our business is there to make more sales to our customers and make more profits. Those suppliers are there to help us make more money by offering more and different offers to our customers.

But here's what comes out of all of those meetings, and this is what all the entrepreneurs are afraid of: work, work, and more work. Somebody has to write the promotion, somebody has to put it all together, somebody has to do all the thinking; and that somebody is often you, if you're the one who's working on your marketing and you're putting all your focus in that one key area — product development, working on new sales copy, everything it takes to get those new products and services into the hands of as many people as possible. That's work, and a lot of entrepreneurs are afraid of work. They're afraid of responsibility. It reminds me of the quote that says, "What's the best thing about being self-employed? It's the fact that you're your own boss. And what's the worst thing about being self-employed? The fact that you're your own boss!" A lot of people just aren't very good at being their own boss. They want to lie around too much, they're not as productive as they could be; they're afraid of commitments, obligations, deadlines, and stress, and they never work as hard as they should. These meetings are a format for you, so you've got to have them every week. Your staff is going to show up, your suppliers are going to show up, and you've got to do something right during those meetings, besides tell jokes or talk about the football game last weekend. By the way, we also have fun at our meetings; I try to keep it lively. We make jokes, we crack up, we have fun. If it's not fun, why do it? You've got to enjoy the people you work with, and so we keep it lively.

But we're all there to make money; the staff is part of our revenue-sharing program, so they're getting a piece of every dollar that comes in. A rising tide lifts all boats as they say, so it's a win-win situation for our staff. They know that the key to getting a bigger paycheck is to do everything possible to make that cash register ring. So every week I've got to show up with three or four different things we can plan, because that's my responsibility. I'm trying to practice what I preach and it keeps me on my toes, but I always walk away from those meetings knowing my to-do list keeps growing. Many entrepreneurs are afraid of that; they want to run and hide from all the pain and pressures. They don't want those self-imposed deadlines. But if you'll do this, you'll keep your business moving forward; you'll get into the habit of realizing that all the money you want to make next month and the month after that comes from what you do every week in planning and preparing the mailings that will go out to your existing customers. Then there are the new mailings that are designed to attract new customers.

We use direct-mail almost exclusively, by the way. That's our favorite medium. It's just a wonderful feeling to be in total control over the media. But right now, today, after I'm done writing this chapter, I've got to get on the phone and negotiate with the publisher of some publications that we're going to advertise in; she wants us to sign a year's contract, and she wants to negotiate all kinds of things. God, I hate that. Once you discover the thrill of direct-mail, it's hard to go back. Direct-mail is a medium you control completely. You control the print, the mailing, the mailing list — it's just wonderful. But whatever media you use, you've got to plan; you've got to keep things organized.

Here are some of the ways to use this eighteenth secret to make millions of dollars. First, plan new promotions on a regular basis. Those plans can be kept in journals; that's all I do. I get up, drink a couple of a pots of coffee every morning, and get high on caffeine. That's when I do a lot of my great thinking. There's no phone, no fax machine, no distractions. It's just me and my journal full of ideas. I write a lot of different ideas down. Many, if not all, are combinations of ideas I've worked on in the past. It's always nice to have an arsenal of all kinds of ideas that you're working on, and just to think and to make the commitment to do new projects.

Once you make the commitment, figure out how to do it. What happens is, you create these self-imposed deadlines. Now, the deadlines are very stressful sometimes, but I believe that deadlines are the entrepreneurs' best friend. You're always going to do more when you're committed to your deadlines. You're going to show up in that meeting every week with your staff; you can't get into the habit of planning things, and then just erase them off the board. You know there's an obligation here — that if you're in charge of the marketing of your company, which I'm telling you is the area you *need* to be in charge of, don't delegate that. You may have people within your company who are working closely with you, but don't delegate it. That's your commitment to the company, that's your contribution to the company, and you've got to work your butt off and make sure you're planning all this stuff. Then it's up to you to fulfill that stuff. Now, here's one of the things we do that I just have to share with you, something that really can make you a lot of money. We do this all the time to help motivate ourselves to do more.

First, we plan a mailing and a basic promotion, and then we write some kind of small lead-generating direct-mail offer. It can be a postcard, or a small direct-mail package that stays under an ounce — a small package that's designed to just get people to raise their hands. We plan that mailing, we get it out very quickly, but it takes about a week to ten days from the time we plan it until the time it actually goes out. Now, during that period while it's going out in the mail, we're busy working on all the fulfillment materials, because we know we're going to get leads from a group of customers who'll raise their hands and say, "Yes, send that to me," so we're obligated there. We bring in a ton of leads from people who want the free report, the free CD or whatever; and now, we've got hundreds or, in some cases, thousands of customers who have raised their hand. The pressure we feel is out of a sense of obligation to our customers, knowing that if we don't get it to them quickly it's going to be a bad thing;

every day that you don't get it to them, you're sending negative messages to your customers. You can't do that. When somebody sends for something you owe it to them right away.

So we scramble like crazy to put it together. We do this with all kinds of things. Many are pre-publication offers where we make customers special deals on products that we tell them aren't *finished* yet, and that's true. What they don't know is that many times the products don't even *exist* yet, so it's not that we're lying to people; we're saying, "Look, we're going to give you a pre-publication rate. You're going to get it for 50% off the regular price. But it's not finished yet." Then we get a bunch of people who order, and now the sands of the hourglass start dropping. The timer's on; we've set a deadline, we've promised it to the customers in 45 or 60 days, so we've got to do it. We do that with tele-seminars, seminars, and workshops, too. We offer things that aren't yet finish, and sometimes things that we don't even quite know exactly how we're *going* to finish. There are questions that remain to be answered, but we go ahead and make the commitment, and there's magic when you do this right. I know it sounds a little scary, but it comes with confidence and experience, and pretty soon it becomes a fun way to stay creative and challenge yourself to do more and go higher. You make promises to your best customers, which you only have the haziest of notions of how you're going to fulfill, then you scramble like crazy to fulfill them. As you do this, you'll develop more confidence, and it'll become fun; it's more like a game.

I've had this happen to me so many times now that I can speak with some real authority on this. All the answers of how you're actually going to pull it off and keep all the promises you've made — they come in the midnight hour. Right before the deadline you start thinking about things where I am absolutely, positively convinced that, if it wasn't for the deadline and the commitment that you've made, you would never, ever have thought about. Yes so many entrepreneurs are trying to run and hide from pressure, responsibilities and obligations! I'm here to tell you that the secret to making millions of dollars is to put more pressure on yourself, to take on bigger responsibilities, to set higher goals, to try to achieve *more*, not less. Sure, there are going to be hard times, but you're going to get more done and you're going to end up with a feeling of tremendous satisfaction. You're going to make millions of dollars that your peers will never ever make, and you're going to feel so incredibly good about yourself at the same time.

Secret Nineteen:
Become Part of a Mastermind Group

The nineteenth secret that we use to make millions of dollars is that developed our One Hundred Million Dollar Roundtable group. This is a group that's made up of like-minded, dedicated entrepreneurs who are in the same basic market that we're in; we all serve the same customers. We work together to create new products and services, and then jointly sell those products and services to our own customers and keep all the profits ourselves. It's a powerful way to work together. In this chapter, I'll show you how to put your own group together — and it's worth the effort, because it can make you a huge sum of money. You'll make more money faster, you'll achieve great satisfaction in the process, and you'll make some friendships that will last for life.

Our group gets together on a regular basis to brainstorm new ideas, to teach each other new things, to help each other out; and I've learned so much from this group over the years. They've helped me to sharpen my skills; they've helped me to develop my knowledge for marketing, business, making money and generally being an entrepreneur. They've also helped me move in totally new directions that would have been impossible without them. Millions of dollars have come pouring into our business because of my involvement with this group, my level of commitment to the group, and the way that we've implemented all the things that our group has created collectively.

At the same time, some of our members have come and gone, so it's funny how we've gotten so much benefit out of this — while some of our members have received *zero* benefit from it. I believe it's more about what you do with all this that counts, and we've done a great deal with it; we've developed all kinds of new products with the group. The group has helped me map out certain strategies; whenever I've had problems I've just gone to the group, and I've freely opened myself up to these people and shared my problems with them. They're entrepreneurs just like I am. Some of our members, like Russ von Hoelscher, Don Price, Alan Bechtold, and Michael Penland — these guys have been doing it longer that I have. Things that I don't know how to solve, they've solved, and that's a powerful thing; sometimes we just become vapor-locked, we become confused and frustrated, and we need help from other people who have gone where we want to go, who have solved the problems we want to solve.

I just can't stress enough how important this is. Napoleon Hill talked about the power of the mastermind group, and that's really what we've achieved here with our One Hundred Million Dollar Roundtable. It's a mastermind group in every way. I honestly consider these guys to be my best friends, and I hope they think of me in the same way. We're all looking out for each other; that's what the group's all about. We have only one rule: that none of us can undercut each other on the prices of the products and services we create as a team. We're not going to play that game. We're all selling information products, and those are the products we get together to create. Information products have huge perceived values; in other words, the amount of money it costs to develop and reproduce them is very low compared to the amount of money that we sell them for. The perceived value is high, the profit margins are huge; but then what happens is, you sometimes get people, say on eBay, where they're selling this stuff too cheap. I think it's totally wrong to do that; one of the great benefits of this business is, you can sell things for huge profits, and you *should* sell them for huge profits. People will value the materials you develop and you'll sell more if you sell them for higher amounts of money.

Other than that, the competition between us is actually a good thing. All our members are doing something a little different; there are ways that we all differentiate ourselves. That's what marketing is all about; we can all serve the same market and even carry the same products and services, and still do enough things differently within our own group, with our own marketing, with the way that we serve our customers, so that we'll completely separate ourselves from each other.

We started out with just three members: my wife Eileen, Russ von Hoelscher, and me. Then we attracted new people who liked working with us, people like Alan R. Bechtold and Jeff Gardener. Every year we picked up a few new members; lost one, picked up two. We like working with each other, for the most part; there have been very few problems. The bigger the group has gotten, the harder it is to keep it all managed, but also the bigger the group has became, the more products and services we've created together. Now, I don't want to paint a false picture for you: There have been some challenges, and there have been some times when it's been tough to work together as a group. But the benefits and advantages of this group have far exceeded the challenges. Real friendships have developed out of this, people that I love and care deeply about, folks that I enjoy working with. Whoever said business and friendship don't mix — well, they were right, and they were wrong.

Here's where they don't mix: You can't really take pre-existing relationships and mix in business. I think that's an absolute disaster; for every time it works, there are probably 100, 500 or 1,000 times when it doesn't. The thing to do is to make friends with people who are already going in the same

217

direction you want to go in, who are already serving the same type of people you want to serve. Their businesses are very important to them, and your business is very important to you. Your relationships are built around you helping them get more of what you know that they want, which is to build their business, and them doing the same thing for you. Being an entrepreneur can be a lonely experience. We're surrounded by a world full of people who, God love them all, have the employee mentality. A true entrepreneur is a rare thing. The way most people think about work is completely different than the way most entrepreneurs think and feel about the work they do. It makes us unique. The people in our worlds don't understand us; they see us working long hours, and they scratch their heads and call us workaholics. People just don't understand what being an entrepreneur is all about. So it's great to have people in your life who are like-minded, who are moving in the same direction you're moving in, who understand you, who truly are your peers. The support, the understanding, the appreciation, the respect, the guidance that can come from those people — that's what true friendship is all about.

Another great reason to form these relationships, besides the facts that you're moving forward in new directions, and getting ideas that you wouldn't have had you not been part of the group, is the fact that customers love it. Our customers are exposed to all the members of my group, and that's one of the reasons why some people have joined the One Hundred Million Dollar Roundtable — just so that they can do joint ventures with us and reach out to our customers. Then they get into it, and it has other benefits and advantages for them; but the customers like the fact that we're bringing other people to them that they can trust and develop relationships with. The customers see us as big thinkers because of this. Initially, they were kind of surprised that we were working with other people in our marketplace; most of our customers are locked into this whole idea of competition. When they see us working together as a team with other companies, it actually becomes inspirational to them. They're initially shocked by it, but they develop relationships with all the members of the group and we all work together as a team.

What that does is help us create new joint-venture opportunities that are automatically created out of the friendships we develop — and these are long-term opportunities. They go on and on, unlike most joint-ventures, which are shortsighted, one-time affairs. The more you trust your partners — the more you enjoy working with them — then the more you start looking for bigger and better things to do together. You do one joint-venture, you make a lot of money together, and now all of a sudden you're asking each other, "What more can we do together?" Joint-Venture Number 3 grows out of Joint-Venture Number 2, and Joint-Venture Number 10 grows out of Joint-Venture Number 9, and you keep moving forward. You keep trying to do bigger things. The synergy that comes from different people working together, the ideas that emerge for products and services that serve your customers in the highest way, is a great thing. All the members are looking out for each other; all the members realize there's tremendous value in them helping to share their best ideas with you, knowing that you have ideas you can add to it that will help improve the whole thing. All of us realize that together, we really do achieve more, which is one acronym of the word "team" — Together, Everybody Achieves More. Again, there may be some hard times that you have to go through. There are some personality struggles; there are some bad situations. People wonder how we've kept this thing going year after year. Well, not all of our members have stayed with us — some just had to go. People come and go, and we've changed directions several times, and we're doing different things now.

But the group spurs us on; it keeps us moving forward, and we're constantly searching for bigger and better things we can do. We all end up helping each other realize our dreams here, and strong friendships are built around our businesses. Those are the best kinds of friendships, by the way. Our businesses are important to all of us. They're like our children; they're extensions of ourselves, they're the magnifications of the dreams and the ambitions we've had — to do and become more and have all these wonderful things in our lives. Being an entrepreneur can be a lonely experience. But the people in our group are like-minded entrepreneurs who really do understand us, and they become our friends; they help us build our business, as we're helping them built theirs. There's a respect that's developed when you have people you like to do business with, who you trust. You start looking out for them and they start looking out for you; and if you think about it, that's what friendship really is. It's about respect; it's about having something in common with the other person. So, whoever said friendship and business don't mix, they were absolutely wrong. The key is that the friendship must be built around the business, rather than the business being built around the friendship.

Our businesses are more than just ways to make money; they're our livelihoods. So friendship becomes a powerful force if used correctly, if you find the right partners. Here's how to do that. First, put together what I call a "hit list." If that name has negative connotations for you, call it something else. It's just a list of people you want to joint-venture with. These are people who are doing big things, who are moving in the direction you want to move in, who are going where you want to go, who've already achieved what you want to achieve. The bigger the list, the better. You should spend some quality time putting it together, and then you should start writing letters to that list on a regular basis.

Just stay in touch with the list — you're not asking them for help; you're not asking them for a damn thing. You're wanting to *give* them something, to serve them somehow. This is how some of our current Roundtable members became part of our group: they just sent me letters. Here I am, dealing with all the challenges of my business, going through all kinds of problems and headaches and hassles, and many times it just feels like there's a new problem everyday — and suddenly I get a package in the mail, and it's unlike all the other crap I'm faced with that day. It's something positive; it's a gift somebody sent me. A book, a cassette, a CD — something that really stands out from all the negative things I have to deal with. It's just a little letter that says "Hey, T.J., I wanted you to have my new CD," or "I wanted you to have my new report, and I really like what you're doing."

When somebody in my position gets something like that in the midst of all the other crap that they've got to deal with, all of a sudden you've elevated yourself head and shoulders above all that other stuff. You stand out. That's how I've met some of my joint-venture partners, and that's how I would recommend that you do it; just send something to that list on a regular basis. What you're trying to do is show them that you're somebody they should be working with. You're not asking them for anything; instead, you're offering to give them something. Give them the rights to sell a report, a cassette, or an audio CD or DVD you've done. Give them something of value. Give them a new book you created; give them some kind of a gift and then let them know, in a very soft-sell kind of way, that you're available for any kind of joint venture, or to help them with a project they're working on. It can be just that simple. If there's one thing that entrepreneurs have in common — and we take a lot of crap for this — it's that we all have strong egos. Sometimes having a strong ego can be a bad thing, but here's my justification for why I think it's good, in general, for entrepreneurs to have strong egos. We're faced with more adversity than most people; we solve more problems than most people ever solve; we have to struggle constantly to get where we want to go. It's hard to stay in business year after year; it takes somebody with a very strong personality, with a very clear idea of who they are and what they're trying to accomplish. Those people tend to be very prideful individuals; they're proud of their businesses, proud of their success.

It's great to receive a letter in the mail from somebody who says, "Look, I've been watching you for years; I love what you're doing. I want to offer my help in any way I can, and I want to be a part of your team. Here's a report that I just did; you can have it, if you can use it as free bonus materials for something you're doing or whatever. If you ever need me for anything, don't hesitate." You give them your phone number, and once every couple of months, you make sure that the people on your hit list receive some package from you. Maybe you gift-wrap it; maybe you just do something to separate yourself, something to show that you can offer the value that they're looking for. We're all looking for people who are winners, people who are doers. Those people reveal themselves by the actions they take, and the directions that they're moving; those are people that we want to be around, people who are doing big things and moving forward. We're all looking for people we can catch on the way up, too.

A lot of entrepreneurs are very smart in that area. They want people who are on the move, but haven't already gotten to the top yet — because sometimes when people do get to the top, they become very difficult to reach. They're extremely busy, it's harder to get their attention, it's harder to get their interest, it's harder to work with them. They become prima donnas and their egos get too big. And so, we're all looking for people that we know are future superstars but haven't actually gotten there yet.

Those are the people who, as they move up, we can move up; as they're doing big things, we can grow with their business. I'm always looking for folks like that; there are so few of them out there, and that's the honest-to-God truth. I wish it were different, but it's not. I wish there were more people out there that who were doing big things, instead of just talking the big game, but unfortunately they're rare.

If you're the kind of person who's doing big things, moving forward in the direction of your dreams and looking for joint-venture relationships that are going to be more than a one-shot deal, then naturally you're going to stand out — but you've still got to do things to attract attention. So develop the hit list. Put 50 to 100 good names on it, market to it on a regular basis, and soon you'll start putting your own group together and you'll start being a part of other people's groups. Remember, you're not asking people to do anything for you; you're offering to give them something, and as a result you will attract the best people, who can help you in the way my group has helped me. My advice to you is to go after them; court them, just as if you were a man going after a woman that you like.

If you were that man, you'd do certain things to attract a woman you really wanted. That's how you should go after your joint-venture partners. Most people will never use this secret, sadly, and there are reasons for that. Most entrepreneurs are locked into this fear of competition. They're small thinkers. They can't see the big picture. They're too independent, too stubborn, too afraid of joining a group and facing the headaches and the hassles they know come with it. And there *are* some headaches and hassles; I don't want to paint a false picture for you here. You have good times; you have bad times. There are positive aspects and negative aspects of a masterminds group. It can be tough to work with the same people over and over again.

Some people are just too egotistical for this; they're too

223

antisocial. A lot of entrepreneurs are too, because they're rebellious. Hey, that's part of what gets them started in the first place! That's what did it for me. I was very rebellious. Throughout my teen years I was one of those kids who was headed for a bad end — until I learned to channel my rebelliousness in positive directions. A lot of entrepreneurs are like me. They don't want to work with people, and they can't take the first step toward doing so. They don't *want* to take the first step. But you've got to, and I suggest you do it in a positive way. Just send them things you create on regular basis; send them little gifts, send them stuff that proves you're different from everybody else, offer to help them, offer to be there for them; and don't do it just once. Put them on your hit list, keep sending them things six or eight times a year, and you'll be surprised at the number of people who will want to work with you. You'll separate yourself from the crowd, and ultimately you'll end up becoming a part of a group of like-minded people who have what it is that you want, who are moving in the same direction you're moving, who can help you on your path to getting whatever you want and going wherever you want to go.

That's what we're all looking for. I just can't stress this enough to you: This is something that has made us millions and millions of dollars, because we've used the group. That may sound bad, maybe, but it's true. I've used their talent, their knowledge, their skills, their abilities to do all kinds of wonderful things for our company that have made us millions and millions of dollars. Now, in exchange I've tried to be there for them, I've tried to do things for them, I've tried to help them; so you see, it's not a bad thing. They use me too! What's bad is people who take and take and never want to give a damn thing. We all know people like that. We all know entrepreneurs we can't work with, who just want you to reveal your best secrets — but then when it comes time for them to share something with you, they clam up. You can't work with people like that. But if you find people you *can* work with, and you use them and let them use you, you'll make a ton of money. Every time we have seminars, we bring in our joint-venture partners; every time we to do tele-seminars, we bring in our joint-venture partners. The group helps us. They become part of every project we do, and it means less work for us. We get a lot more done, and when they have a project they need our help with, we're there for them.

So the door really does swing both ways. It's a synergy that's created from you and all the individuals in the group working together; you'll end up making a lot more money, but you'll also end up enjoying the high level of satisfaction and joy that comes from true friendships. You're working for people who understand you, who appreciate you, who respect you, people who are looking out for you as you're looking out for them. Ideas will come out of this group that never would have had you not been part of the group. You'll move in directions you never would have, probably, if it weren't for the strength of a group of people saying, "Let's do this together." They help you move in new directions, they help you achieve new things, and you'll help them — that's what friendship's all about. You'll end up making a ton of money together. People on the outside will scratch their heads and wonder how in the world you're able to do everything you're doing, and a large part of it will be because you're using ideas you got from your group. You're developing all kinds of products and services that were only created and developed because you were working together as a team; you're helping each other stay motivated, helping each other move forward in a certain direction. You'll try to do all kinds of things to help the people you're working closely with, and they'll try to do all kind of things to help you. The more you work together, the more you'll create, and the more you create and work together, the more money you'll make — it all ties together.

I want you to think very carefully about this. When we get

together at our free three-day workshop, I'm going to pound this secret into you. I am going to encourage you to either get involved in someone else's mastermind group, or to go out there and use some of these ideas I've shared to create your own powerful group, which will help you make huge sums of money and achieve the kind of joy and satisfaction that most entrepreneurs will never realize.

SECRET TWENTY:

Constant, Never-Ending Product Development

The twentieth secret that we used to bring in $10 million in less than five years (and another $100 million since!) is constant, never-ending product development and promotion. It's your intimate understanding of what the people in your marketplace want, and your ability to give it to them in the form of the products and services that you develop, that can make you more money than anything else. It sounds simple, and it *is*.

Now, I'll admit that within that simplicity, there are a few things you have to learn. It can, in fact, get very complicated at times — but you can't let that throw you off. As a matter of fact, you need to keep going back to the simplicity of it all. Every time it gets a little complicated, every time it gets a bit frustrating and challenging, keep going right back to the basics. Understand that it's all about your core understanding of your customers — what they really want, why they're really buying from you. Take that knowledge to heart, along with the ability to continue to develop products, services, and combinations of products and services, and the question is not, "Will you get rich?" The question is, "When and how much?"

How rich will you get? That depends upon the price you pay to learn all this and to develop it, and the amount of time and effort that you put in to it, especially in the beginning, as you're sharpening your skills. It also depends on how big and rabid the marketplace is. There are some marketplaces where people just buy like crazy. I personally think the opportunity market is absolutely exciting. I wish there were more people in it. I know that may sound funny to you, but if you understood it like I do, you'd see that's not something I'm saying just because it sounds good. I honestly wish there were more people in this marketplace, because a rising tide lifts all boats. When you're doing things like I am with 100% direct-mail, you wish there were more mailing lists you could mail your offer to. We need more serious players in this marketplace, more people willing to get involved at a serious level like we are, who will help us develop this marketplace and make it even bigger.

The ideas I'm sharing with you will work in any market, but I think you should work in the marketplaces that are most rabid, where people are happy to fork over huge sums of money for the products and services you offer. With so many people, I run into this claim, "I want to make millions of dollars." But then I ask them what kinds of ideas they have for businesses, and I see the potential just isn't there. Every one of their ideas is either for some local business, so they're not thinking big enough; or they're thinking too big, and they're not niched out enough. The market that you choose is the Number One thing; it's got to be a niche market.

I call the opportunity market the second largest niche market in the world; the first is probably the diet market. By niche market, I simply mean that the people within the marketplace all think alike. These markets offer very profitable psychographics — which is fancy way of saying that the people in the market are thinking alike, they behave the same way, they're all looking for the same types of thing. It's a marketplace that knows absolutely zero demographics. There are people within the opportunity market who are doctors and lawyers and successful business people, and then at the other end of the spectrum, you have people who are completely illiterate. That's not a judgment on them; it's just an observation. Their reading skills, if they're even able to read, might be second, third, fourth grade. That's a terrible thing, but we run into it all the time in this marketplace. Everybody from welfare recipients to people who are already worth many millions of dollars come to our seminars and buy our programs. We've made a fortune by simply understanding these people, really getting a handle on all of the emotional reasons that cause them to spend huge sums of money and continue to do so.

For years I did nothing but analyze the market, to get a real hard-core, knowledge of who they are, why they buy, what it is they're looking for. I kept asking myself that question over and over. I met them at seminars, spent a lot of time with them. I also analyzed the reasons why I was a good customer of this marketplace for so many years. I thought very carefully about what was behind my insatiable desire to make millions of dollars back in the mid-1980s. Sometimes there are answers, sometimes there aren't; sometimes there are just theories. But the more you strive to get to know your customers at an intimate level, the more you think it through. Spend hours thinking about all this, and it's all going to come back to you, hundredfold. The key is to understand them at this core level: why they buy, the emotions behind the marketplace, the techniques of your very successful competitors. This last concept is especially important. Study only your top five or ten competitors; the rest don't have a clue. There's nothing you can learn from them, except maybe not to make the same mistakes they're making.

So find the people who are doing the very best, the ones who are making the most money, and get on the other side of the cash register. Become their customer, get on their mailing list, let them send you everything they're doing. Study it from a conceptual, entrepreneurial place, rather than as a consumer;

look for the common denominators. The more you do that, the more you'll get a trained eye. The longer you do it, the more you put yourself into it, the more work you do behind the scenes, off the clock — the more you just put yourself into it 100% and study it from every angle — the more you're going to become an expert at these things. Some of them are hard to put into words; we're dealing with emotions here, human emotions that cause people to buy and rebuy. They cause them to get so excited that they'll wire their money to you. They'll FedEx their money. They'll jump in the car and drive over from a few states away just so they can beat the postal system and get it to you quicker. We're talking about things they can't even begin to explain to you themselves; they don't understand why they buy, and that's one of the reasons why focus groups are such a joke. Big companies put people in these focus groups and ask them a million questions, as if the customer really understands what's behind their insatiable desire to buy things. They don't; it's up to *you* to know. Some of it's tough to put into words because we're dealing with emotions, and emotions are irrational in the markets that will make you the most money.

A lot of what drives those markets is whatever causes people to give up their money in exchange for your products and services. Sure, it's an insatiable desire, but what's behind it? The answer to that question is in a great book by the Nobel Prize winner Eric Hoffer: *The True Believer.* All you have to do is read the first chapter of the book — that's it! The first sentence of the first chapter says it all. It says that it all starts with a frustrated person. What's behind most of the insatiability in the marketplace that causes people to spend huge sums of money? Frustration — these people are frustrated, unhappy, unsatisfied. That creates the want. Every book on marketing and selling tells you that you have to give people what they want. Well, what *is* a want? It's an unfulfilled desire. There's a gap there, there's something missing, and the people who are most unhappy are often the ones who end up spending the most money because they're dissatisfied.

We've taken a lot of flak over the years at M.O.R.E., Inc., because many of our customers are senior citizens. I've taken a lot of personal criticism for it. People think we're taking advantage of seniors; they think we're somehow targeting them, and nothing could be further from the truth. There are magazines that reach out to the senior citizen market, and we stay completely away from them. I don't want anybody to make any argument that sounds like we're there to take advantage of the elderly. Honest to goodness, the real reason why a lot of senior citizens gravitate towards the business-opportunity market has everything to do with this frustration factor I'm talking about here. I know; I watched my own father go through it. I watched my stepfather go through it. I've talked to dozens of my customers who happen to be living in their golden years right now. All their lives, they had a job that provided them with great things. They were getting their needs met through those jobs, their feelings of importance and self-worth stroked, the interaction they needed with other people — and then they retired.

Now there's a huge hole in their lives — and after six months of playing golf or five years of watching TV, they long for something to fill this hole. They're miserable. They want to do something with their lives; they know they've got to stay active. There's a part of them that knows that the more they're able to move forward and keep that hope and excitement alive, the better — they know that's part of what life is all about. I've seen it. I know that there are exceptions to this, that I'm generalizing about something where human beings can be very complex. But whenever you have a marketplace where people are spending a ton of money repeatedly for the same basic types of products and services — well, you know that underneath it all is a huge emotional void. It's all based on emotions. That's the best part about being human — though maybe some people would say that's the worst part about what we all are as human beings, too. I know that there are plenty of people taking advantage of other people's emotions. Don't do that — but what I *am* asking you to do is create products and services that give your customers the highest amount of value. Don't sell them crap just because you can. It's wrong from an ethical point of view, and you don't have to do it. There are plenty of things you can sell them that are good and solid, that really do stand the greatest chance of helping the most people get what they really want.

I want you to think about this frustration factor — because the more you realize just how unhappy and miserable people are in your particular market, the more you'll be able to speak directly to their unhappiness. We do this by telling the customers about all the pain and the frustrations, the confusion, and all the emotional and mental and even physical turmoil that we went through on our quest to make millions of dollars. We're upfront about that. By telling our story, we let them identify with us; they know that we feel the way they feel. We create that bond with them.

You've got to understand your marketplace in an intimate way; nothing can replace that. If everybody is your market, nobody's your market. A lot of entrepreneurs have crazy ideas that they're just going to sell something to everybody, and there are a lot of companies out there, pushing biz-ops, that try to tell you that they have products and services for everyone — and that's just not true. Even if it *was*, it would be ineffective. The more niched your market is, the better. So strive to know your market: who they are, how to reach them, where to reach them, the best way to reach them, what they want the most, and how to give it to them. That's the golden secret to getting rich. Then constantly search for the newest and best ways to give your customers more of what you know they want the most. Spend some time thinking about this. Get up in the morning, if you're a morning person; drink a couple of pots of coffee like I do. If you're a late night person, stay up late, where it's just you and you're alone with your thoughts, and you're looking at this from a more conceptual standpoint and thinking it all through, writing all this down. Your answers will continue to improve; they'll get deeper and deeper. We all start out with shallow things, but the more you think it through, the more you *will* think it through. Your answers will become better, and the better your answers are, the better you're able to create things that truly give people what they want.

There are some really good reasons why you've got to create a constant, never-ending stream of newer and better products and services. First of all, people always want something that's new and exciting. One of our websites is WhatsHotRightNow.com. We created that site because we know people are always searching for the next thing, the newest thing. They want to know what's new. If you don't give those things to your customers, if you're not constantly trying to offer them something new, someone in your marketplace will. They're going to give that money to somebody, so they might as well give it to you. That's especially true if you're committed to creating products and services that offer people great things, solid programs and products you can be proud of — and that they can be proud of, too. That's another the key to selling people repeatedly — you can't rip them off. You've got to produce quality stuff so they'll gladly come back for more. You think that makes common sense? You're right; it does.

And yet, there are a ton of companies out there that don't have the slightest clue about any of this — especially companies in the opportunity market. How do I know that? Because I study them constantly. I'm on their mailing lists, and believe me, they don't do a good job of staying in touch with their customers and building relationships with them. I can tell, because I have an educated eye; I've been doing this for so long now. I can instantly spot all the things they're doing wrong. As far as I'm concerned, most of the companies in my marketplace are like this, and I wish it wasn't this way. Everything they do seems to be so fly-by-night; they're thinking about making sales, not developing customers. That's sad, and it's stupid, because your existing customers are open to your marketing messages. They'll get a hundred pieces of mail in their mailboxes in a single week, and they're more apt to answer your mail than they are to answer those other ninety-nine product pitches, because they *know* you. In some ways, there's so much money on the table just waiting for you from people whose skepticism has been minimized. Their sales resistance has been lowered, the ice has been broken, and they trust you. All you have to do is keep coming up with newer and better stuff to offer them.

People always ask me, "What should I sell to my customer?" That's a good question. It's one that you should keep asking yourself — and I'll give you a clue here. You keep selling them more of the same types of things they bought from you the first time. Variations on a theme. You've heard the saying, "familiarity breeds contempt?" I think that's true only in extreme cases. I think what familiarity breeds is apathy. People are looking for things that are new. It's part of that emotional kind of thing that we've talked about. Little kids have it. If you want to understand their emotions, look at little children and how excited they get about different things, and how they respond to excitement. Look at animals — dogs especially — and how they respond to excitement.

Emotions are a basic part of who and what we are in general. They're also a part of what makes us the highest that we can be. The love we feel for people, our willingness to take a bullet for those we love, to put ourselves in harm's way, to do all kinds of wonderful things; that's a higher part of us. It's complicated and hard to put into words, but it's something for you to think about. Think about it a lot, because that's the key to building bonds with people that cause them to come back again and give you more of their money, and be happy to do it. You're not manipulating people or ripping people off, or lying to them, as long as you're creating high-quality items that really can help them go from where they are to where they want to be at the fastest pace possible. You're doing them a service by offering them all this new stuff. The more you offer them, the more money they'll give you.

I have a great quote from Dan Kennedy hanging up here on my wall, and it's something I'd like you to think about, too. Highlight it here, and come back repeatedly to take a look. It's only four words. "Consumption expands with usage." The more people buy, the more they *want* to buy. Look at collectors; if they collect guns, do you think three guns are going to be enough for them? No, they want thirty. If they collect cars, do you think just having one or two is enough? No, they want more; they're insatiable. That's a quality that we all have, and some have it worse than others; and some can't control it in the darker aspects of life. We all have this insatiability, and in a positive way it causes us to do more, become more, achieve more, reach for higher things. It's that insatiability that causes people to continue to open their wallets up to you.

Now, here's one of the best suggestions I can give you when it comes to developing products: Do the sales letter first. If you can't, at least do the sales letter while you're creating the product. The big mistake I see so many entrepreneurs making is that they put all their time, effort, energy, and focus and into developing wonderful products, and when they're finished they're completely exhausted. When it comes time to develop the promotional materials to sell it, they're running on empty. So

235

when you create the sales material first, or while you're actually developing the materials that are a part of the product or service, that's best. That's when you're excited! There's a certain edge that comes while you're in the heat of the moment, while you're excited about whatever it is that you're creating. You capture that excitement through your sales material, and what's selling is transference of emotions. The more sold I am on something, the more sold *you're* going to be. The more excited I am, the more I have the ability to get *you* excited. It's a transference of emotions, and the last thing you want is to take all the energy that should go in to the promotional materials, the sales letters, the order forms, the question and answer sheets — and waste it. You want to channel as much of that energy in to the promotional stuff as you do to the product.

Every day, you should do a little product-development work — every single day. I woke up this morning at 6 a.m. Sometimes I sleep late on Saturdays; but not this morning. I was out of bed at 6 a.m. because I had all these great ideas in my head for a sales letter I was working on, and I had to get out of bed. For two and a half hours I wrote until my hands hurt, and I cranked that copy out and got it while it was hot, and I haven't even begun to develop the product yet. Actually, it's going to be for something we'll introduce at a seminar. When it comes time for the seminar, most of my work will already have been done — it will all be downhill from there. But see, this is something I'm excited about right now, and I don't know a whole lot about this new opportunity that we're promoting. I know just enough to get people so pumped up that they'll gladly shell out the fee to come to the seminar. While I was so jazzed up and so excited, I couldn't even stay in bed to sleep in this morning. I captured all that on paper, and I hope to do it some other mornings now, so I can get a big batch of really exciting copy where I analyze all of the reason why I'm excited, the reasons why this opportunity is unique, the reason why it stands out head and shoulders above everything else. I came up with a list of thirty-four reasons why this opportunity beats every other, and I wrote about it with passion because I'm excited. The more excited I am, the more I'm able to get other people excited. Of course, sometimes the more you know, the less excited you get. See, sometimes people want to understand everything before they develop everything. I think there's real strength in getting it while it's hot. Capture all your emotions, whether you're doing pitch tapes or sales letters or whatever. You've got to capture that emotion.

One of the reasons you need to do constant, never-ending product development is that you want to stay sharp. The knife can never get rusty; and if you're constantly spending a good portion of your time every day working on it, it won't. I don't care whether it's a half-hour or three hours or four hours, do it every single day. I like to do it seven days a week, because I don't want to get rusty at all. This is how skills are developed. You hear writers and artists talking about it all the time; they practice on a regular basis because they want to keep their skills honed. This is very similar; so whether you're writing sales copy or developing or producing a product, whatever you're doing, keep doing it. Your skills will improve. There's going to be some pain involved as you learn these new skills; but once you master them, your confidence is going to soar. You're going to find yourself enjoying things that used to cause you a lot of problems, because it was tough and there were a lot of things to learn, and it was new; those are the things that are going to give you the greatest satisfaction down the road.

You're just going to have to take my word for that for right now. Just be willing to do what other people aren't willing to do: Pay the price, learn how to do all of the things we've discussed in this and other chapters, and when we get together to spend good, quality time at our free marketing workshop, we're going to talk about these things. I'm going to encourage you to pay the prices you have to, because constant, never-ending product development and promotion is a golden secret that can make you super-rich, and I'm going to help you do it. I'm going to do my very best to help you realize this tremendous advantage that can make you huge, never-ending streams of money for the rest of your life.

SECRET TWENTY-ONE:
Rework Your Past Promotions and Materials

The twenty-first secret to making millions of dollars is to rework the same sales letters, to keep redoing the same products, and to keep rerunning the same promotions. Now, I've already talked about this a little, and I don't mean to sound like a broken record; I just want you to understand this. So many people don't get it. They don't understand that you can keep reselling the same basic things over and over again. It's a trick of the trade that a lot of people in the trade just never pick up on. If you do, you'll have a major advantage over the other competitors in your marketplace, because most are simply not selling enough new things to their customers. One of the reasons is that they just don't realize how easy it is to keep repackaging the same things and calling them new. Of course, there can be some element within your package that makes it look new; it has a new look, it has a new feel, there's some new angle to it. You're not ripping people off; you're giving them exactly what they want, which is old things with a new twist.

Look, everybody wants new stuff; there's no question about that. However, the newer it is, the more unestablished it is. Nobody wants to be the guinea pig, the first one out on the dance floor. People need stability, the peace of mind that what they're buying from you has an established track record. It's proven; it's not just something you dreamed up out of thin air. Customers like this; they like the message, in general, that what you have for them is established, it's rock-solid, it's proven, and yet they *also* like the idea that you've found some way to make it even better — and that's all you have to do. Keep finding ways to put a facelift on everything, make it seem like it's new, and it *will* be new to some extent.

If this sounds manipulative, I'm sorry; it's just something that everybody who's making the most money is doing. Maybe some of them don't want to tell you about it, because it does sound slightly manipulative, but really it's not. Look at the cars that keep coming out year after year. Every few years they may change the basic design of the model, but most years they're just doing tiny things to give it the appearance of something new. It's just the same old stuff over and over, and that's what people want. You've got to realize just how insatiable people are, and you have to realize the things I've talked about in my other chapters about the emotional qualities in play here.

People buy for emotional reasons, so don't try to think all this through too much from a logical standpoint. There's all this irrational behavior that goes into the best marketplaces, the ones that can make you the most money in the shortest time in the easiest possible way. These are markets that are driven by emotions; people are irrational in their behavior, and that's fine, it's good. The only time any of this becomes bad is when you're not committed to delivering products and services that offer good, solid potential. When you're just out there selling crap that doesn't stand a snowball's chance in hell of giving people the benefits you're promising them, that's when it falls apart.

I think it's kind of funny how the same customers (and God love them all, I try to take good care of my customers) end up coming to our seminars repeatedly. People ask us, "What's the seminar about?" Well, it's just like the last seminar we had; and the next seminar we do will be just like the last one we had before that. And, yes, there's always the appearance of something new, and there's always something new we're introducing; but the basic, core seminar continues to be the same. We say the same things; listen to all the tapes of our seminars, and you hear the commonality woven throughout.

The same thing is true for all our major competitors. The reason we do this is twofold. First, that's what the customers want. All of us are in business to serve our customers, to give them more of what they want; and what they want are variations on the theme of what they bought from us the last time. The second reason you do it is because it's easier to do it; it's faster. You can keep coming up with new stuff again and again, so you can get all that pressure off your shoulders that it has to be somehow totally different than what you gave them last time — because I promise you, it doesn't have to be. Once you have a library full of things that have worked for you in the past, it's easy to keep giving them variations of the same theme. That should be something you look for towards the future. You work your butt off creating all this new stuff, finding out what works the best, experimenting, getting some things established; and then, after a certain numbers of years... well, it's not that you can just coast. I don't want you to even think like that. You can't just take it easy; but it does become easier, there's no question about it. Just keep pulling up the same old sales letters, rewrite them a little bit, and boom — that's all you have to do. Once you understand at a core level what it is that really turns your customers on, it becomes so easy to do the things that used to be difficult for you.

Once you get to that point, you can do in two days what used to take you twenty days. It'll be a whole lot easier, and it'll be a whole lot better. Some of this involves simply pulling up old computer files and rewriting, and we do our share of that. That can all be done while you're relaxing on the couch in front of the TV at night; it's no big deal. Rewriting is actually my favorite part of the job. The writing part is difficult for me, because I put so much of my energy into it. The rewriting part is easy: you've got your feet up, and there's the TV, and you're half watching some stupid TV program. In my case I'm with my sweetheart at night, and we're spending some good quiet time together. I've got my laptop, and I'm very quietly rewriting the same things we've done in the past.

When you're in the writing mode, you're able to get so much done, so fast, because you know exactly what your customers want. There's a power here, and you can acquire it. It's on the other side of that learning curve, so it'll take some effort, but you've got to know that it does get easier. There is a quote from the late, great Joe Cosman that goes something like, "What was once difficult is now easy," and when I first heard that I thought, "God, that Joe Cosman is such a wise man." And he is, but it turns out that he was rephrasing a concept that was already very old. Because I collect quote books, one day I ran into that quote. It was from the King James Version of Bible. It wasn't said exactly the same way, but six hundred years before Christ, somebody expressed the same sentiment: that the things that are difficult for you right now are going to get easier and easier if you keep working through them. Once you build up an arsenal of sales letters and promotions and products, they can make you money for the rest of your life.

One of the things I wrote to myself a few days ago — because I'm trying to practice this principle myself, and I keep journals where I try to think these things through and I write notes to myself so I can go back and remember them — was "never create anything ever again; you've got so much stuff that can and should be recycled." I love to create new stuff, I honestly do, and I think a lot of entrepreneurs are like me. But the truth is, we've got all this other stuff that's worked for us over the years, and you're a whole lot smarter if you'll rework the old stuff and try to incorporate your need to create new stuff into that, so that you blend it in with the old. It's the best advice I can give you for making millions of dollars, and it all boils down to the same basic emotional reasons that cause your customers to buy and rebuy from you. Now, it's true that your customers do go in and out of emotional heat. They get hot for things and they get cold, but the core reasons that cause them to buy and rebuy don't change. The same basic selling messages keep working over and over again: the same themes, the same benefits, the same type of offers, the same types of products and services. You do have to get people while they're hot, and not all your customers are going to stay hot; but the more you offer people, the more they'll buy from you in general, and I feel that you can't sell to your best customers enough. You have to keep going back to them again and again. As long as you're providing good value, there's nothing wrong with it; you're actually doing them a favor.

People are going to buy from you, or they're going to buy from your competitors. They would much rather buy from you and from the people you recommend. There's a trust built up there, so you might as well be there for them. At the same time, they want old stuff with a new twist — and they trust you to provide it. That means you can keep stamping out the same stuff over and over, as long as there's a new angle to it. Let me repeat: people want more of what they bought from you the first time; they want the same basic benefits and advantages in the items you provide. They'd rather buy from you and the people you recommend than anyone else. Remember, a lot of this is emotional. What you have to do is get a very good conceptual view; you have to think this through as much as you can from the top down. Keep swipe files of other people's sales material, and of course keep everything that you've done in the past. I have boxes and boxes of stuff that we've done previously, and it's nice just to be able to reuse it again; it's a fast, simple way to be creative. You get leverage on all the hard work that you do once. It's a great way to do something once and keep getting paid for it forever.

This is true especially if you're in the information publishing business; that's one of the greatest advantages that we have. We do something once, and we can get paid for many years. If I were to die next year or ten years from now, the people working within our company could just keep stamping out the same basic things, if they're smart — and I know they are. Of course, they suffer from the same thing most entrepreneurs suffer from. They want to keep coming up with new stuff; it's almost like we think there's something wrong with stamping out the same old stuff. But there's nothing wrong with it at all! Remember, one of the reasons you do it is because that's what your customers want; all of us are in business to serve customers, to give them more of what they want. If it's too new, they don't want it, because it makes them more skeptical; they want that old stuff with the new twist. You've got to think conceptually, to look for patterns and themes, test as many new ideas as you can; and then you find out what works the best, and keep coming back to those things. You keep incorporating those things in the new stuff that you're doing. You've got to always look at where your biggest sales and profits are coming from, the promotions that work the best, and keep asking yourself, "Why?"

Now, I want to tell you this: you'll never come up with a *real* reason. Remember, all this is driven by emotions, and emotions know no logic, so trying to apply logical answers to emotional questions just isn't a good idea. But you do develop themes and theory, once you understand the marketplace at a very intimate level. You'll come to realize that one of the things about the opportunity market that causes people to rebuy so much is simply this: they want the fastest, simplest and easiest way to make the most money with the least effort, and if you can do it all for them, or promise to do it all for them, then so much the better. This is one theory that I've developed. It may sound cynical, but I don't care; I know it's true. There are exceptions, and there are theories within the theory, but usually they want to get super-rich, even though most of them are like I was back in the 1980s. I could barely put a roof over my head or pay my bills, and I had no knowledge and experience; but I still had an overwhelming obsession to get rich. That's who the people in the opportunity market are in general. There's no logic behind it. It makes no sense. Certain skills and knowledge have to be developed to get rich, and although it's possible to get rich quickly, usually you have to put in some time and work, effort and energy. I stumbled around for years before it happened.

There is a compelling emotional reason why people buy, and I would suggest that you study your biggest competitors closely; forget the rest. Study and identify the promises and benefits they're communicating to their customers. Try to determine the general selling ideas that they're using; what are the promises behind the promises? Just identify these things, think these things through, and keep some journals. Look, all of this may sound easy right now, as I express it to you — and it is. For me this is easy, because I've been doing it for twenty years. But there were years when it was all very confusing, and I kept lots and lots of journals, and I studied my customers intensely.

Until you develop your own style, you have to steal other people's style. You have to copy what others are doing until you can get a feel for it yourself; it's like training wheels. Training wheels are the best way I can think of to learn to ride a bicycle, because you get the feel of it without falling, and then eventually the training wheels can come off. Well, the training wheels that we have are all the great sales letters, promotions, products and services that other people are using. Get on the other side of the cash register, and start looking for ways to steal an idea here and an idea there. Now, you don't want to copy what somebody's doing exactly; that's plagiarism. We've had people do it with us. Did we go after them? No, we didn't. We didn't want to spend years in court and waste our time; we're moving forward. We're willing to walk over a few hundred dollar bills as we move forward in the direction of our dreams. What do we care? People who plagiarize aren't long-term players anyway. You don't have to be afraid of them, because they have nothing within themselves that will allow them to become any type of threat to you. So don't plagiarize, but model after ideas other people are using, and then find your own way to incorporate them and package it all together.

There are shortcuts, simple secrets, and proven strategies that do give you leverage. Stealing a little from everybody is one of those things, and eventually you're just going to steal from yourself. See, that's the thing I want you to think about: you start off by studying the marketplace, looking for the people who are making the most money, finding out what they're doing, studying and identifying and quantifying those exact methods, benefits and the advantages they're offering, what's behind the basic pitches. You have to look at it all from what I call the other side of the cash register, because if you're locked into this consumer mentality, you're never going to see it. You almost have to think of yourself as a consultant, a consultant for yourself, and your job is to study all this stuff. So you're able to get into this mindset where you can start really identifying all this, and you'll see things; it does take a trained eye. Part of that trained eye is to not think like a consumer. *Think like an entrepreneur.*

Once you see all this, once you study it, once you get a feel for it, then you start copying from the best people out there. You develop a lot of stuff, and you develop a sense of confidence, and you start making a lot of money. With that comes a feeling of confidence; your experience level starts increasing, your skills start developing, and after a while you'll have so much stuff that you've done that you'll wake up, like I did. I've lost years of my life, because I was so absorbed in my work, and so absorbed in creating all kinds of new products and services for the customers. I wake up and look in the mirror, and I'm ten years older. What happened was, I created such an avalanche of different products and services that now I can just spend the rest of my life, if I want to, reusing ideas. I'm striving to do that more and more, because why work harder if you don't have to? If you can get so much more done faster, you're a fool to spend a lot of time doing something you know you don't have to. I'm practicing what I preach here. After a while, you're not really stealing from competitors anymore at all; you're just stealing from yourself. You just continue to find a way to hone it down more and more, and boil it all down. Pretty soon you develop this confidence that comes from knowing exactly what your customers want, and you know exactly how to give it to them, and you can just keep taking the same themes, the same things that you've done over and over again, and find new ways to give it a new spin, a new look, a new feel. There's always something new that you can incorporate; and then that becomes your new theme that you develop.

People wonder how in the world you're able to get so much new stuff out there; but you'll know the secret. You'll know the trick of the trade here, which is Secret Number 21. You'll know that all you're doing is reworking your past sales letters, products and promotions; and if you do this, you can make a huge sum of money in the easiest way for the longest period of time.

SECRET TWENTY-TWO:
Join a Coaching Program

The twenty-second secret that we used to make millions and millions of dollars is the five years that we spent in a great coaching program, Dan Kennedy's Platinum Group. This is something that changed my life forever, and I want to share some ideas with you here that I know can not only put millions of dollars in your pocket, but can also help you experience a lot more of the joy and satisfaction that can come from making money.

Dan Kennedy is a marketing genius. He's brilliant when it comes to his ability to teach people the things that can turn small sums of money into a lifetime of huge sums of money. He's dedicated, he's committed, he's passionate, he's knowledgeable — a very, very smart marketer. In 1995 or 1996, when we'd already been his customers for a few years, he invited us to join a new group that he was thinking of starting. He was putting a meeting together just to see how it would go, and of course a bunch of people showed up, and most of us ended up joining right then and there. It was called the Platinum Group, and it was a decision that changed my life. Just the fact that Eileen and I said "Yes" to being a part of that group made us millions of dollars; and it taught us some things that I want to teach you right now. Again, some of this stuff sounds like common sense, but it's not. There are so many people who never ever figure these things out, and I'm going to tell you why that is. I really believe I have the answer to this, because some of this isn't that difficult; but as Mark Twain said, "common sense is a very uncommon thing."

Now, here's how being a member of Dan Kennedy's Platinum Group changed my life forever. First of all, it helped me become the marketer I am today. It sharpened my skills. I learned from all the other members. I became much more serious about marketing. I got some of my biggest wealth-making ideas for our company. Eileen and I sat in those meetings for five or six years. Many times, right during the meeting itself, I would come up with some revolutionary idea that I never would have had had we not been sitting there, had we not made the commitment. First of all, it let us break away. Whenever you break away a little, it always helps you — to just get away from the day-to-day grind. It's a good experience to do that on a regular basis. We met four times a year, mostly in Phoenix, but sometimes in Cleveland and a few other cities. It was just an amazing experience for me personally to meet and get to know other marketers who were doing big things in their business.

There's a synergy created when people get together to help each other, and you can never pour your heart into helping someone else without helping yourself. Eileen and I tried to contribute to this group; we tried to encourage the other members, and tried to help them in their quest to make more money and build their businesses. The meeting was pretty simple. Dan would have some things to teach us in the beginning, usually, for a couple of hours; and then, just taking turns, we'd get up and make a little presentation that we'd prepared to teach the other members the best ideas that we'd discovered since the last time they'd seen us, just a few months earlier. Sometimes we would volunteer, sometimes Dan would hand-pick us. Nobody wanted to be the first, sometimes, and sometimes everybody wanted to be the first, just to get it over with — because you're under some scrutiny. You got up and you shared your best ideas, you told the other members what you were working on, and then they'd offer you suggestions, both positive and negative. There was some positive criticism, and there was some teasing. The group spurred us on, we spurred each other on, we gave each other a hard time. We tried to encourage each other to learn and do more and be more, and use some different secrets that the rest of the members were already using to make huge sums of money.

A lot of entrepreneurs just don't want to be a member of a group, and I can't blame them. We tend to be extremely independent; one of the reasons why we become entrepreneurs is so we can do it our way. We don't want to be part of anybody's team. We want to boldly carve our own paths, do our own thing, create our own destinies. I understand that, and I think it's a great thing. However, things happen when you're involved in a group of like-minded entrepreneurs, people who are trying to build their businesses just like you are, people who have the same goals you have, who are trying to do big things, who are equally as committed to becoming the very best that they can be so they can achieve everything that they dream of achieving. When you're around those kinds of people, they'll inspire you, they'll motivate you, they'll persuade you to do better and to step it up a notch or two.

That's one of the greatest things we got out of the situation — though admittedly, just to be candid with you, not everything was great. That happens to me at seminars all the time. I try to go to a few seminars ever year where I meet other marketers who are on their way up. Some of these people have been doing this a lot less time than I have, as far as years go. I've been doing this since 1988 — I've been self-employed since 1985 — and I'll run into people who've been self-employed just a few years. They're in the same type of business we're in, they've only been doing it a short time, and yet they're making huge money. It makes me jealous and envious in a positive way. Whoever told you jealousy and envy are wrong — well, they were right, and they were wrong. There's a good form of jealousy, a good form of being envious. You meet people who are on the same path you're on, doing big things, and they'll help you realize you can do more. It's one of the best things about being part of this group and other groups I'm a part of right now, like my One Hundred Million Dollar Roundtable group.

The friendships that you develop from people who are doing the same things you are can be tremendous. You'll get ideas you would never have developed on your own. There are all kinds of subtle variations here, and there's plenty to learn. You'll deepen your knowledge, you'll get outside your box, you'll broaden your horizons. There's a whole world out there, and the danger of being too absorbed in your own work is that you can become provincial in your thinking. You start getting locked into a certain way of doing and thinking about everything, and you actually close your world off. You've got to widen your view; you've got to meet new people and experience new things. Too many people attracted to direct-response marketing are what I call "hiding out from the world." One of the reasons they're attracted to direct-response or Internet marketing is because they want to be left alone. They're stubborn, independent, egotistical, and want to do everything through e-mail. They want to avoid a lot of the headaches and hassles that most business people have to go through, and that's one of the cool things about direct response. It can be a perfect business in terms of the things that most business people have to do, because you don't have to do them. You don't have to meet with people, you don't have to go face-to-face with anybody, and you don't have to do any personal selling.

But what happens is, you become so addicted to this kind of business that you close yourself off from the rest of the world.

You become socially retarded, difficult to work with. Other people around you are doing big things, and they're moving in big directions, and part of the reason they are is because they're affiliated with a group that's helping them do, become and have more. They get new opportunities they would have never been exposed to, new ideas they would have never thought of on their own. This is one of the greatest secrets I have to teach you. I understand what it is to be an entrepreneur: you want to do it all yourself. I understand how difficult it can be to be part of any group. Lots of entrepreneurs, including myself, can be anti-social. You spend hour after hour behind a computer screen, day in and day out. You get absorbed in your work; and ironically, you lose some of the skills that are essential in helping you make money!

Too many entrepreneurs are too independent; they're small-minded and paranoid. They're so worried about other people stealing their ideas that they don't want to share them. They're afraid of competition, they're afraid of opening themselves up to others, they're afraid of getting cheated or ripped off. I just want to say that you *do* have to open yourself up. Yes, you'll get lied to and cheated and misled; there are people out there who are total jerks. That's one of the reasons why when we find good joint-venture partners, we stick with them. We try to do everything we can to keep doing more and more business with the same good partners, because good partners are hard to find. Sometimes the only way to find them is to go through a bunch of bad partners.

I want to emphasize that being part of a group of like-minded entrepreneurs is a powerful experience. It can make you rich, you'll learn more, you'll sharpen those skills for making money and marketing, and you'll experience a deeper form of knowledge. You see, there's a difference between just knowing something and really understanding it at a deep level. When you're working with a group, you're sharing your ideas with them and they're sharing theirs with you; this will help you understand things at a core level most people never get to understand. It's hard to do that on your own; it's hard to pick all the stuff up in books. You'll discover new ideas; you'll find yourself going in new directions and into new areas you would have never gone into if you were just by yourself. You'll find yourself wanting to do more.

I've shared with you the good part about being jealous and envious. We can see all these other people out there, and they're just kicking butt. One of the benefits of being part of Dan Kennedy's group is that we were all supposed to be totally honest about the amount of money we were making; we were supposed to share numbers that normally you don't share with other people. Now, I'm sure some of the members did hold back; it's only natural. We didn't. We were just out there, very vulnerable, and the group responded to that; people saw that in us and they liked us. It was a good experience, and these are people that I respect. The helped me a lot at a very deep level.

Among them were people like Reed Hoisington, whom I'll never forget. My wife is a smoker, and at that time Reed was too, and so during meetings I would go out there to be with my wife while she was smoking her cigarettes, and there would be Reed. He's a seasoned veteran; he's got about ten years on me as far as business experience goes. He's already made millions, and he'd already made all the mistakes I was making at the time — so he saved me from some future mistakes, and he helped shape my thinking a little. Some of the things he told me while we were outside helped me a great deal.

You know, there are so many people who have already gone where you want to go. They've solved all the problems you're trying to solve, all those things you just get so overwhelmed with. They can help you out of those things; they can show you answers that you would never come up with on your own. They can support you, they can guide you, they can help you shape your thinking. That's what the members of this group did. I had a great opportunity to get to know Joe Polish, Kendra Murphy, Bill Glazier, Rory Fatt, Ron LeGrand... the list just goes on and on. Man, it was just such a positive and powerful experience in my life — and I recommend that you get involved in something like this. Too many people are locked up in their own little world, and there's such a big world out there for them, with all kinds of newer and better ways to make money that are faster and easier than you can imagine. By opening yourself up to a group of like-minded people moving in the same direction that you're moving, folks who've got the same high goals that you have, you're going to find things that you would never, ever have found on your own. You're going to discover shortcut secrets that they're using that will become your shortcut secrets. You're going to deepen your commitment to your business, and deepen your commitment to the development of your marketing skills.

Now, if you look in the dictionary under the word "power," you'll that see it means the ability to act. It's your capacity to take action. When you're trying to do everything by yourself and you're locked into your own little world, totally absorbed in your own thing and not realizing that there's a wider world out there, not trying to connect with others who are also moving in the direction you're moving in — well, you actually limit your ability to solve problems. You limit your ability to latch onto new things and strengthen your skills, and you become limited. One of the ways you get more power is by networking with other people. One of the reasons I love going to seminars has nothing to do with the stuff they're teaching. Now, every once in a while, I'll pay very close attention to what a speaker at one of these seminars is saying, and I do take notes. Some sessions are more important to me; but mostly what I'm doing is hanging out in the hallways, meeting people who are on their way up. I love that more than anything else. I love the look in the eyes of a newcomer who's ambitious and excited about the business, because it helps me connect with that part of me that was the same, back when it was new and fresh. It's a great experience, because there's a chemistry here that we all have as people; and if you get it right, you can have a lot of fun and you can make a lot of money.

Of course, if you get it wrong, it ends up being a waste of time for you and everybody else. Other people had an opportunity to join Dan Kennedy's Platinum Group. Remember, Dan had the first meeting where a whole bunch of people showed up, and many of them joined the group — but some didn't. We had other members who came in and out; they were just in it for a year, and then they were gone. They thought they were too busy to be part of the group. They saw the group as something that would cost them money rather than *make* them money. Now, Eileen and I spent about $10,000 a year to belong to this group — it costs more now — and that included the travel expenses. We thought it was kind of pricey, at first. But at the same time, there was something inside us that told us it would be good for us, and it turned out we were right. We made literally millions of dollars because of the new ideas and directions we got from our participation.

Now, this is going to sound bad, but it's the truth, so I might as well tell. As part of our commitment to the group, I was forced to sit there in those meetings for two or two and a half days. Now, if you knew me, you'd know that I'm energetic. I can't sit down, I can't stand still, I've always got to be moving. I'm just that way; maybe I've got attention deficit disorder, I don't know. I just know that I constantly have to move, and I can't stand it when I'm standing still. Even when I'm writing copy, I'm walking around with legal pads; I write and walk at the same time. That's how I write some of my best sales letters.

Well, when you're part of something like the Platinum Group, you have to behave a certain way. During those meetings, while I was trying to be a good member and contribute to the group, I was forced to sit there and be still. It drove me crazy. I was always scribbling away on my legal pads, and I'm sure the other members of the group thought I was just taking notes. But here's what was really happening: I was coming up with all kinds of ideas for making money. Some of them produced millions and millions of dollars for us in a short time.

So find yourself a great group of people to hang around with — people who are trying to do big things, who can coach you and help you learn how to dream bigger yourself. Most of the folks you know aren't going for their dreams; they're not doing big things. They're coasting through life, asking for very little. They're the employees of the world, working only for money or security. Even if they're attracted to business, too often they just want to do little businesses in tiny markets. If you want to get rich, you need to find a better group of people than these to work with. You don't have to let all those other people go; they provide certain levels of support and guidance, but you've *really* got to be around people doing big things with their lives. You've got to meet with them, and get to know them over a long period — and you *can* do this. There's no excuse not to. There are plenty of seminars you can attend. Once you get involved, you'll realize that there are lots of shortcuts these people can point out for you. As a member of the right group, you really can learn more and sharpen your skills, and experience a deeper form of knowledge and create all kinds of new ideas that can help you make huge sums of money for the rest of your life. As you do, you can experience the tremendous satisfaction and joy of getting to know other people — good people who are doing the things you want to do.

SECRET TWENTY-THREE:

Find the Right Joint-Venture Partners

The twenty-third secret that made us millions of dollars is our joint-venture relationships with other marketers. We see so many entrepreneurs trying to do it all on their own; they never open themselves up to the resources available through other people. You always hear that the secret to getting rich is using OPM, "Other Peoples' Money." But it's also using OPR, "Other Peoples' Resources." There's plenty of help available to you; and there are millions of dollars just waiting for you if you'll simply do joint ventures, as we've done. In this chapter, I'm going to show you how simple it really is.

Before I go any further, I want to emphasize, again, that you need to shed that "Entrepreneur Hero Myth," the idea that you can go out there and do it all on your own. Nobody gets rich by themselves; that's one of the biggest misconceptions out there. Study those people who supposedly made it big alone, and you'll see that there are always plenty of folks behind the scenes, making it all happen for them. I want to convince you of this; I want you to see it, and catch the vision that all the personal help, support, guidance and secrets you need in order to make millions of dollars are out there, right now. All you have to do is find joint-venture partners who have the things you don't, and help them while they help you. It's so simple; in fact, it's too simple for most people. They just never get it, and that's their loss — and your gain.

THE BLUE JEANS MILLIONAIRE!

Nobody ever gets rich by themselves, and other people will gladly help you make money if you can help them get something that they need. You joint-venture so you can make more money faster and easier. That's one of the main benefits. Another is that you'll discover things during a joint venture that you would never have discovered on your own. You'll make money that was unavailable to you before. One of the big reasons why people don't joint-venture is because they don't understand that. They're small thinkers. They think a joint-venture will cost them money, and they don't want to share money with other people. But if you do it right, the money you create with your joint-venture partner is brand new money. Sure, you split it with your partner, but it's income you wouldn't have made without them. Small-minded people will never understand that, and again, that's their loss and your gain.

Here's how easy it is: in most cases, you do absolutely nothing but lend your endorsement. You provide a list of customers, and you're providing your credibility along with it. You've got an established relationship with the people buying from you, and now your joint-venture comes along and they put together all the promotional materials, they develop the products and services, they do all of the customer service work — and you collect 50% of the profits. So think about that; this is money for nothing! Now, there's your endorsement, of course, so if your joint-venture partners screw your customers, it's going to reflect badly on you. But even those deals can be fixed.

I'm not going to pretend that some joint ventures don't turn out negative. It happens. We've had joint-venture partners who have screwed over our customers, and we didn't know it until later; in fact, we had that happen recently. We brought in a new speaker for a seminar, and we checked him out as much as we could. Then he ends up screwing our customers by not giving them what he promised. There's a class-action lawsuit against him right now; we've apologized profusely to the customers who did business with him, and they've accepted our apology. They know it's not our fault. So yes, one of the reasons why people don't joint venture is, they're afraid of getting ripped off; they're afraid that some joint venture partners are going to withhold money that should be theirs, or they're going to end up cheating the customers, as what happened to us. Out of all the joint-venture deals we've done, that's the only time it's really happened. I don't want to paint an unrealistic picture; we've had so many positive experiences with joint-venture partners, and only one terrible negative experience, and then a couple that were fairly unpleasant. Some people you can work with, some people you can't.

Now, what's the perfect joint-venture? It's pretty simple, really — despite the fact that some people seem to want to make it hard. You've got to look at joint venturing for what it really is. It's a partnership; it's just two people getting together who want to do business together. That's the way it was with Russ von Hoelscher and us back in the beginning. He was our first joint-venture partner; he liked us, and we liked him. He started out being our consultant; the same is true of some of our other joint-venture partners. We got to like them, they got to like us, and we started doing some deals together. No big deal. With Russ, it was a seminar; then we put together our *$2,500 Weekend* program, and later he helped us develop other information products.

After every single deal that we did with Russ, we wanted to do more. We're talking about a friendship here; we're talking about all the best that business and life has to offer — doing business with people you respect and appreciate, people who appreciate you. There's a mutual friendship and kinship, and it's just about good, close personal relationships. It starts out, essentially, because you have something they want; that could be a mailing list of people who trust you, it could be a hot-selling product, service or promotion, it could be technical know-how, it could be some type of experience they lack, it could be certain systems you have in place, or it could be money or resources. You've got something they want and they've got something you want, or something you lack, or something you value greatly. It could just be talent and energy, or even just time.

Just to give you a an example of how loosely these things can be structured: one of the things I love to do is find people on their way up, people who are extremely ambitious, who are very smart, who have all those qualities I had 20 years ago. Every once in a while you can find one of these people, and I have; I have some relationships going right now with people I've found on their way up. All they're looking for is an opportunity, but they're willing to work their butts off; they're willing to sacrifice long hours. They have a respect for us experienced entrepreneurs, because we've been around for so long and we've done so many things. Now they're looking for any kind of deal they can do with us, and they say "Yes" to everything we ask them to do, and they're helping us with a lot of our projects. We're just doing business together, that's all. That's all a joint-venture is. It's just people coming together to do business. When you put together the things you have that they want with the things they have that *you* want, the result can be a huge explosion of wealth. We've made millions of the easiest dollars in the world through these joint-venture relationships. They're so powerful.

I told you about Russ von Hoelscher, who was our first joint-venture partner. Russ helped us get into seminars; he helped us develop information products. He made me want to be a good copywriter. He used to come to our house; we'd pay him $2,500 for the weekend, and basically he helped us with all our promotions. He wrote the copy, and I admired his ability to do that so much. I would watch him do this; he'd be working away, and I'd be feeding him ideas and stuff, and we'd be talking things through. But I watched him, and there was a voice in my head, every single time, that said, "God, I'd love to be able to do that too." This was the late 1980s/early 1990s. Russ would leave, we would typeset all the sales copy that he'd written and send it on out — and suddenly the cash register would start ringing, and we'd start making huge sums of money. Yeah, we paid him $2,500 for the weekend, but the copy he wrote at our kitchen table produced a lot of money for us, and that woke me up. But, I wonder: what if Russ hadn't been there? What if I would have tried to do it all on my own?

That's one of the great things about joint-venture relationships: You connect with people who have already achieved the things you want, or who are on the same path you're on. And then, when you do achieve some success, you look for other people on their way up. You catch them before they become difficult to work with, before they have a whole battery of people who protect them and protect their time, so that you can't even get your phone calls returned. Unfortunately, that's a sad fact in my life, too. I have a strong desire to help people, and yet I have gatekeepers; and very often, the gates are locked. Hey, there's only so much time in a day; you've got to keep your focus where it's needed, where it's going to make you the most money.

The first joint-venture deal that made us millions of dollars was with Russ. Then, Alan Bechtold came along, and we made $12 million in total sales within a handful of years; the money just came rolling in. He had something that we needed desperately, which was technical know-how. Alan's an electronic marketer. We first got involved in computer bulletin boards back in the early 1990s, showing people how to make money with these bulletin boards. Then the Internet came along, and it absolutely exploded with growth. We were right there in the beginning, because we had a true expert who was helping us every step of the way. If we'd tried to do this on our own, we would never have made that $12 million, ever. It would never have become a reality — except for the fact that we had an expert, somebody who was deeply committed, somebody who was capable and competent, who had all the expertise. Alan had all of that. He'd been marketing online since 1983, back when the Internet was only available to techno geeks with inch-thick glasses and the bow ties and pocket protectors. Alan is anything but a nerd, but he *was* one of the very first electronic marketers, and when the Internet came along he was one of the few people capable and competent enough to carry us through.

I already told you that Russ got us into seminars. If it weren't for him, we would have never done our first seminar. We were absolutely terrified; we were frozen in terror, in fact. We were so scared on September 22, 1990, when we had our first seminar, that Eileen and I wouldn't even get up to speak to the crowd. We were just too insecure, too frightened of our own shadows. But thank goodness for Russ; we got through it. Then, a couple of years later, we decided to have a series of small seminars, where we brought in just a small group, and even *those* scared us. If it weren't for joint-venture partners like Russ, we would have never gotten into seminars. Alan got us into the websites and the Internet. Russ taught us how to develop information products, and that has been so powerful for us — to develop these products that reach out to the customers, to express ideas that really can help them get what they want, and to build relationships with people. When you strive to help them, people appreciate it; they respect you. It's helped us develop these solid relationships that we have with our customers. People listen to us on these programs, they come to our seminars, and they come to our tele-seminars, which Dan Kennedy got us started with. When Eileen and I first used Dan as a consultant back in 1993, he told us about tele-seminars —

and we had one immediately.

These are the things that have helped us make millions of dollars that we would never have made otherwise, had we not had these relationships with people who had already figured out the things we needed to figure out. They had the ideas we lacked. All we had was the ambition; we were willing to do whatever it took. But thank God for our joint-venture partners, because they're the ones who helped us to do these things.

Don Bice got us into e-books and mini-websites back in the late-1990s that made us millions of dollars, and I think we paid Don maybe a couple of thousand dollars, maybe not even that much, for just a few hours of his time. We recorded it, transcribed it, and in those three hours he gave us secrets that made us millions of dollars. We would never have had that without him. He helped us get through it all. Chris Lakey — if it weren't for him, there would have been no Mall of the World. That's one of the greatest things that we've developed so far; it lets people sell more than a million of the hottest-selling, in-demand products on the Internet. It was a major undertaking, and if it weren't for Chris, it never would have happened. Jeff Gardner got us involved in Internet advertising, and Eric Bechtold got us into advertising co-ops. Russ got us involved in eBay, a whole new area for us, and he also got us into real estate. There's a whole marketplace out there of people who are making, collectively, hundreds of millions of dollars, helping other people get involved in real estate. It's very technical, very specialized; it's something where I would have thought, "There's no way we could ever do it." But Russ showed us how. He helped us through the fear, that and being involved with my One Hundred Million Dollar Roundtable group, as I've tried to express to you earlier in this book.

There are so many things that we've done as a group that I would never have done on my own — and so much money that we've been able to generate because we're working together. We're helping to strengthen each other, we're helping to take each other in new directions — and unless you're totally unlike me, you need all the help you can get. Even if you're somebody who doesn't have the same kinds of insecurity issues that I've had all my life, even if you're a totally confident person who's 100% secure in yourself, you can still benefit from the help other people can give you. There are so many ideas out there you could be tapping into, if you just had a group of people to joint-venture with.

Now, remember, this doesn't have to be that complicated; here are some easy joint-venture relationships for you. The easiest ones are when you have a mailing list and they have a product or service; you sell their product or service to your mailing list, and you split the profits down the middle. That's so easy and simple. You don't need a contract; you agree to do it, and you just do it. Number Two, you have a seminar, your partners come and they sell their products or services to your customers, and you split the profits. There's nothing complicated about that. You don't need a joint-venture program to tap into that deal, and yet people make millions of dollars with that secret alone.

Here's a third idea, and this is the one I love the most; out of all my joint-venture deals, I get the most pleasure from this one, and I wonder why more people don't use it. There are plenty of people out there who *are* — that's how we got the idea — but why more people don't tap into it is beyond me. Here it is: Simply work with a group. It could be one other person, it could be 10 people — we've had as many as 14 and 15 people involved in some of these projects, where we all come together to co-create or jointly create a product, and then we jointly promote it to our individual customer groups, so we keep all the money ourselves. We've used this one secret to produce hundreds of information products, and when I say hundreds, I'm not just exaggerating. We've done literally hundreds of information products where all we do is get together on the telephone and record the phone call. These are programs where once we produce them, we're free to sell them to our own customer groups in any way we want to, and we keep 100% of the money, so you don't have to worry about royalties and such.

Lots of people just don't do joint ventures because they're cheapskates and small thinkers. Well, here's a joint-venture deal where you can keep it all. We've not only created product together, but we've also created sales material together, where we get together and one person will be responsible for loosely creating some raw sales material, and the rest of the group will work on it. We've produced some very powerful sales letters that have yielded millions of dollars in total revenue that way. There's a synergy at play when you're working with capable, competent, talented people who have the appropriate experience and knowledge. The ideas all of you come up with together are far greater than anything you'd come up with on your own, and therefore the revenue is bigger than it would otherwise be. That's money you create together. Joint ventures don't cost you money — they *make* you money. You and your partner are baking a bigger pie, so there are bigger pieces of the pie for everyone to enjoy. It's brand new money. That's an interesting concept that small thinkers will never get, and it's one reason they don't joint-venture more. The other reason is that they're fearful. They're afraid of competition, they're afraid of getting ripped off; and yes, it's true. Bad things do happen sometimes.

One of Dan Kennedy's rules is to never joint-venture with anyone unless they can give him several references they've joint-ventured with successfully in the past. It's a good rule of thumb, one I should follow more myself — but of course somebody has to be the first one out on the dance floor, too. And sometimes references don't mean a damned thing. This partner who ripped us off a few years ago in our seminar had references. His references turned out to be nothing more than shills. It just goes to show that you can't escape all problems. There's always some risk involved here.

Recently, we've been working in this new area of real estate, so we're interviewing all these real-estate experts and creating products based on those interviews. I got ahold of a guy in Florida, because we sent out some mailings to some of the big, heavy hitters in the business, and different people who have websites on the Internet that we really like. There was just something wrong with the deal. I just didn't like him; I was talking to him and trying to work things, and the entire time I was talking to him, I was thinking in the back of my mind, "This guy is just like my brother-in-law." I just couldn't get that out of my head. My brother-in-law's a good guy, but he's a pain-in-the-ass to work with, and I would never want to work with him.

There has to be a certain chemistry there. Sometimes the only way to find good partners is to go through a lot of deals until you find the right few. One of the reasons you keep doing business with the same partners is because you find people you can trust, people who are competent, people who won't let you down. They watch your back and you watch theirs, and that mutual friendship just spurs it all on. It makes you want to do more with the people that you've done successful deals with in the past. So, I think it's important to look for long-term joint-venture partners. You're not always going to find them, but you should think long-term. Find the best people you can, try to keep doing repeat business with them, and after every single venture you ask your partner, "What can we do next?"

The more you trust them and the more they trust you, the more both of you are able to let down your guards, get rid of all that paranoia crap, and stop worrying about getting ripped off.

Secret Twenty-Three: Find the Right Joint-Venture Partners

You're able to share more freely, and there's great synergy that comes through all of this — great ideas that none of you would have ever thought of had you not had that joint-venture relationship, had you not had that friendship. You watching each others' backs; you're helping each other build your businesses. This is just such a powerful thing, and I want you to tap into it. When we meet at our free workshop, I'll stress to you just how important this is — especially if you're a person who suffers from some of the same challenges I've suffered, especially insecurity.

I'm not ashamed of it now, because I've worked through it. The fact is that for some reason, I was always an insecure child; I had issues, particularly feelings of low self-worth. It's taken a tremendous amount of work for me to get through all that crap, and I'm still dealing with some of it to this day. Maybe I'll be dealing with it for the rest of my life — but I certainly don't let it stop me, and my joint-venture relationships with these other people have helped me to get past some of it. Any time you're trying to take on new things, especially if they're big things, you're going to deal with all kinds of fear, anxiety, and worry, unless you're a better person than I or you don't suffer from insecurity at all. If that's the case, then my hat's off to you. I don't understand what it's like, but I'm always happy to meet people who have natural confidence in themselves. As for me, it's been a slow train coming. My joint-venture partners have been there every step of the way. Every time we look at a whole new area filled with more questions than answers, filled with all kinds of uncertainties, filled with new skills and knowledge that has to be developed, where we have to start almost from scratch — they're there.

Together we go through some of the bumbling around in the dark, when we're looking for the light switch and trying to figure everything out. There's the confusion and stress that comes from entering new areas that you really don't know much about. You only have the vaguest ideas about how you're going to put it all together, and, man, every step of the way, as we've gone through that, we've had a team we've done it with. I don't think that makes us worse people. In fact, I think that's one of the reasons why small businesspeople stay small. They want to do everything on their own, and they're afraid to get help; they're afraid to reach out to other people, and I'm here to tell you that there are plenty of people out there who *want* to reach out to you. They're looking for things you have. Even if you don't have any money or experience; there are plenty of people like me who are looking for people with talent, even if that talent is undeveloped. They're looking for people who have ambition, hunger, drive — and so I would encourage you to put together a list of people you want to joint-venture with. I call mine my hit list, and I've talked about the importance of it. Then, once every month or every quarter, send them something you're doing: a report, a book, a personal note. Ask them for ways you might be able to help them. Give them one of your products and say, "Look, if you're looking for a free bonus, use this." Extend your hand to people, without asking them for anything in return. The result: You're going to separate yourself from everybody else, just because you've asked what you can do for *them*. Your phone will ring. You'll get through to people, because of your unique approach.

Most everybody else just wants something from these people. It's always, "What can you give me, what can you do for me?" When you achieve some success and you get up there and people know about you, your whole life is filled with people who want something from you. When you run into somebody who's offering you something at no cost with no strings attached, asking how they can serve you, how they can contribute to your projects and your business — well, those people are going to stand out head and shoulders over everybody else. If you're the guy trying to help, as you *should* be, people are going to come to you, they're going to be attracted to you; and *that's* how to find these joint-venture relationships. All it takes is just a few joint-venture partners to do a few different projects, and you could put millions of dollars in your pocket.

The money is out there for you, right now, and joint venturing is the way to get it. It's the fastest, easiest, and simplest money that you'll ever make in your life, so I would encourage you to get started with this, to think it through very clearly. From the get-go, if you'll just use joint venturing as part of your overall strategy, you'll make more money — but you'll also achieve a level of satisfaction and joy that comes from building relationships with people, that enriches their lives and yours, and helps all of you make huge sums of money that would never have been otherwise available to you.

SECRET TWENTY-FOUR:
Focus Totally on Your Marketing

The twenty-fourth secret we used to make millions of dollars is called "Operation Money Suck." Now, I didn't coin that phrase; it came from a brilliant marketer and copywriter named John Carlton. He's the one that first came up with the idea, and introduced me to it. Operation Money Suck. It's such a simple idea, and yet most business people just don't do it. If you will, you'll make huge sums of money. This really is part of the secret to getting rich, and just like many of the ideas that I'm sharing with you, it's so simple that it's easy to overlook. It's easy to complicate things, and I'm telling you, it's not that complicated. Of course, the more money you get, the more complicated things can be. It's like chess. There are only six basic chess pieces, and each one can only move so many different directions. When my son Chris first taught me how to play chess, he was nine or ten years old. We sat down, and in an hour and a half we were playing chess together. It's no big deal to learn to play chess.

The big deal is how you study that game. I had a friend, Gayland Bohler, who was a chess master. His IQ was off the charts; Gayland could have been a Mensa member, but he was too independent for that. All he did was study the game of chess. He was writing this huge manual, and he kept a chessboard or two around his house all the time, and he would play chess with himself. The guy had dedicated a large part of his energy to it,

273

and his focus was wrapped around this game of chess — and yet it's a simple game, ultimately. There are all kinds of intricacies, and many, many different strategies, and the good players always think three or four moves ahead. Good players can whip you in an instant if you're a novice. Well, that's exactly the way it is with this game of marketing. It's easy to start out with, and you can master it; you can become so good at playing it that millions of dollars come to you automatically after you've developed some skills.

There's a saying that marketing takes a day to learn and a lifetime to master, because you can constantly learn new things about it. You'll never know it all, and yet the basics are simple; I've covered all of them at least four or five times so far in this book, and I'll cover them again. I get criticized a lot for being redundant; and yet, I feel that it's absolutely necessary to keep coming back to the basics, because things *do* get confusing. They get frustrating, they get challenging; and you always have to realize, as difficult as it may be at times, that the more money you want to make, the more difficult it's going to be. But you always go back to the basics, and you always remember just how simple and how easy it can be when you get back to the root of it all.

Operation Money Suck is a very basic idea, one that you should make part of your personal philosophy, and here it is: you simply stay totally focused on the things that bring you the most money. That's exactly what Eileen and I did. I became a marketing expert; marketing became my top priority, and it was all that I thought about. I lost many years of my life totally obsessed with becoming a great marketer, and I realize that now. Some people talk about the lost years; people who become alcoholics and drug addicts lose large periods of their time in this fog, this drug-induced coma that they put themselves into. Well, see, that's the way it is with me; I absolutely lost years of my life, which went by so fast because I became so absorbed in my work. I became so focused on becoming a marketer to the point of total obsession. I'm not trying to say that that's a good thing; I just want to say that one of the secrets to our success is that I fell in love with all of the aspects of marketing, which is simply getting and keeping customers — that's it. Remember that no matter how difficult it gets the most important thing is getting and keeping customers. I continue to ask myself even now, "How can we attract and retain more customers?" That question lives inside me all the time; it's part of who I am.

We find whatever it is that we look for in life, wherever our focus is. If you go out tomorrow and buy a brand new Lincoln Continental, then you're going to start seeing Lincolns everywhere. You're not really seeing them right now, even when you're being passed by them every day on the highway. There are Lincolns everywhere; Eileen and I have one ourselves, and I see them all over now. Whatever kind of car you drive or whatever you're interested in the very most, that's where your awareness tends to go. So just home in on this one burning question: "How do I retain and attract more customers?" As part of that, ask yourself, "Where's my next dollar coming from? What new promotions are people really interested in my marketplace? What's hot right now?"

Recently eBay became very, very hot, and by the time you read this book it may be completely cold. There might come a time when you read this and wonder, "What the hell was eBay?" Well, at the time that I'm doing this it's very, very hot; it's in all the magazines, in the newspapers, on TV. The Internet was that way in the mid-1990s too. When the Internet first came on the scene, it absolutely exploded — it was on every TV program, every news program, in every magazine, in every newspaper. There was just such a buzz. So many people were so excited about this thing, and it created such a stir that we made literally millions of dollars by just tapping into it. We were totally focused. We knew that this was something hot. We knew that we could take all the things we were doing and blend them with this hot thing that was already in the news, that was so exciting to people. We found that just by adding Internet to anything that we did, sales instantly bumped up 30 to 40% or more. We had conversion rates that were so phenomenal — from taking a group of leads and then converting them over to some of the websites we did on the Internet — that when we told seasoned veterans what we were doing, they actually thought we were lying to them. Like the big fish story: "Oh man! You should have seen the one that got away. Wish I would have had a camera with me before we ate that fish!" Yeah, right. That's how these seasoned marketing guys were with us. We were telling them, "We're converting over 50% of our leads to $1,000 sales!" and people were going, "Bull, you're lying to us, you know you're not doing that, nobody converts 50% of their leads." Well, we were doing it. We were doing it because it was hot.

So Operation Money Suck is about always looking for those things that are hot, and putting your total focus on what's going to be the next deal. Where's the next deal going to come from? That's how I spend my lost years, just totally absorbed in learning how to become a marketer and develop product. Eileen made it possible for me to stay focused on the marketing because she ran the business for the first fourteen years. She did a phenomenal job; she's a great manager, she makes it look easy, and I focused all my time on product development. I'm always looking for the next exciting thing, developing the products, and writing advertising copy — learning the secrets, learning the art of it, the skill. It really is a skill more than anything else. I've thought of writing copy as an art; and I think it's an art form the same way selling is an art form. Selling is basically just transferring your emotions. I feel so strong about something that when I communicate it to you, because you're open and receptive and interested, you can't help but feel the way that I'm feeling. You pick up on my emotions; you get excited about it because I'm excited about it. You start believing in it very strongly, because you accept my beliefs and I transfer my emotions to you. That's what selling is, or at least one strong definition of it: learning how to become a great marketer, staying focused on this Operation Money Suck, and finding ways to stay totally focused on all the things that bring you the most money. You're going to have to develop some of these skills. You're going to have to spend your time learning how to do these things, and thinking and dreaming and planning and scheming about newer and better ways to compete in your marketplace. It's fun.

Most business people aren't doing this; they're doing what I call "putting out the brushfires" in their business. They believe in this whole Puritan ethic of hard work; I don't know where it comes from, and I don't mean to be sacrilegious here, but most businesspeople have bought into a lie. And here it is: "Just be the first one to get there in the morning, and be the last one to leave at night." You've heard that before. They go into their businesses every day and try to wear all the hats. They spend their whole day putting out brushfires, because in business there's always something to distract you. There's always some problem, or somebody who needs help with this or that. Sometimes when I have to go into the company offices, I try to escape as fast as I can. I don't want to say hi to anybody, because then somebody's going to ask me, "What's your opinion about this?" or "What do I do about that?"

Because I really care deeply, because I'm committed to the business, naturally I'll spend five minutes with this person, fifteen minutes with that person, thirty minutes with that person; then there's this problem, there's that problem, and pretty soon three or four hours have gone by. I've gotten sucked into this huge vortex, all my energy is drained, and I haven't been staying focused on the few things I need to stay focused on that are going to bring in the most money for our company. That's what you need to do. You need to be the architect of your business; you need to work *on* it and not necessarily *in* it. Spend your time working on new promotions, new campaigns, and let somebody else manage the whole thing. This occurred naturally for the first fourteen years of our business. Eileen ran it; she's a great manager, she put her team together, and if it weren't for her I would have ran them all off a million times, because I didn't have the necessary maturity and the patience. I expected more out of them than they were able to deliver. It was all my fault.

She was a good manager, somebody who can work with people. Entrepreneurs tend to be lousy managers. Most are great at doing things that bring in the money, but they're not great at all the things it takes to keep the money or retain customers. We love the hunt; we love the chase; we love new ideas and all the action, and the excitement of moving from this field to that field, and what's next and what can we do now. That's the thrill of being an entrepreneur, and it's great. It's the most wonderful thing in the world. But managers tend to be people who have more common sense; they're more stable; they're more mature. Usually, they're focused on the day-to-day part of the business and on building systems. Eileen was a great manager. All those years I watched her do it, I always thought to myself, "I can do a better job." First of all, she didn't put in the kind of hours I thought it took to be a good manager. I was very critical, sometimes right to her face. She would go in and spend a few hours a week in the office, and that's it. She had key people she worked with, and they were *her* managers, and then those key people worked with everybody else in the company. Whenever problems occurred, she was right there on top of them. She has a lot of common sense and she's a natural leader. She's a very stable person, very mature; and I tend to be the exact opposite. I'm driven by my emotions. I'm impulsive; I'm immature. I tend to be a loose wire sometimes, or a loose cannon, and I'm very passionate about the company. I love what we do; this is our baby. So for years I'd watch her go in and work a few hours a week and come home, and of course she had other things she was interested in. She's more normal and a lot saner than I am. I just always thought, "Man! I could do a better job of running the company than you!" and so when she stepped down because of health reasons, I stepped up, and now I'm the president and the CEO.

My God! All those years I thought, "By God, I'm going to run that company, and I'm going to do this and do that," and what did I do? I ended up almost blowing the whole company up! Two and a half years later, I almost drove the company into bankruptcy, and I'm trying to help you to *not* make these same mistakes. I've got a good general manager now. The best ones don't cost you money: they make you money. Whatever it is you pay them, they make up for it in all the ways they help you squeeze more profits out of the business; they keep it running better, they help you retain customers. See, that's what a good stable staff of employees does when they're well trained, a system's in place, and there's good communication. You've got processes for weeding out the bad ones and rewarding the good ones and keeping them there, and it's good for customer service.

A lot of entrepreneurs just don't realize that. They want to make the most money, but they look at employees as a cost rather than an investment. They're always looking for ways to cut back, and they usually look at the employees first. Many entrepreneurs are resentful of employees, because they don't realize that employees are different from us. This isn't a criticism of employees, because we all need them in our businesses. Employees tend to be the salt of the earth, but they're not necessarily in it for the same reasons that we are. You can't expect them to ever feel the way about the business that you feel about it. You can't expect them to work as hard as you. They're interested in doing a good job, enjoying their work, getting a steady paycheck, and they have lives outside of the company, in most cases. They are the ones who don't tend to create problems.

A good manager is worth his or her weight in gold. Find somebody to take care of that position, and then you can perform Operation Money Suck, which is to stay totally focused on the marketing. Let other people do everything else; become a marketing expert, read and study, and think about this fascinating subject. It's so exciting. If you really think about the basics that tie every business together, you'll see that it's all about marketing. It's attracting new customers who are most likely to become the best customers, and then all the things you do to keep them coming back to you for years, rather than going to all your competitors and doing business with them. It's so simple and yet it's such a fascinating subject, because there are amazing intricacies here. It's both easy and complex — and what I would like for you to do is think about it as a game.

I love this great quote from the late, great Robert DeRopp: "Seek above all else a game worth playing and play the game as if your entire life and sanity depended on it, for it does." Well, I think making money is the greatest game on earth. Marketing is the way you play the game. There are all kinds of ways to attract new customers; there are all kinds of ways to keep those old customers coming back. You've got to stay open, you've got to stay receptive; you've got to be willing to put in the time, pay the price, learn some of the skills necessary, some of the knowledge you need to know. To do that, find good people to run the day-to-day part of the business for you, the stable part of the business, and don't be afraid to pay these people good money, because a good manager is not going to cost you money — they're going to *make* you money. Most entrepreneurs are lousy managers, and even if you have the skills necessary to be one, there are things you can do that will help produce more revenue than managing. So even if you *can* manage, that doesn't mean you *should*. That's what Operation Money Suck is all about. Your entire focus should be on making more sales and more profits, period. I'm looking forward to meeting with you face-to-face and helping you to learn how to do all this so you can make a great deal of money.

I want you to experience the joy and satisfaction that comes from working on your business, not in it. It really is fun and it's creative; it's work, and yet it's the kind of work that gives you a deep level of pride and satisfaction, and makes you millions and millions of dollars.

SECRET TWENTY-FIVE:

The People You Work With Make All the Difference

The twenty-fifth secret that made us millions of dollars is surrounding ourselves with the very best people we could find. These people made us a ton of money; but also, and this is the key point here, they enriched our lives in so many other ways beyond the money. It's about a lot more than just the money. It's about the enjoyment that you get from working with people you care about and respect; it's the great feelings from having people in your life who are moving in the same direction you're moving in, people who are equally as passionate and committed as you. It's other entrepreneurs who really understand you, and people who understand your business because they've been working with you year after year. It's other people who are looking out for you while you're looking out for them, and it's these relationships that can make you millions of dollars; but also, and I think this is just as important, they can give you a tremendous amount of personal joy and satisfaction. You're going to find yourself doing and becoming more because of the people you surround yourself with.

A business is a lifestyle, and so having people in your life that you're working with, where they're part of your business and you're part of theirs, is a great thing. I know it's been a recurring theme throughout this program, but it's worth talking about again, and there's more to tell you about this whole subject. It's very important, and I hope you'll get it, because a lot of people don't. *You're always going to do more because certain people are there in your life and in your business.* You're going to move in directions that you wouldn't have explored had it not been for these people. You're going to discover many new things through the synergy of working with them that you would have never have discovered otherwise; and it's these relationships, which never show up on a balance sheet, that will become your greatest assets.

Which is why so many people don't talk about this — they don't understand it. They look at people as a cost, not as an investment. They're always looking for ways to cut costs instead of adding to the investment. Look, we've made millions by working with certain groups of people. I've talked about that repeatedly in this book, and I can't stress it enough. We've done everything possible to find good, capable, competent, talented employees, joint-venture partners, suppliers; and then lawyers and accountants, bankers, consultants and other professionals. We've done everything possible to find and hang on to the very best of these people. They've ended up making us a lot of money rather than costing us money, and that has a lot to do with our attitude towards them.

When you find the right people, do everything possible to treat them with the respect they deserve. Overlook their minor faults, because people will always let you down — just like you're going to let other people down, too. There's no way around that, and one of the reasons why more people don't use these principles is because they can't work with other people. They're too demanding; they expect too much from them, or they're just jerks. I hate to say this, because I don't want to offend anybody, but sometimes the things that it takes to become a great entrepreneur, the skills or the abilities or the character traits, are the very things that cause us to not cash in with principles like Number 25 here. We're stubborn, we're independent, we're power-trippers, we're control freaks, we're people who love to do everything our own way. That's why we become self-employed in the first place: so we can tell our boss to take that job and shove it, and so we can have all the freedom and independence to build our own little kingdoms. Sometimes that makes for people who are very anti-social; they're rude, obnoxious, extremely opinionated, very stubborn, independent. They're not team players. This has been a really hard road for me, and it may be a hard road for you; but I'm telling you, it's also the very best thing you can do. Hindsight has given me 20/20 vision here.

There's another side to this that's very important. It's not just about using other people's talents and resources; there's what I call "the emotional side." I work with people on a daily basis whom I care about very deeply. I even love some of them, and I feel connected to them at a deep level. In some cases, I've worked with them for years; and even with those I haven't, there's a connection there, and I honestly believe they feel the same way about me. I know that if something bad were to happen to them tomorrow, I would be completely devastated. That's how I know how much I care about them, and I'd like to think they feel the same way — though that's beyond my control. In any case, those strong feelings I feel for them have helped me in many ways. I feel committed to these people and I want to do more; I want to work harder. I take my work more seriously, I'm trying to contribute to them, and they're trying to contribute to me. I end up trying to do many things to help them, just like I'm trying to help you right now with this book. I'm going to end up doing and becoming more through working with all of you who invest in this book, just by trying to do everything I can to help you. This is how it is with all my joint-venture partners. It's how it is with my suppliers and all the people that I work with; I'm constantly trying to do more to help them and to contribute to their businesses. I'm sure that I fail as often as I succeed, but at least I'm trying.

Hindsight is 20/20. When I look back at the early years, I know that it's my relationship with my wife Eileen that was (and still is) a major influence on my success. Eileen has inspired me. She ran the company the first 14 years as we built this thing together; it was our baby. We started it from Day One, and we struggled along. The business benefited from our marriage, and our marriage benefited from the business, and not everyone can or should work with their spouse — but here's the thing. I feel so sorry for people who aren't getting the support from their spouses that they need. Before I met Eileen, I was with another woman for a few years, and she ran down every moneymaking idea I had. She just tore them to pieces; she was extremely unsupportive, very negative, very critical, very angry with me for the few things I did in the beginning that absolutely bombed. She was just so unsupportive; and I run into people like that all the time.

A lot of my very best clients have spouses who are unsupportive, who are dream-killers. Now, I'm not trying to make this a man-woman thing; there are plenty of female entrepreneurs who are married to guys who are unsupportive. But traditionally it's a man who shows up at our seminars, and he's open and receptive and there to learn; and his spouse has her arms crossed the whole time. She's got a scowl on her face; she wishes he would give up his dreams to make a lot of money. I understand this from a personal perspective. When I was with that woman, I was going from sales job to sales job, and eventually I went to work for this company whose CEO produced an informational tape a lot like the products I do now. Well, on that tape he said something that altered the course of my life. This is something that I would never say to you, because it's a pretty bold statement — but I just want to share it with you. This is him talking, not me.

The tape was a direct sales opportunity that went out to all the brand new recruits in the company. On the tape he said, "If your spouse or significant other in your life isn't fully supportive of you and what you're doing with your career, and where you're moving with our company, then you must do one of two things right now. You must either quit and go do something else that doesn't involve straight commission — or you have to get rid of her or him." I thought that was pretty damn bold. He was very clear about it. You either get rid of them right now — just leave them, go, get rid of them, move on, find somebody else in your life, or be single until you become successful — or don't do this. Man, that hit me like a ton of bricks! I thought about it, and I'm glad he was so blunt. I wouldn't be that blunt with you. I don't want to be responsible for anybody's marriage; I don't want anybody calling me up and saying, "You told me to get rid of her!" But that guy did it for me, and I got rid of this gal shortly after. A little more than a year later, I met Eileen.

You never know how valuable something is in this world until and unless you have something else to compare it to. That's one of my biggest beliefs. How *can* you know how valuable something is unless you have a comparison? When I met Eileen, she inspired me. She has multiple sclerosis — she's had it since she was 23 years old and she's 50 at the time I'm writing this, so she's had it over half of her life. It's a terrible disease. When we met, I had a little carpet-cleaning business; and the entire time I was dating her, whenever I'd work when she wasn't working, she would want to come with me and help. Here's this little bitty gal — at that time she couldn't have weighed more than 100 pounds — and she has this life-threatening disease, and here she was lugging around these carpet-cleaning buckets. I fell in love with her on a carpet-cleaning job. She inspired me so greatly, because despite her handicap she was right there moving sofas, working her butt off, just doing all kinds of things — anything, whatever it took.

THE BLUE JEANS MILLIONAIRE!

I was in the process of quitting smoking at the time — and how I quit smoking involved carrying a basketball with me everywhere I went, and I knew all the basketball goals behind every church and every school, every park, and I would stop and play basketball all the time. There was a basketball goal right near Eileen's house, at the back of this church, and we would walk over there and I would shoot baskets. This is when we were first dating, and I would tell her about my dreams of getting rich, of making all kinds of money — and not only was she *not* critical, she was buying it all! There was something about my dreams that really sparked something in her, because she had her own dreams. She got excited about some of these ideas, she was open and receptive, she was going with me on these carpet-cleaning jobs and working her fanny off; and I thought, "Here's the woman I can do something with. Here's the woman I can build something with." That relationship was the catalyst for me. I feel sorry for people who have unsupportive spouses; I think it's a terrible thing. I won't tell *you* to do what the guy told me on that tape — but I'll tell you that I listened to him.

It's not my nature to be that bold. I don't want to take responsibility for your marriage or your relationships. All I can say is, his message hit me like a bolt of lightning. I knew he wasn't talking to me; it was a tape that he did of a speech he gave to a group, but he was still *speaking* to me. He said, "If your spouse is not supportive, get rid of them or leave this job now, because this job is a straight commission job. It requires you to take enormous risks; you've got to step out." Now, they had sales reps in that company who were bringing in a quarter of a million dollars a year, so it was a proven opportunity, and it helped me. Shortly after that I read Harry Browne's great book that he wrote in the early 1970s called *How I Found Freedom in an Unfree World*. It's a little dated, and he's updated it since, but it's still a wonderful book. You might want to check it out. In that book, Harry talked about the value of finding someone in your life — a significant other you can work with, somebody who will believe in you, somebody who will get excited about the same things you're excited about, somebody who's willing to do whatever it takes to support and help you. There's nothing that could be more important. As I've told my wife many times, "Everything that I have, I owe to you." And then she, of course, says "Can I get that in writing? You know, just in case we ever get divorced." Well, I'm putting it in writing right now, baby — here it is!

I know that a lot of people call themselves "self-made millionaires," but they're full of it. It's always about the people behind the scenes. Get rid of the whole idea that these entrepreneurs are out there doing it all on their own, because they aren't. They've got people who believe in them, people who support them, people who fill in the gaps and all the missing pieces, people who are strong in the areas they're weak in. They've good suppliers who are more like partners, good joint-venture partners who are looking out for them, a good, stable staff behind the scenes — you know, the rhythm section of the band. My piano teacher once told me that as long as you have a good rhythm section in a band, a really solid rhythm section with musicians who really know what they're doing — whether it's rhythm guitar, rhythm keyboard, the bass guitar, the drum — then you can have a lead singer or a lead guitar player who sucks, and the band will still sound good.

I think that's the way it is with a lot of entrepreneurs. I'm not going to name names, but you all know who they are. They're in the news constantly, and they want you to believe it's all about them, that they've got some magical ability that makes them special — and I think nothing could be further from the truth. Those people are just like me. They've surrounded themselves with the best people they could find. It's the smartest business move you'll ever make, and whoever said love and money don't mix, I think they were right in some situations — but they were wrong in others. I told you about Eileen. I fell in love with her on a carpet-cleaning job, and she was right there with me from Day One, and we did this together. We also fought a lot, and in the early years I did a lot of things I regret. I was a jerk — a total, immature, irresponsible, impulsive, egotistical jerk. If it weren't for Eileen, I would have destroyed the company many times. She's my opposite in so many ways. She's very stable and has a lot of common sense, whereas I tend to be impulsive and emotionally driven about everything. If it weren't for her, I would have run off all the great staff I inherited when she stepped down from the company in 2001. By that time I was mature enough to take the reins, but if it weren't for Eileen, it would have never happened. Why more entrepreneurs don't figure this out is beyond me.

It's the people in your life who make all the difference, and it's the people you surround yourself with in business who can make it all happen for you. Sir Isaac Newton, the great English mathematician and physicist, once said, "If I have seen further, it is only by standing on the shoulders of giants." I've had so much help from so many giants, people who are so much better than I am, people who are so much smarter than I am. There have been so many people over the years who have helped me in so many ways, and you've got to find that in your life too. I want you to think about all of this very carefully. It's a recurring theme here, and it does make sense, and if all the entrepreneurs were doing this, then that would be one thing — but they're not doing it, and that's the whole thing. So many entrepreneurs are simply not doing this at all. They're trying to do everything on their own. They're very difficult to work with. They're cut off. They do it because of fear, for one thing; they're afraid, and they don't view people correctly. They see people as a cost rather than as an investment. People are always an investment if they're the right people, if they're the good people — and if they're not, get rid of 'em as fast as you can. I don't want to paint an unrealistic picture here. We've had plenty of things that haven't worked for us, we've had plenty of things that have gone wrong. It hasn't all been roses — and even the roses have had their thorns.

It's not easy to work with people all the time, and you have to develop a philosophy that involves just accepting them for who they are, not being overly demanding of them, looking at their strong areas and trying to fit them in to the right places. Everybody has their strengths and weaknesses. Sometimes people who are really strong in certain areas are also weak in other areas, and there are problems and challenges that you have to face when you're working with them on a regular basis. That's one of the reasons why people don't do it more: they want to avoid all of those problems.

Well, I'm here to tell you that the good far outweighs the bad, and one of the reasons we keep working with the same individuals again and again is because there's a trust, a relationship developed, and that makes you want to do more with them. They want to do more with you, too, because you're looking out for them also. The door swings both ways. So think about this concept; it's very, very powerful. It's about a lot more than making money; it's also about the enjoyment you get from working with people you care about and respect. It's a wonderful thing that can not only make you huge sums of money for the rest of your life, but also give you the most extreme joy and satisfaction that you'll ever experience in your business.

SECRET TWENTY-SIX:

Concepts First and Details Last!

The twenty-sixth and final secret I have to share with you is very simple, like everything else I've shared so far — and yet it's very profound at the same time. I call it "Concepts First and Details Last." You've got to think it bigger, and yet you have to see things as simpler than ever before. You must develop a strong personal philosophy that keeps you moving forward at full speed, no matter what the obstacles are. This philosophy, which is made up of your core beliefs, will help you achieve bigger results in less time. Too many people get bogged down in the details. Concepts First, Details Last; don't even worry about how you're going to do things. Instead, spend your time thinking about the "why" to the thing; spend your time working on your goals and developing all the reasons why you want to make millions of dollars, and think about all the previous other wealth secrets I've shared with you in this book.

Much of what I've covered here is conceptual in nature. You still have to figure out a way to do all these things, but the more you focus on the details, the more you're going to get bogged down — the more you're going to become overwhelmed, frustrated, and confused. If you keep going back to the reasons why all these things work, or the general nature of the basics of what we talked about, you're going to be fully empowered. You develop your belief system, the things that help to guide you; and one of the things that I hope you've gained from all of this is an understanding that none of this is easy. There are people out there who want to totally mislead you when it comes to getting rich; they want to tell you that it's a snap. But they're liars — and surely there's a part of you that knows that you can't just make money that easily. There's a price to pay for it. Now, the point is that once you fall in love with the ideas I've shared with you on this program, and once you become passionate about marketing, once you become passionate about product-development work and all the things you do to attract and retain customers, *then* it becomes fun or challenging. It becomes interesting and exciting; it becomes a way of life, so you're willing to do more than the average person. And when you are, that's when you're going to develop the skills necessary to make millions and millions of dollars.

That's when it becomes more like a lifestyle or a hobby. Some of the things that are very difficult for you to learn will give you a tremendous sense of pride and satisfaction, once you learn them, like you can't even imagine right now — a feeling of confidence and power because you've mastered these things. People tend to place the largest value on the things we pay the biggest price to gain, and some of these skills can make you millions of dollars, just as they have for me. If everybody had these skills, then everybody would be making millions of dollars, wouldn't they? And if everybody was rich, why would *you* want to be rich? Part of the attraction of getting rich is the fact that it's the trophy, the prize, the catch, the goal that we set out for; it's the way we keep score, the way that we rise above it all. It's not just egotism. You can always look at your net worth and know how well you're doing, but what I've have done is kept journals over the years. I've thought through my own personal philosophy, my own concepts and my own beliefs — and I want to share with you some of the core ideas that have helped me achieve my success. I've got 39 powerful, core ideas that have served me and have helped me to be, do and have more of what I really want. I'd like for you think about these 39 ideas, and maybe some of them can be part of your core philosophy as well. These are part of my belief system and part of my guidance, the things that help keep me moving forward.

Number 1: Go as far as you can see, and when you get there, you'll be able to see even farther. So many people are confused because they're trying to figure it all out too fast; they want all the answers *now*. They want to try to figure it all out before they get started. Forget that: go as far as you possibly can, take it as far as you can take it, and when you get there you'll be in a better place. You'll be more knowledgeable, you'll know more, and you'll be able to see even farther. So don't think that you have to have it all figured out; you don't. You'll figure it out as you go.

Number 2: "He who flies the highest can see the farthest." That's what conceptual thinking is all about. When you're detail-oriented, you tend to see everything from the bottom up; you get bogged down in the minutia. When you think conceptually, you're thinking from the top down; you're able to see it bigger and think it simpler. So set your goals very high, and see the simplicity in everything we've shared here. Making millions of dollars doesn't have to be that complicated when you stay focused on the basics, when you don't worry about how you're going to do everything. When you set your goals high and keep it simple, that's the one thing that's going to separate you from all the other people who are working with you. You're going to be able to see things from the top down and know just how simple all this is. So fly high, and always answer that question, "How high is high?" What are you really capable of doing; how far can you go? Set those high goals; don't be afraid to do that, and you'll see even further than most people.

Number 3: You must develop the heart of the lion and the mind of the fox. For years now I've had a little fox and a little

295

lion, and I keep them where I can see them at all times. I've thought a lot about that: the heart of the lion, the mind of the fox. The fox is a cunning animal, and you've got to be a bit like that in business; you're always on the edge, you're always aware, you're always looking around, you're always watching people's actions instead of just listening to what they say. You realize that people are self-centered by nature; the more you have, the more people want to get it. So you've got to be on guard; you really do. I've talked a lot here about working with other people; well, you've got to be careful too. And then you've got to have the heart of the lion: the lion is bold and audacious, the king of the jungle — and it does take a little bit of audacity.

One of my greatest stories is the story of Solo Flex. The guy who founded that company was a jet pilot who flew high rollers back and forth to Las Vegas, mostly to and from L.A. or San Francisco. Over a period of time, he got to know some of the regulars. They'd get up to the cruising altitude, he'd flip it over to automatic pilot, and he would go spend forty-five minutes or an hour talking with these people. They got to know each other well. So here he is, at age fifty or so, and he's making pretty good money; he has a six-figure income coming in, he's a chartered jet pilot, and one morning he just seized on this powerful question: "What makes these people any different than I am?" The answer to the question was: audacity. These people were just audacious; they were bold. That's it. They were no smarter than he was, they were no better looking than he was, they had no more special abilities or talents; it was just audacity. They each had the heart of the lion, and that's what some of this really does take. You've got to suspend all of your fear and go for it. Don't be afraid to fall, and just keep getting up every time you *do* fall.

Number 4: In every business deal, always assume there's something, or a series of somethings, that the other party is holding back from you. You have to be careful — that's sort of like the mind of the fox. Always be careful; always. I've tried to hold nothing back from you in this book, but I promise you, in every deal you have to assume that there's something that they're not telling you. Just assume it, even if it's not true. It'll help you stand guard; it'll help you be very careful. Here's an example: once upon a time, Eileen and I needed the help of an attorney. I'll never forget this: he was asking us to sign this contract that would have made him many, many thousands of dollars, and he was trying to scare us a little. We were in trouble; we needed some fast answers, and he was, I remember, using high-pressure tactics on us. Eileen and I were in his office, and I recall watching him very carefully — and I saw a little bead of sweat start rolling down his face as he was waiting for us to sign this contract. I got up and left his office, and Eileen followed me; and we didn't sign the contract. Pretty soon, we drove off and we found another lawyer who turned out to be a great person who worked with us for a number of years. The other guy was trying to use a number of tactics on us, trying to manipulate us, trying to scare us. Look, you've always got to watch people, watch them carefully. Always think that they're holding something back from you; then you'll be on guard.

Number 5: You've got to work on yourself as hard you work on your business. These ideas are simple, really. If you go back and reread this book, you'll see that there's nothing all that complicated about what I'm sharing, and yes, a lot of it's redundant. That's because a lot of these ideas are really simple by nature. It's all about working through the fears and the insecurities, and all the false and limited beliefs that have held you back. That's going to be the challenge; that's going to be the determinator of how you use these secrets, whether you go full force and use them to make millions of dollars, or whether you hold back. It's about dealing with yourself and it's setting higher goals; it's about working through your fears and insecurities; it's about deciding that you're going to go for it, even if you don't have it all figured out. So work on yourself; write down a list of all of the things you're afraid of, all the things that have held you back up to now, and be completely honest with yourself. There are plenty of good books out there that can help. One of the best books I can recommend was written in the late 1980s by Susan Jeffers; it's called *Feel the Fear and Do It Anyway*. I would encourage you to get that book. You've got to work on yourself constantly. If you're not making the kind of money you want to be making, then there's something that's stopping you; and until and unless you work on yourself, you're never going to figure it out.

Number 6: Work *on* your business, and not *in* it. You've got to be the architect of your business; you have to be the general of the war. You can't be on the front lines. I would advise you to find other people to manage your business, so you can focus all your time on all the things that are necessary to attract and retain customers. Work on it, look at your business in a conceptual way, and you see the simplicity of it.

Number 7: See everything from the top down, and not the bottom up; that's what concepts are all about. They let you see how simple everything is — and it really *is* simple. I've tried to share that with you throughout this entire book.

Number 8: Self-discipline leads to self-confidence. You've got to force yourself to do the things that are necessary, that will make you the most money. You have to force yourself to learn these new skills of being able to write copy, develop product, do things that make you a great marketer. A lot of times it doesn't feel good, and even when you get good at it, you still have to force yourself to do it. You'll have moments when you're on fire, when you're so excited, when it's not work at all. You'll have moments when it's fun, it's interesting, it's challenging, and the energy is there and you just want to do it all, and it's easy. Then you have other days when it's very, very difficult.

Remember: the professional does it when they don't feel like doing it. You don't just do it when you feel like doing it, you do it all the time. You discipline yourself, *force* yourself to work. I got up at 5:00 this morning and wrote copy until my hands hurt, finishing up a sales letter. Some days, it just comes flowing out of me; today it didn't. Today I had to work at it. I've been doing this for twenty years now and it's still work, although sometimes it's a great pleasure. So, you've got to take the good and the bad, and the more you do to force yourself to do the things that you know are in your best interest, the better you're going to feel about yourself — and that does lead to self-confidence.

Number 9: This Jim Rohn quote became my mantra, and I want it to be yours: "Don't wish things were easier; wish that you were better." So many people want things to be easy. When life gets tough, they fantasize about an easy life. Jim says, "Look: just wish you were better, because if you were, you wouldn't be faced with such obstacles." That's one of the cool things about growing and developing, and it's one of the ways I can see true growth in myself. I meet entrepreneurs who are on the path I've been on for 20 years, and I see them struggling with things I used to struggle with. I see them going through problems I used to live with — but they're not problems for me anymore. I see them getting upset about things that used to destroy me; but those things don't bother me now, and I know it's because I've gotten better. I've practiced what I've preached, I've put in the hours, I've done the work, I've developed the skills. You've got to do it too. Wish that you were better, because if you *were* better, you wouldn't have such problems. You'd be able to solve some of the things you can't solve right now.

Number 10: It's always better to have a valuable resource and not need it, than to need it and not have it. That's true with

299

so many things. A valuable resource can be great people in your life, or it can be money in the bank; it could be products that you've got waiting in the wings, all kinds of promotions that you can rework. It can be certain things that you've learned. It's always better to have that resource and not need it, than to be in a position where you need something and don't have it. Just think about what that can mean for you, and think about what a resource is: something that offers you value.

Number 11: All that glitters is not gold. That's one of my most important concepts. There are all kinds of distractions out there, all kinds of things you can get into, and there's lots of different kinds of glitter; but you've got to think about what's most important all the time, and realize that some of that glitter is just fool's gold.

Number 12: A quote from Robert DeRopp, a great philosopher: "Seek above all else a game that's worth playing, and then play it as if your entire life and sanity depended on it, for it does." I think the greatest game on Earth is the game of business: the money acquisition game, learning all the things I've talked about in this book that have to do with developing product, attracting customers, separating yourself from every other competitor in your marketplace, continuing to do business over and over with the same clients, who continue to give you more and more money for larger profits every time. This is a great game, so play it like one!

Number 13: One day at a time; let go, and let God; this too shall pass. Yeah, I've had to learn that. It's easy to get overwhelmed; but all you've got to do is just worry about today, and let tomorrow take care of itself. If you're putting everything you can into today, you're fine. Think of it as a brick wall, a solid brick wall that's your whole life, and each day is one of those bricks, and think about what you're doing with it. Most people are just heaping those bricks outside; their lives are directionless. They're going nowhere, they're achieving nothing, they're not doing anything big with their lives. They're taking that brick everyday and just throwing it onto some great big pile. I want you to think about this: Don't worry about the future, take care of today, let the future take care of itself, and don't get overwhelmed. There were things, back in the early-1990s, that used to cause me to almost have a heart attack. Here I was, in my late 20s, early 30s, and my chest was hurting and I'd get so angry — but now those things don't even bother me. I've learned to let it go, and you've got to, too. That's one of the things I see in all these up-and-comers who are on the same path: I see them getting so bothered about things that used to bother me, and there's no need for that. Just let it go.

Number 14: You must be willing to lose a few (or many) battles so you can win the war. You have to decide what war is to you, but be willing to lose a few battles; be quietly effective. Don't worry about fighting every battle; you're going to wear yourself out. Just be willing to stay focused on your goals. Nothing else means anything.

Number 15: The "why" to do something is always more important than the "how." That's where concepts and goals come in: knowing why you want to make millions of dollars. I *know* you want to make millions; only a fool would invest in this book if they didn't. You've got to ask yourself why. You'll figure out the "how to do it" if the "why to do it" is big enough.

Number 16: "Selling is serving" — that's a Ray Kroc quote. Well, a lot of people don't want to be salespeople. Salespeople have a bad rep. A salesperson is somebody who's offering something that's worth so much value that the money they're asking for in exchange should pale by comparison. Their whole focus is on serving, whatever serving means to your marketplace; focus on that. That's what selling really is.

Number 17: A successful life is a series of successful days. Take care of today and tomorrow will take care of itself. Everybody's worried about the future; well, you don't have to be, as long as you're taking care of every single day, right here and now.

Number 18: You've got to be willing to do what nobody else wants to do. You see, a lot of this is difficult, in the beginning especially, and that's not popular. If you want to go out there and buy some, well, there are magic programs where people are trying to tell you how simple and easy it is. And it *is* simple; that's part of what this last principle I'm sharing with you is all about. You've got to *keep* it simple. But you also have to be very disciplined; you have to be willing to put in the time, put in the work, put in the effort, and you've got to be willing to do the things most people aren't going to do.

Number 19: Keep your eyes on the stars, and always let your reach exceed your grasp. You've always got to be pushing for more to answer the questions, "How high is high?" and "What are you really capable of?" Set your goals high; keep dreaming big dreams. When you keep your eyes on the stars, you're willing to endure the problems and challenges that stop some people. There are going to be speed bumps on your road, so keep dreaming those big dreams. Don't be afraid to do that.

Number 20: Don't drive down the road with one foot on the gas pedal and the other on the brake. Too many people are trying to be so cautious all the time that they're afraid to drive. Look, race car drivers will tell you that the secret is to just stay totally focused on the road ahead. That's it; that's all you've got to do. Keep your eyes right on the road, and just go for it. Just drive; don't hold back.

Number 21: The things you tell yourself about yourself are the most important things. You're better and stronger than you think you are. Keep telling yourself good things about yourself. Don't listen to your inner critic; don't listen to the exterior critics in your life. Write down all the things you're the best at, that you're strong in; and that goes back to what we talked about in Number 5. Work on yourself as hard as you work on your business. Be your own best friend. Life is too short to go through it by second-guessing yourself, criticizing yourself and tearing yourself down.

Number 22: Business is a combination of art, science, sport, politics, and war. Think about those concepts. It's creative, it's artistic; it's also scientific. There are principles at work here, and I've tried to share them with you in this book. These are the same principles that have made us millions of dollars. It's also a sport, and there are ways of keeping score. It's somewhat political; sometimes you can't always be direct with people. It's like war too; it's a battle. Try to keep that in your mind all the time. It's not just about making money. You noticed I didn't use the word "money" in there at all. It's art, science, sports, politics, and war; those are the concepts to keep you moving forward.

Number 23: Marketing is like chess. The masters of marketing are always thinking three steps ahead at all times. Remember, chess is pretty simple; there are only six basic pieces, and a few basic moves for you to learn. Once you have those moves down, that's it. Marketing is like that too.

Number 24: Making money is the greatest game on Earth. Play it, and keep playing it. It's not just something you do for the money, it's something you do for joy and satisfaction; it'll fill your life up. You'll keep wanting to go for bigger and better things; you'll keep trying to improve yourself and your game. You won't just make money so you can sit on your butt and do nothing. There will be no such thing as retirement to you. There may be semi-retirement, but your business will be about things that you truly enjoy. It's your passion; it's your skill set. It's the greatest game on Earth; play it, have some fun. Remember what DeRopp said: "Seek above all else a game worth playing and then play it as if your entire life and sanity depended up on it, for it truly does."

Number 25: "Fear destroys more people than any other one thing." The brilliant Ralph Waldo Emerson said that. If you really knew you could handle anything and everything that happens to you, what would there be to fear? Absolutely nothing. We're only afraid because there's something inside us that doesn't believe we can handle it. Well, I'm telling you — you *can* handle it. You handle it one day at a time, one brick at a time. You handle it by continuing to go as far as you can see; and then when you get there, you'll see further. You don't need to take it all in at once. Remember that fear is the enemy; you've got to conquer it.

Number 26: This is the thing I say to myself a lot of mornings — like today, when I didn't want to get out of bed. It's a Shakespeare quote: "To thine own self be true." You've got to be true to yourself, true to your goals, what you're trying to accomplish in life. Keep moving forward, in spite of whether you want to or not; just keep doing it.

Number 27: In everything that you do, think it bigger and see it simpler. That's what Concepts First and Details Last is all about. Everybody else is getting bogged down in details; everybody else is focused on all of the little complexities involved in every major project. You can't do it. You've got to think bigger and see it simpler.

Number 28: "You can have everything in life you want, if you'll only help enough people get what *they* want." This is a Zig Ziglar quote. And notice I said "want," not "need." There's a big difference here. You're helping people get what they want. Well, sometimes, what people want and what they need are two different things. That's one of the underlying principles I want to share with you here. It's all about serving. That's where this whole "selling is serving" idea comes from. You're giving people what they want; you're serving them, and if you do that for enough people, you're going to get rich.

Number 29: Keep giving your customers more of what they bought from you the first time. You've seen me say that throughout this book. It's all about variations on a theme. What do people want? More of what they bought from you the first time.

Number 30: Find just a few people you can really trust, who are super-talented in the areas you're weak in, and do everything you can to keep those people on your team. Grab them tight, give them whatever they want, love them, take good care of them, don't let go of them. These people are the most important people in your life and your business.

Number 31: Express yourself fully. Don't hold back. If there's one thing you can say about me with this book, and the audio program it's based on, it's that I've just tried to be myself. I haven't tried to show off. I'm not a professional speaker or writer. I am what I am. Too many people are playing games; they're trying to be perfect, they're trying to be too polished, and they're not being real — and everybody knows that. Whether you like me or not, at least you know I've been real with you. I've been sharing things from my heart; hopefully you'll at least respect me for that. I want you to do the same thing, when it comes to everything that you do in your life. Just be yourself and express yourself fully, and don't hold back. It's the people in this world who really don't give a damn about what anybody else thinks of them that we end up respecting the most. It's the people who are trying to be perfect and polished, who are trying to go through their whole lives pleasing everybody else, who end up getting no respect. I just want you to just take off all the filters; that's what I've tried to do with this book. Express yourself fully.

Number 32: Everything is difficult until it becomes easy. You've got to be willing and even eager to pay the biggest price possible for the things that you want the most. We always value what we pay the most for — and the skills that it takes to make millions of dollars, like product development, copywriting, good marketing skills, everything I've shared with you that has been responsible for the millions of dollars we've made, has come with a price. You'll pay that price and you'll feel good about it. It *will* get easier, but you've got to be willing to pay the price and understand that there's a learning curve involved. I love what Ray Bradbury says: He says that to be a good writer is real simple. What you have to do is write 20,000 pages, and by the time you write those 20,000 pages, you'll have put in the time and work necessary for your writing to be where it needs to be. After you get past those 20,000 pages, you're a good writer. I love that quote, because it expresses what I've been trying to share with you. It's no accident that the greatest direct-response marketing copy writers, the ones who write sales letters that generate millions of dollars, are usually those who have been doing it for at least ten years, and quite possibly twenty years or more. Experience is important; there's only one way you can get it, though. You've got to pay the price and get started today.

Number 33: Fall in love with the few things that make you the most money: product development, marketing, and copy writing. Fall in love with doing those things. They're challenging, fun, rewarding — and the more you love them, the more you're going to get lost in them; and the more your skills are going to develop along with your knowledge and experience. You'll gain tremendous confidence.

Number 34: At any given time you've got to know what the five most important things are in your life. I've got a list right here in front of me; and it's my five things. I know what they all are, and when I read that list I can see if I am on target, if I'm moving in the right direction. It helps you to stay focused.

Number 35: Stay hungry. Remember where you came from, where you are now, and where you want to go. Never lose that desire. I'm just going to assume that you're hungry; you've invested in this book because you got a hunger inside you. It's a good assumption on my part, I think, and I want you to keep that hunger. Sometimes you'll get the success that you've longed for, and you start coasting. You can't do it; stay hungry. That's where playing it as a game helps.

Number 36: Get really good at a few things that make you the most money, then delegate everything else. That's related to Number 33. Just stay totally focused on just those few things that make you the most money. Let everything else go. Find other people you can work through who have skills that can help you fill in all the other gaps.

Number 37: Direct response marketing is math and psychology; that's all. You've got to really understand people — that's the psychology — and then, with every promotion, you need to understand the money math. It's really easy to do.

Number 38: Business is an accelerated lifestyle. You get more of the good and more of the bad. For me, it's been a major roller coaster ride. I've experienced so many wonderful things in business, and it's challenging; it really is. But it's also rewarding and exciting and depressing, and there are things that will break your heart. There are problems and obstacles and difficulties, and it's the best of everything that life has to offer. You get more of everything; you get more of the good, you get more of the bad. It's a wonderful way to live, but keep that in mind; it's an accelerated lifestyle. That will help you deal with some of the pressures you have to deal with.

Number 39: Money and material things are great, but true confidence doesn't come from having things; it comes from handling things. I've got to say that to you one more time. The reason you've invested in this book is because you want to make money. That was me, too; I wanted to become a multimillionaire, and that's all I cared about in the beginning. But money and material things... well, they're great. Enjoy them; they're your trophies, and the more you work hard for them, the more you can appreciate them. That's why it's good to pay the price you need to pay. You hear about people who win the lottery; their whole lives are destroyed, because they're not prepared for the wealth. But once you've paid the price for it, you'll really feel good about it. You'll know you deserve it because you worked your ass off for it. But true confidence, and true happiness also, doesn't come from having things; it comes from your ability to handle things. That's a good place to wrap this book up, one related to the ninth concept I shared. That's the Jim Rohn quote that says, "Don't wish things were easier, wish that you were better."

A lot of people want to make a fortune because they're looking for a perfect life. They've got this image in their heads that they're going to make millions of dollars, and then they're just going to kick back on some sandy beach, somewhere exotic, and everything's going to be perfect. Well, I have my fantasies too, but at least I know that they're fantasies. I want *you* to know that they're fantasies, too. Look, the greatest thing about business and reaching all of your goals is just what Jim Rohn suggested: it's who you become in the process. Life here is limited. All of our lives, we don't know how much longer we have here. This could be your last day; you could have another decade; you could have another five decades. It's who we become in life, through the process of working towards our goals, that's the most important thing, and having confidence means that you're facing all the adversity that comes your way, all the challenges. You're taking charge of your life, you're willing to do the things most people are unwilling to do.

You can make a lot of money, sure, and that's great. But true confidence comes from your knowing, just that knowing, that you have the ability to handle anything that comes your way. Fear is a real enemy of success, but if you knew you could handle anything and everything that comes your way, there would be no fear. I've dealt with a lot of fear and a lot of insecurities; I've had a lot of challenges in my life, and I've tried to share them with you in a very open and honest way throughout this book.

The greatest feeling is *not* just having millions of dollars, it's knowing that you overcame all that crap that was in your way. You've developed some real skills and abilities, and you've tried to focus on serving people and helping people. In order to get your money, you've tried to offer tremendous value to other people, and that's a great, great feeling, especially when those people will use your ideas, your help and support and guidance, to do big things with their lives.

There's no better feeling.

Epilogue:

I hope you enjoyed reading this book. I hope you'll go back and read it more than once; I hope you'll take notes and highlight and underline things, and write in the margins. Think about everything I've shared with you. Live with these ideas. They've made me millions of dollars; they can make you millions too. They can also give you a life that's full of confidence, power, joy and satisfaction. It's about more than just making money. This book can give you everything that you want, and I'm here to help you, so please use me as a resourse.

From time to time – at our own events or those being put on by others in the industry – I get the opportunity to meet my clients and people who have read one of my books. Hopefully we can meet one day at one of these events. I look forward to meeting you, and discussing these things with you in person. This really is a journey, and I want to help you go there. I don't want to just give you my best ideas and leave you on your own to sink or swim; I really, truly want to help you. Yes, I want to make money myself; I'm practicing everything I've preached to you in this book. But I also want to help you. I want to help you with these ideas. It's going to take some work, and I want to guide you — I don't just want to leave you hanging.

So I invite you to meet me... somewhere, sometime. Please reach out through my Support Desk at www.HeyTJ.com or email tickets@heytj.com. Just let me know that you read this book and would like to connect. Even if there's not an upcoming event to connect at, maybe we can share a phone call... a skype meeting... or just agree to stay in touch.

**Let me know what you liked about my book and
I'll give you a free gift to say thanks!**

When you reach out, just let me know you read this book and you'd like your free gift. I appreciate feedback and thoughts... especially if you find value in the 26 secrets I shared with you.

Either way, I look forward to someday hopefully looking you right in the eye and hearing you tell me, "The ideas you shared in your book have made me millions of dollars; it's given me everything you said that it would give me." That's my biggest hope and prayer for you. God bless you. God bless your family. Thank you very much.